PHILIP'S Red Books

MID...H

STOC...TON-ON-TEES

www.philips-maps.co.uk

First published 2008 by

Philip's, a division of
Octopus Publishing Group Ltd
www.octopusbooks.co.uk
2–4 Heron Quays
London E14 4JP
An Hachette Livre UK Company
www.hachettelivre.co.uk

First edition 2008
First impression 2008

ISBN 978-0-540-09276-5

© Philip's 2008

Contents

II	**Key to map pages**
IV	**Route planning**
VII	**Key to map symbols**
2	**Street maps** at 4½ inches to 1 mile
80	**Street maps** at 7 inches to 1 mile
88	**Index**
113	**List of numbered locations**

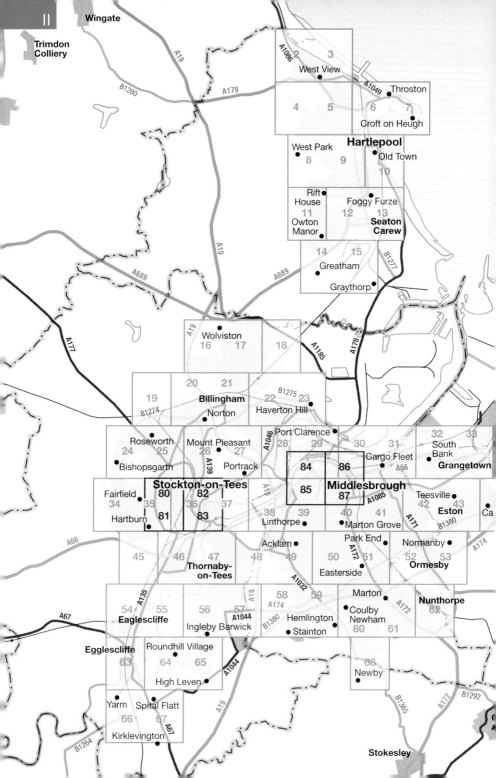

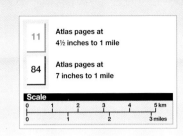

| 11 | Atlas pages at 4½ inches to 1 mile |

| 84 | Atlas pages at 7 inches to 1 mile |

Scale

0   1   2   3   4   5 km
0   1   2   3 miles

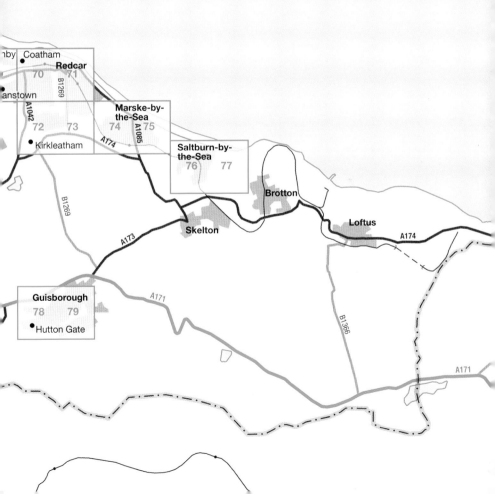

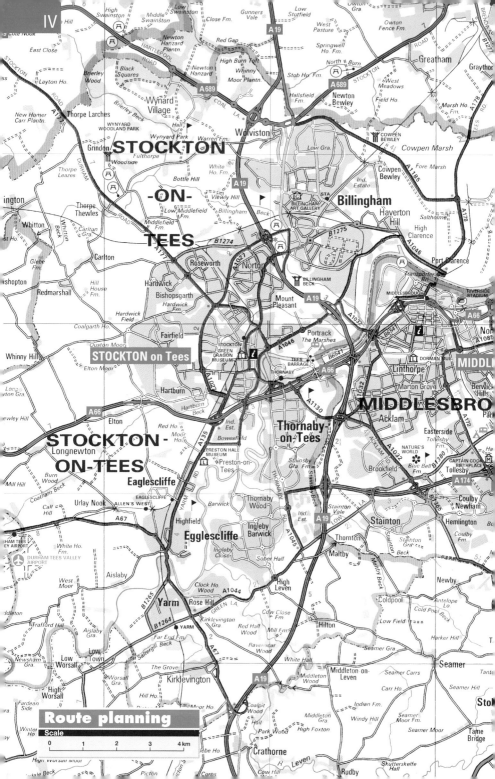

Route planning

Scale

0 1 2 3 4 km

Key to map symbols

Roads

(12)	**Motorway** with junction number
A42	**Primary route** – dual, single carriageway
A42	**A road** – dual, single carriageway
B1289	**B road** – dual, single carriageway
	Through-route – dual, single carriageway
	Minor road – dual, single carriageway
	Rural track, private road or narrow road in urban area
	Path, bridleway, byway open to all traffic, restricted byway
	Road under construction
	Pedestrianised area
	Gate or obstruction to traffic restrictions may not apply at all times or to all vehicles
P **P&R**	**Parking, Park and Ride**
(30) **(30)**	**Speed cameras** – single, multiple

Railways

 Railway

Miniature railway

 Metro station, private railway station

Emergency services

 Ambulance station, coastguard station

Fire station, police station

H **+** **Hospital, Accident and Emergency entrance to hospital**

General features

+ **PO** **Place of worship, Post Office**

i **Information centre (open all year)**

Bus or coach station, shopping centre

 Important buildings, schools, colleges, universities and hospitals

Woods, built-up area

Tumulus FORT **Non-Roman antiquity, Roman antiquity**

Leisure facilities

Camping site, caravan site

Golf course, picnic site

Boundaries

• • • • • • • •	**Postcode boundaries**
— • —	**County and unitary authority boundaries**

Water features

 River Ouse **Tidal water, water name**

Non-tidal water – lake, river, canal or stream

< **‡** **Lock, weir**

Enlarged mapping only

Railway or bus station building

Place of interest

Parkland

Scales

Blue pages: 4½ inches to 1 mile 1:14 080

0	220 yds	¼ mile	660 yds	½ mile
0	125m	250m 375m		½ km

Red pages: 7 inches to 1 mile 1:9 051

0	110 yds	220 yds	330 yds	¼ mile
0	125m	250m	375m	½km

62 **Adjoining page indicators** The colour of the arrow and the band indicates the scale of the adjoining page (see above)

Abbreviations

Acad	**Academy**	Mkt	**Market**
Allot Gdns	**Allotments**	Meml	**Memorial**
Cemy	**Cemetery**	Mon	**Monument**
C Ctr	**Civic Centre**	Mus	**Museum**
CH	**Club House**	Obsy	**Observatory**
Coll	**College**	Pal	**Royal Palace**
Crem	**Crematorium**	PH	**Public House**
Ent	**Enterprise**	Recn Gd	**Recreation Ground**
Ex H	**Exhibition Hall**	Resr	**Reservoir**
Ind Est	**Industrial Estate**	Ret Pk	**Retail Park**
IRB Sta	**Inshore Rescue Boat Station**	Sch	**School**
		Sh Ctr	**Shopping Centre**
Inst	**Institute**	TH	**Town Hall/House**
Ct	**Law Court**	Trad Est	**Trading Estate**
L Ctr	**Leisure Centre**	Univ	**University**
LC	**Level Crossing**	Wks	**Works**
Liby	**Library**	YH	**Youth Hostel**

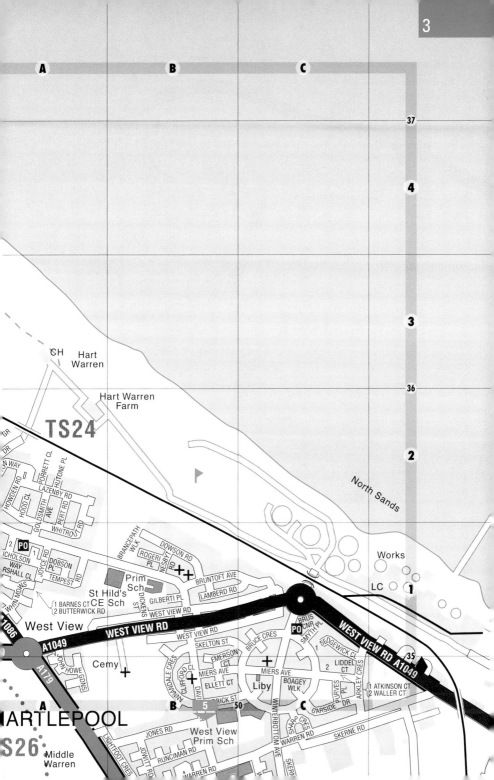

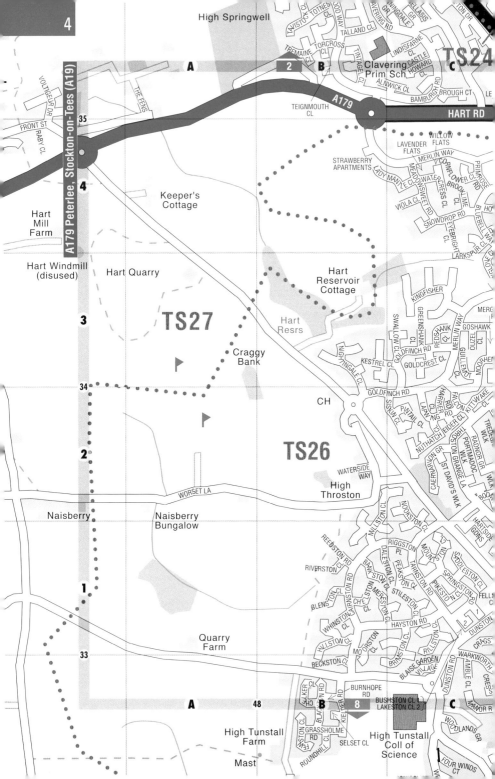

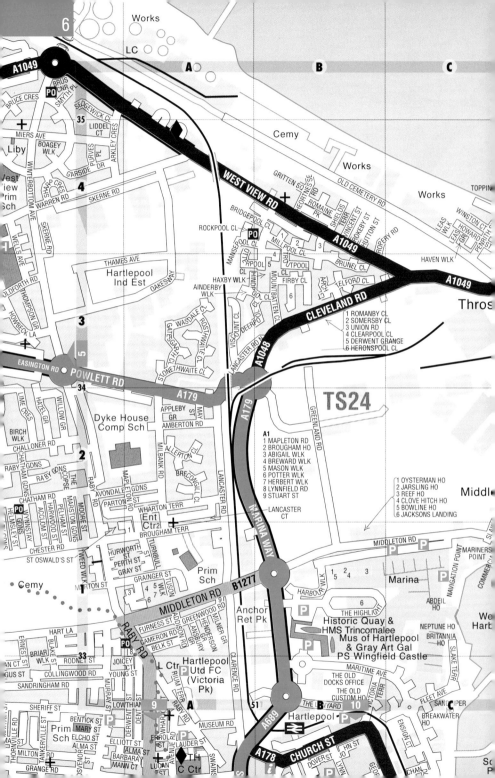

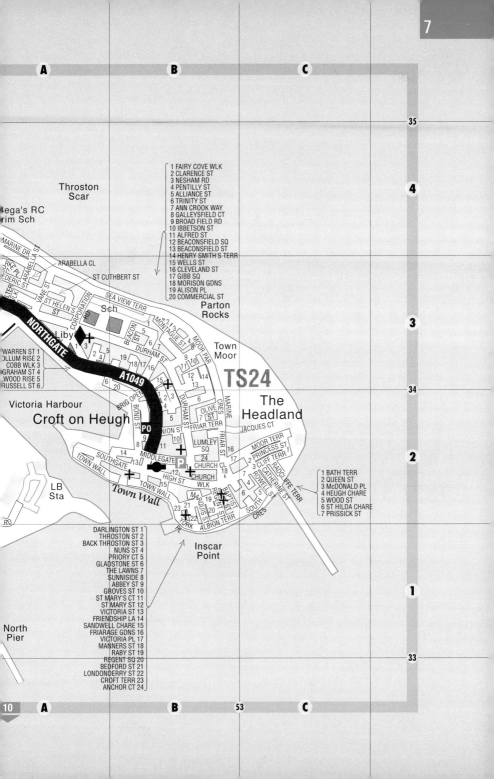

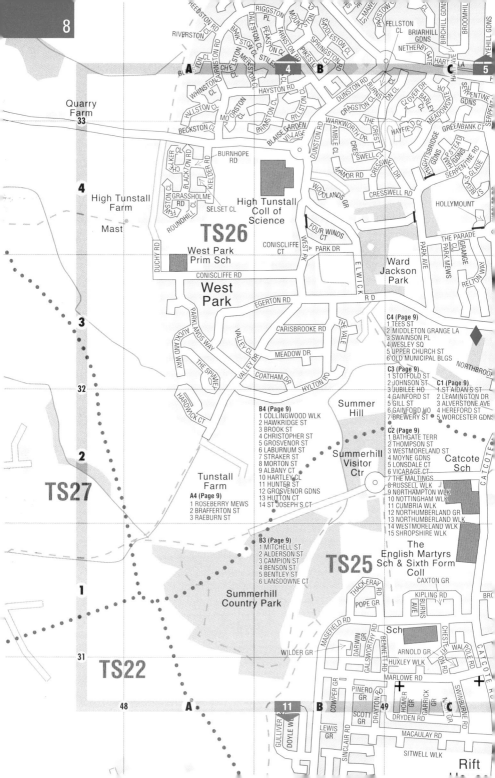

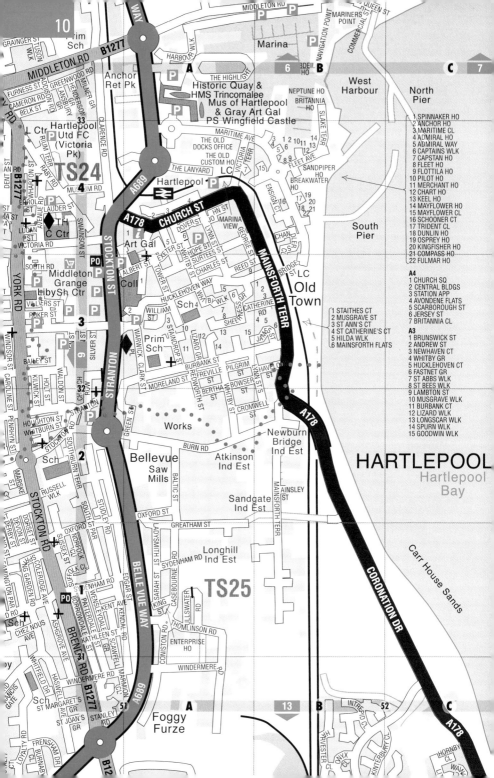

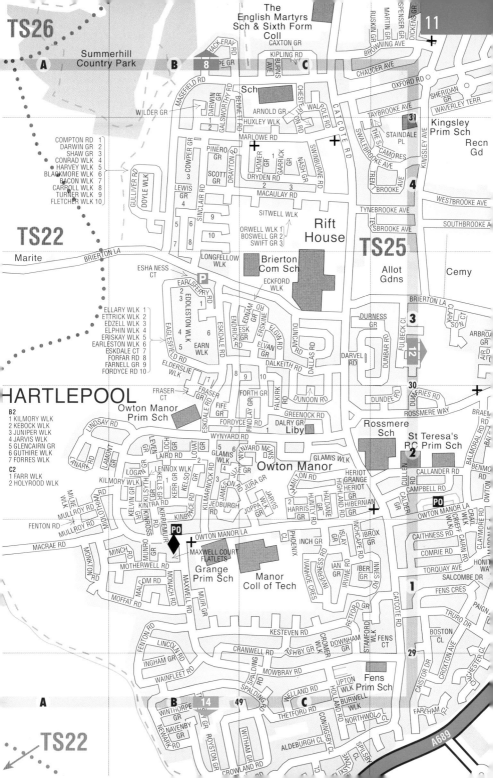

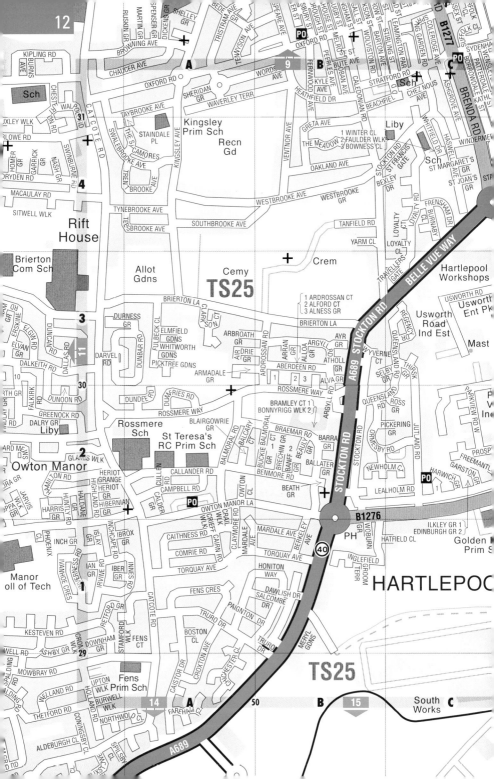

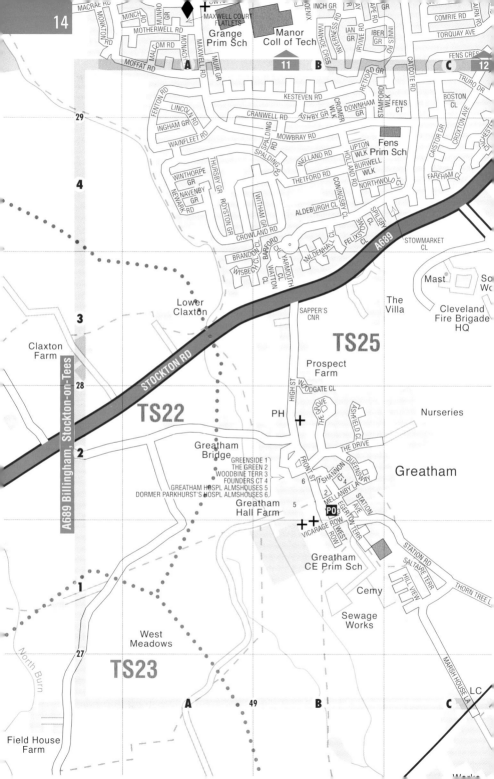

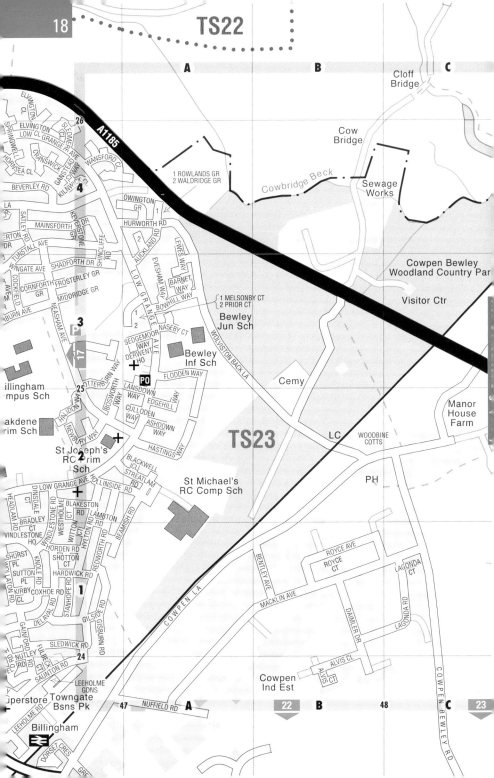

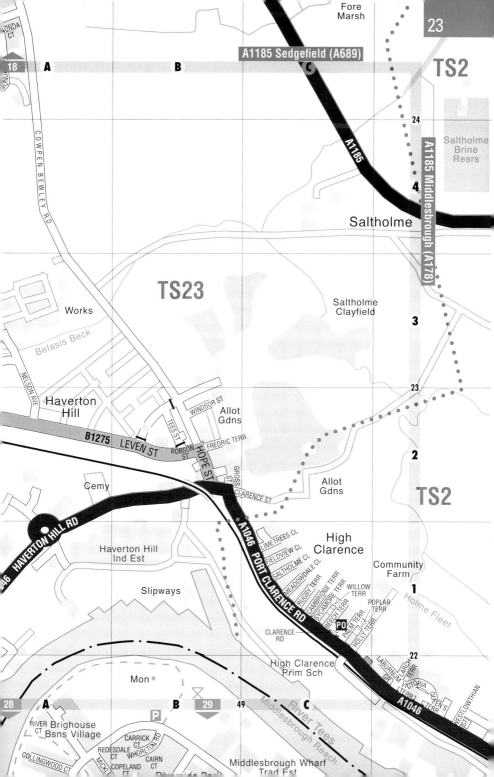

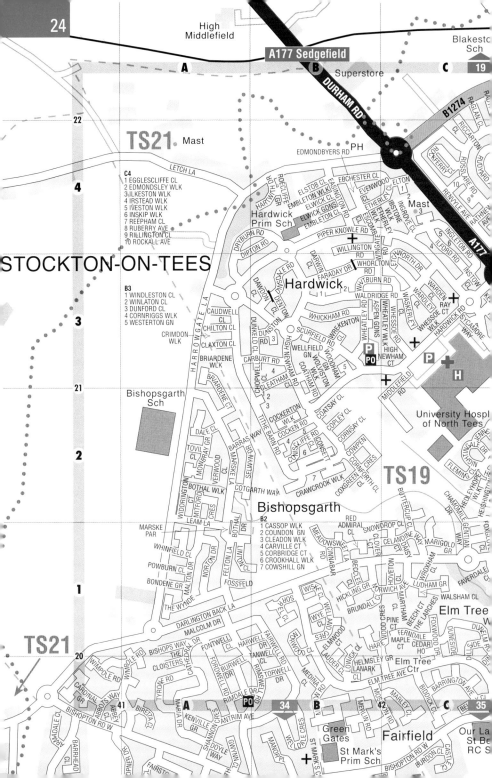

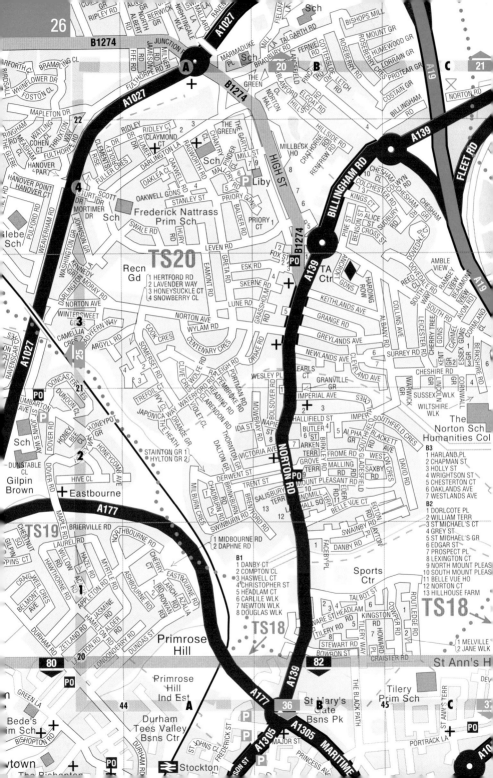

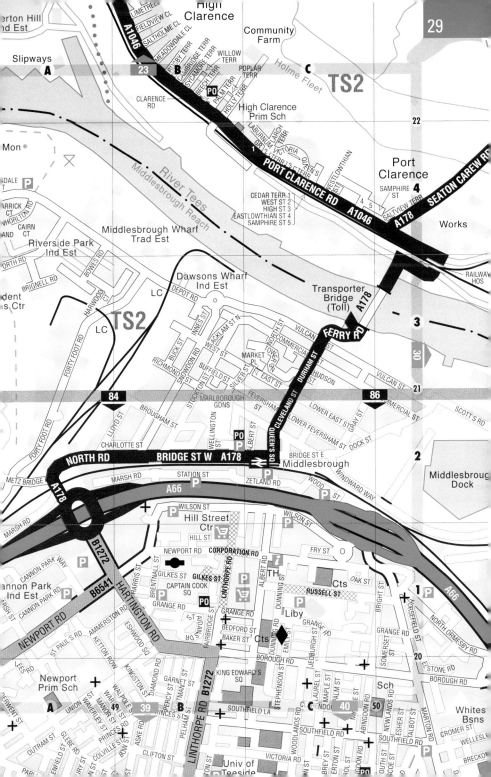

A   B   C

22

4
Teesside Work
Cleveland

Offshore
Base

SMITH'S DOCK RD

DOCKSIDE RD

TS6

3
South
Bank

Cargo Fleet
Wharf

NORMANBY RD

River Tees

Viewpoint
Indicator

KING GEORGES TERR

OLD STATION RD

32

P

PO
NORTH ST

Nelson
Street
Ind Est

21 Superstore
TRAFALGAR
CT

TS3

DOCKSIDE RD

Teesdale Way

TILBURY RD

NORMAN TERR

NELSON ST

A66

EN

Works

A66

HAWTHORN TERR 1

NORMANBY RD

P

ELM
ST
OAK

MIDDLESBROUGH RD

2

HARDWICK RD

WORKS RD

Motor Sports
Pk

SALISBURY
ST

COSTA
ST

STEVEN ST

AIRE ST

PRINCESS ST

P OXFORD ST

NAPIER ST

PYM ST

REDCAR RD

QUEEN ST

Cromwell
Road
Prim Sch

SOUTH TERR

VICTORIA RD

OLIVER

PO

B1513

MIDDLESBROUGH RD

OLD MIDDLESBROUGH RD

DORMER
WAY

BLATCHFORD
RD

Skipper's
Lane
Ind Est

OWENS RD

SCARBOROUGH RD

CROMWELL ST

HARCOURT RD

ANN ST

WARWICK ST

MAXTON R

HAMPD

Cargo Fleet

SOUTH BANK RD

PINE ST

TELFORD RD

WEBB RD

SKIPPER'S LA

Albt
Gdns

SALISBURY

SHINWELL CT

A171

WESTERBY RD

East
Middlesbrough
Ind Est

QUEENSWAY

SOTHERBY RD

MAXWELL RD

E2

METCALFE RD

BRUNEL RD

DAVY RD

RENNIE RD

NEWCOMEN RD

MURD RD

WALLIS RD

SOTHERBY
RD

WEAR

20

AJAX WAY

FLEMING RD

Skippers La
Ind Est

TEES CT

TYNE CT

STADIUM
CT

PARSONS
CT

SKIPPERS LA

STEPHENSON
ST

COMM

A   52   41   B

TA Ctr

C   42   53   Cleveland
Ret Pk

P

Evan
Bsns
Ctr

MERLIN RD

FALCON AVE

HAWK RD

KESTREL AVE

CHERWELL TERR

TEANDALE

PALLISTER
CT

MILLBROOK AVE

COLMORE

LONGLANDS RD A1085

MILFORD

PALLISTER AVE

A1085

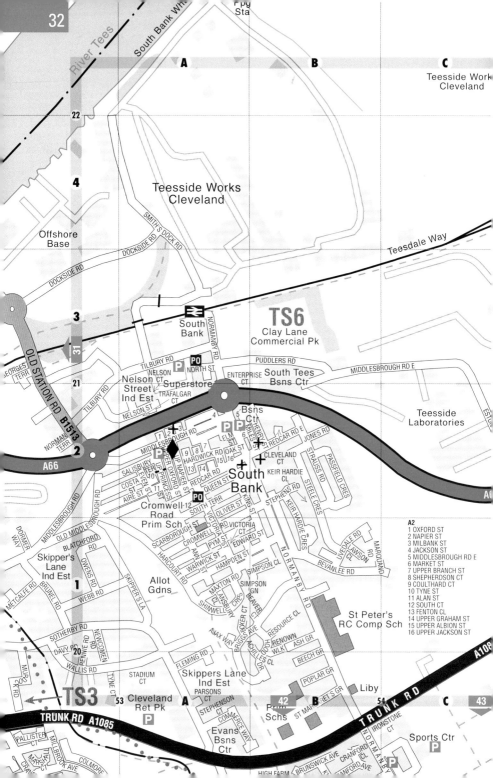

River Tees

South Bank Wh...
Pg Sta

A **B** **C**

Teesside Work
Cleveland

22

4

Teesside Works
Cleveland

Offshore
Base

SMITH'S DOCK RD

DOCKSIDE RD

DOCKSIDE RD

Teesdale Way

3

OLD STATION RD B1513

31

South
Bank

TS6

Clay Lane
Commercial Pk

21

GEORGES TERR

TILBURY RD

NELSON CT

Nelson
Street
Ind Est

TILBURY RD

NELSON ST

P

P0

NORTH ST

NORMANBY RD

PUDDLERS RD

ENTERPRISE
CT

TRAFALGAR
CT

South Tees
Bsns Ctr

MIDDLESBROUGH RD E

ES...

Superstore

Bsns
Ctr

Teesside
Laboratories

2

A66

NORMAN TERR

MIDDLESBROUGH RD

MIDDLESBROUGH RD

P

SALISBURY

COSTA

AIRE ST

ELM
ST

CHERRY...

REDCAR RD E

CLEVELAND
CT

JONES RD

STRAUSS RD

PASSFIELD CRES

South
Bank

KEIR HARDIE
CL

STEELE CRES

REDCAR RD

HARDWICK RD OAK ST

QUEEN ST

UP NAPIER ST

UP PRINCESS

UP OXFORD

Cromwell
Road
Prim Sch

P0

SOUTH TERR

KING ST

STEPHENS RD

KEIR HARDIE CRES

A

7

3

8

9

74

75

76

4

5

11

12

OLD MIDDLESBROUGH RD

DORMER
WAY

BLATCHFORD

OWENS RD

SKIPPER'S LA

Skipper's
Lane
Ind Est

1

HARCOURT RD

SCARBOROUGH

CROMWELL

VICTORIA
ST

PYM ST

EDWARD ST

NORMANBY RD

ESTON RD...

METCALFE RD

BRUNEL RD

WEBB RD

Allot
Gdns

WARWICK ST

MAXTON RD

CANSBURY

SHINWELL

HAMPDEN ST

SIMPSON
GN

SIMPSON CL

BEAVER

LIVERLADE RD

BEVANLEE RD

MARQUAND

LAWSON

St Peter's
RC Comp Sch

SOTHERBY RD

DAVY RD

RENWICK RD

NEWCOMEN

MURD... RD

20

WALLIS RD

TYNE ST

STADIUM
CT

FLEMING RD

Skippers Lane
Ind Est

PARSONS
CT

AJAX WAY

BRIGGS

BOXER CT

ACHILLES CR

RENOWN
WLK

RESOURCE CL

ASH GR

BEECH GR

POPLAR GR

Liby

TS3

53

Cleveland
Ret Pk

P

A

STEPHENSON
CT

COMMERCE WAY

42

ST MAR... S GR

Prim
Schs

B

TRUNK RD

54

NORMANBY RD

IRONSTONE
CT

C

A108

A108

43

TRUNK RD A1085

PALLISTER
CT

MILLBROOK AVE

COLMORE

HIGH FARM

BRUNSWICK AVE

Evans
Bsns
Ctr

CRANFORD...

Sports Ctr

P

A2
1 OXFORD ST
2 NAPIER ST
3 MILBANK ST
4 JACKSON ST
5 MIDDLESBROUGH RD E
6 MARKET ST
7 UPPER BRANCH ST
8 SHEPHERDSON CT
9 COULTHARD CT
10 TYNE ST
11 ALAN ST
12 SOUTH CT
13 FENTON CL
14 UPPER GRAHAM ST
15 UPPER ALBION ST
16 UPPER JACKSON ST

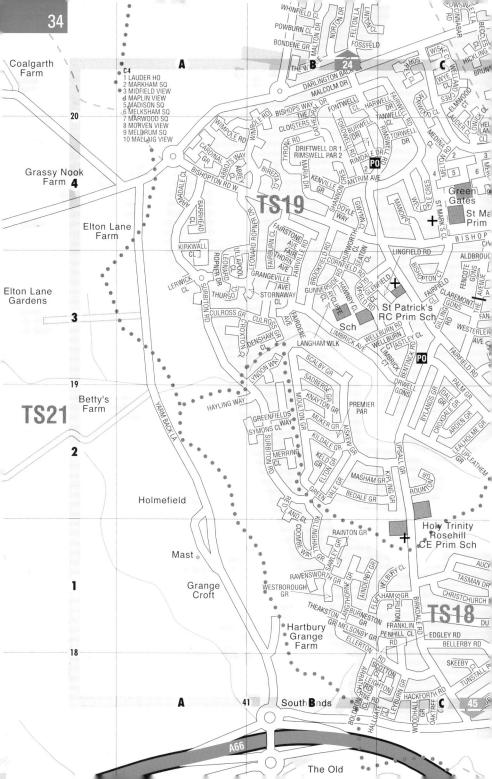

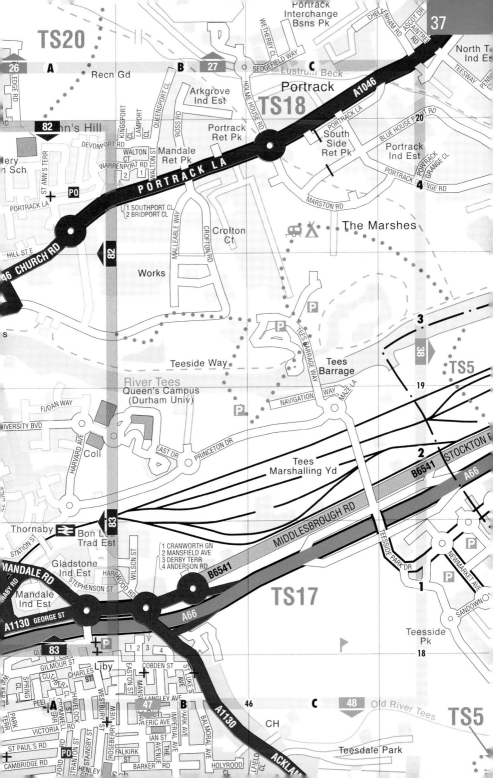

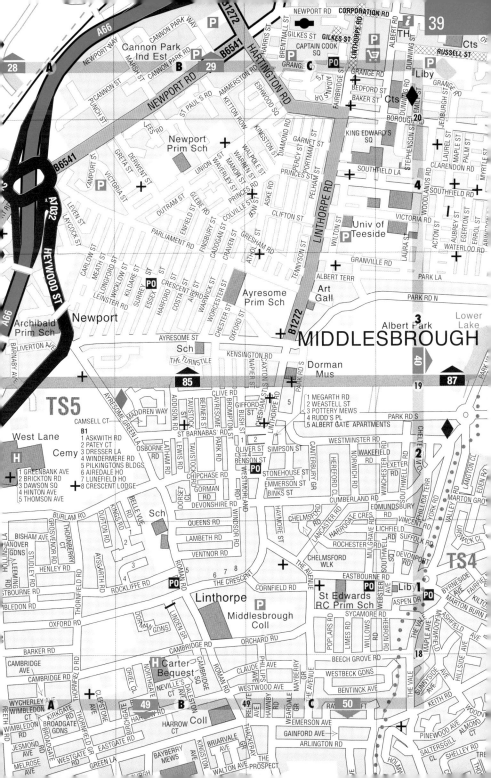

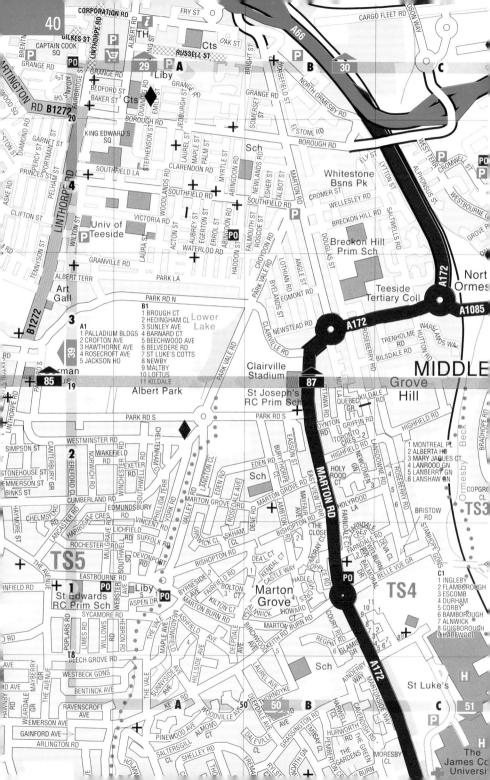

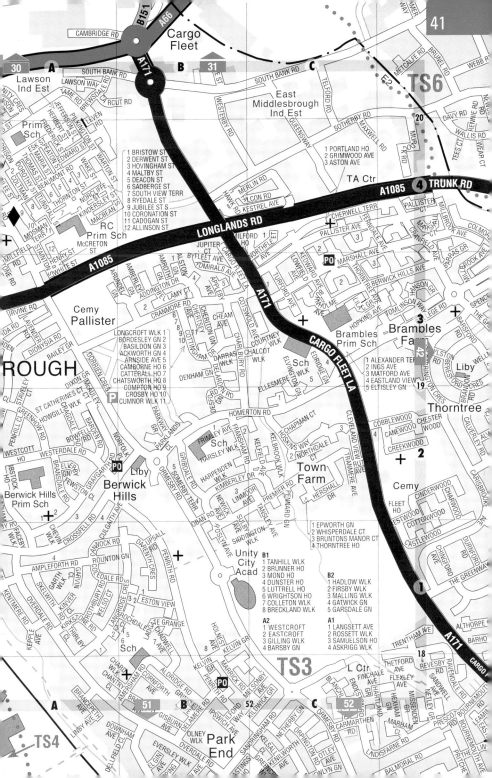

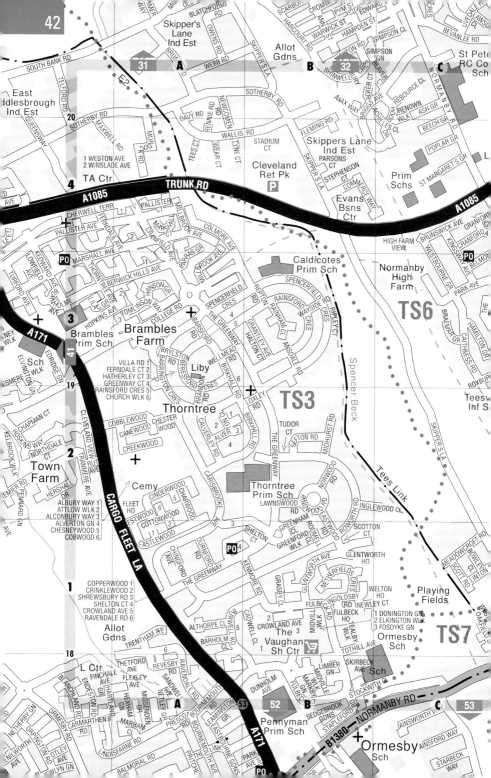

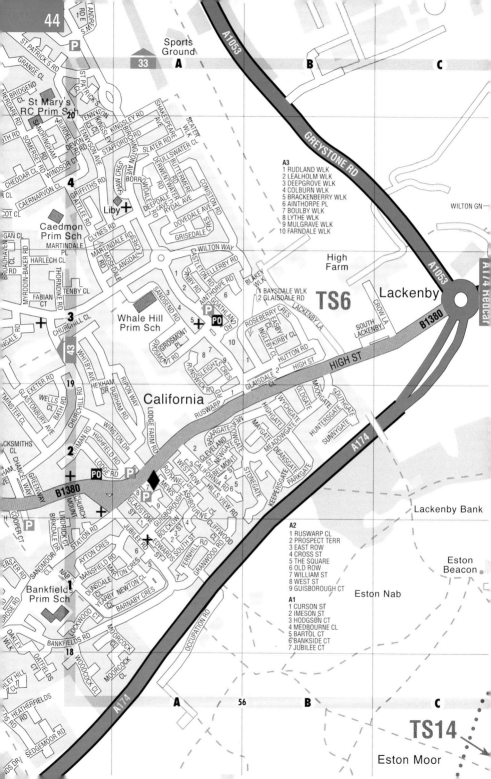

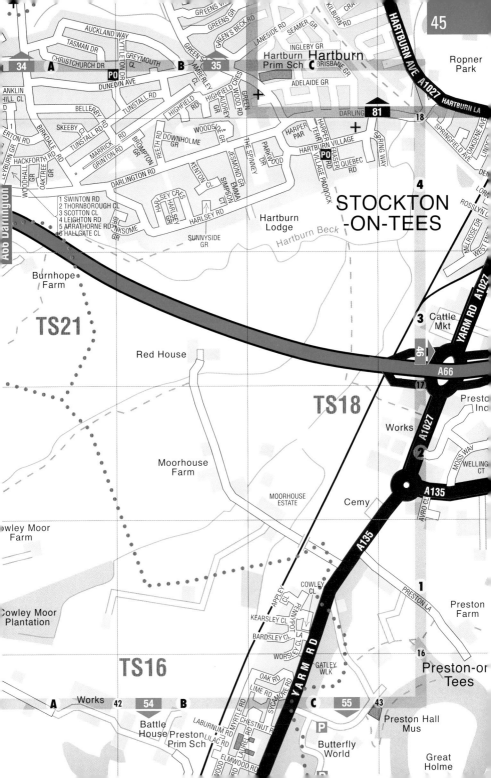

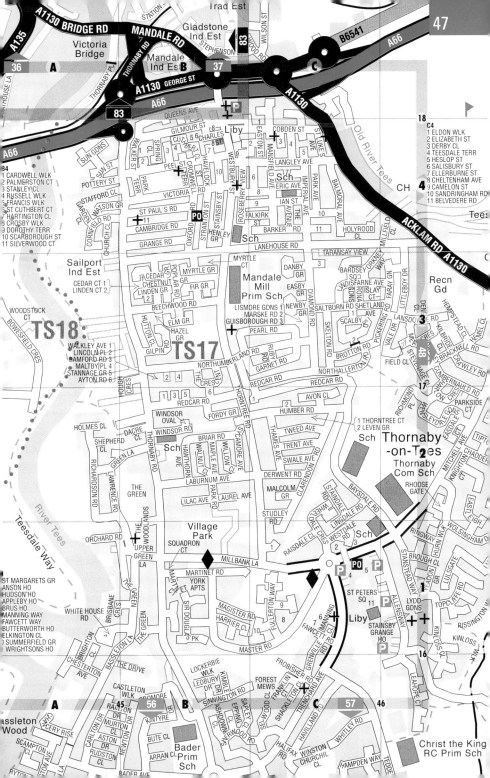

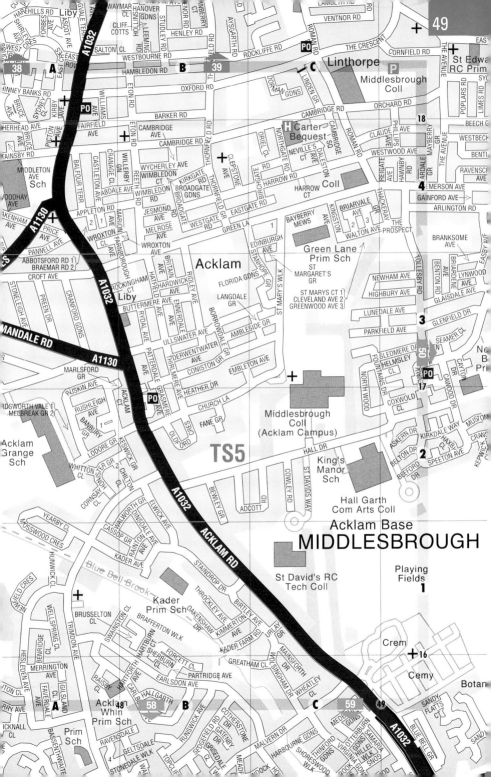

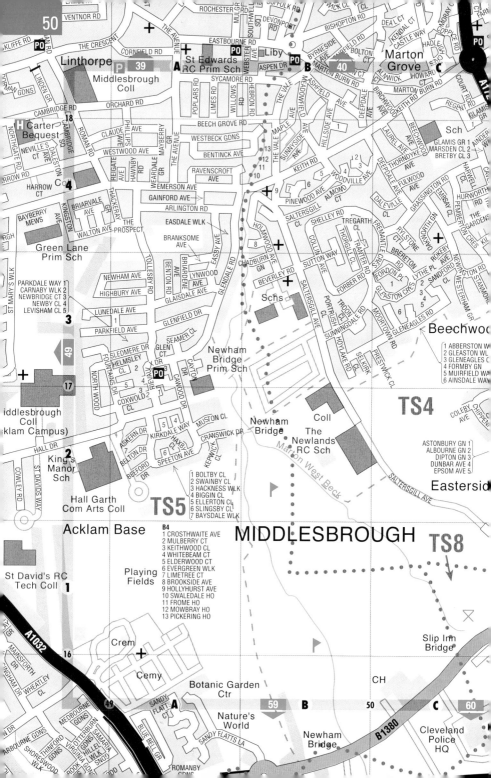

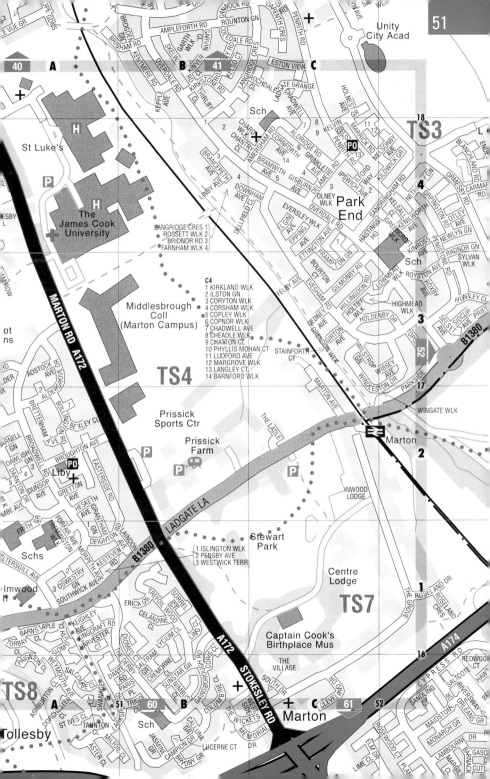

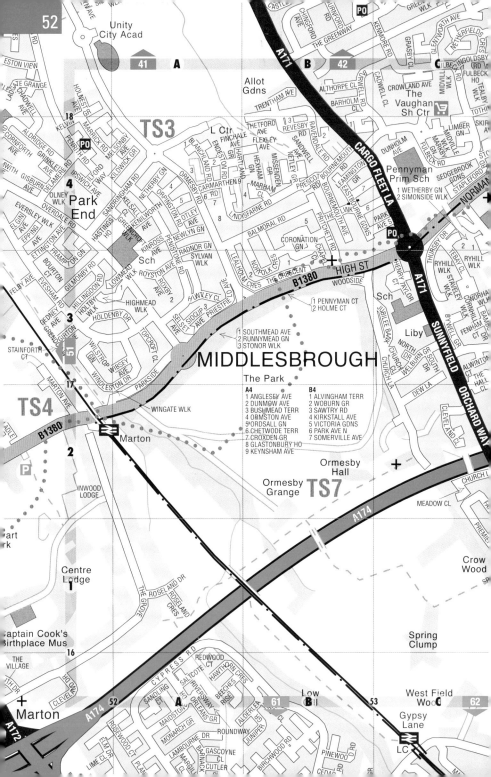

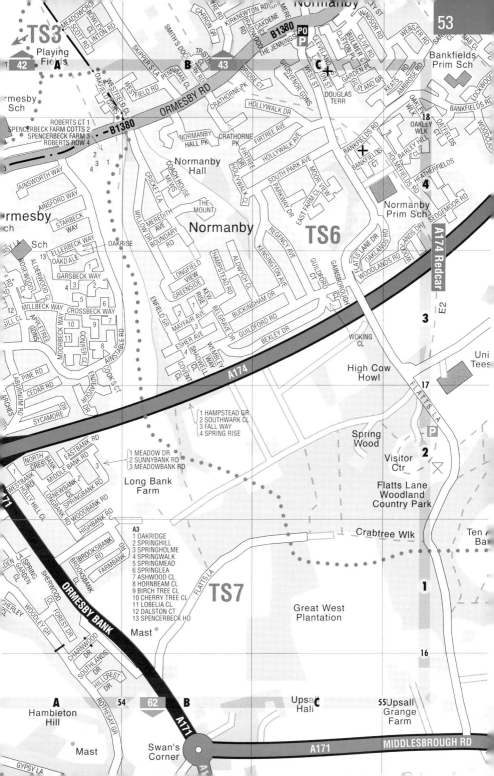

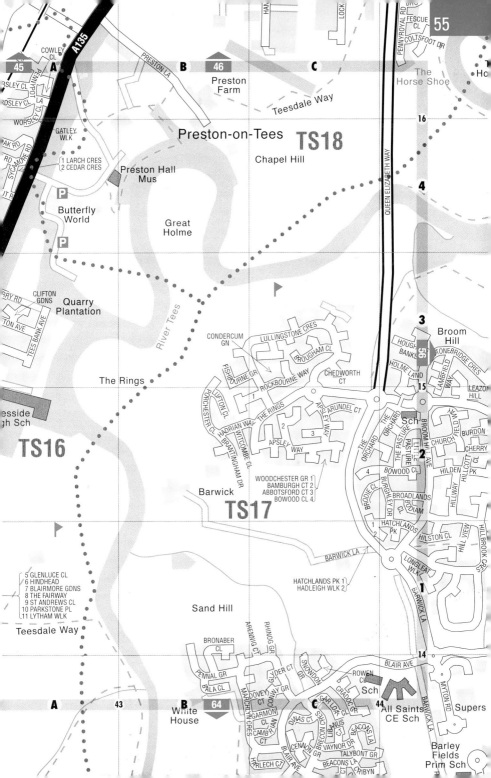

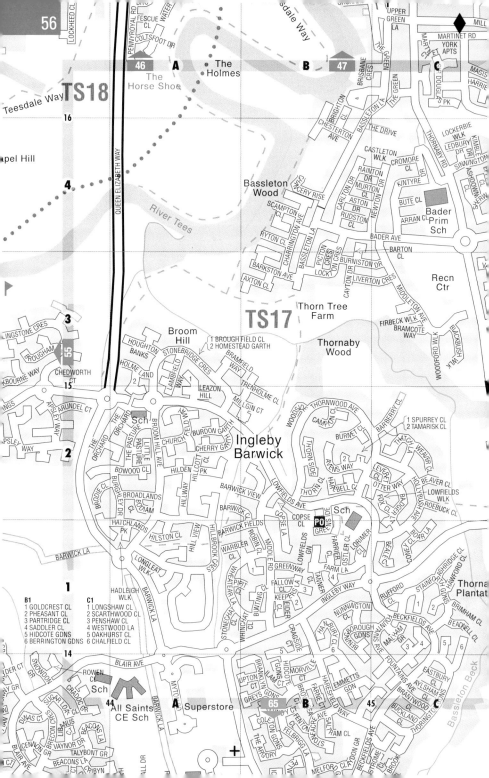

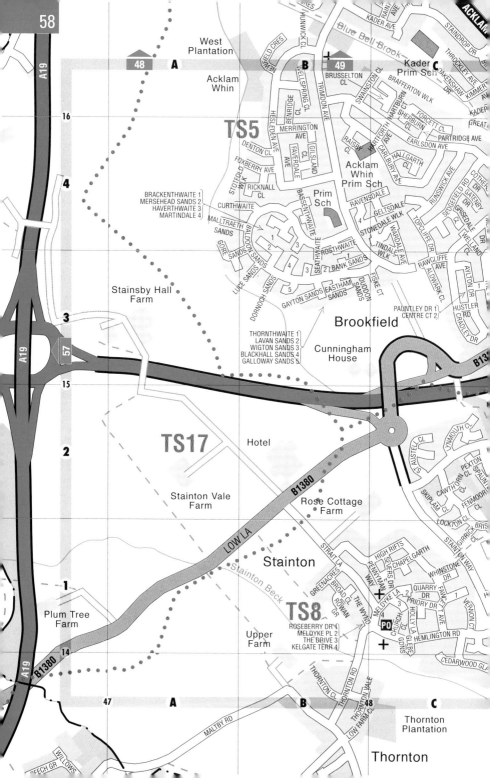

58

A19

West
Plantation

Acklam
Whin

48 A

B 49 C
BRUSSELTON
CL

Kader
Prim Sch

Kader
Prim Sch

TS5

16

4

3

57

15

2

1

A19

BRACKENTHWAITE 1
MERSEHEAD SANDS 2
HAVERTHWAITE 3
MARTINDALE 4

Acklam
Whin
Prim Sch

Prim
Sch

Stainsby Hall
Farm

Stainsby Hall
Farm

Brookfield

THORNTHWAITE 1
LAVAN SANDS 2
WIGTON SANDS 3
BLACKHALL SANDS 4
GALLOWAY SANDS 5

Cunningham
House

PAUNTLEY DR 1
CENTRE CT 2

HUSTLER
CRADLEY DR

B13

TS17

Hotel

Stainton Vale
Farm

Rose Cottage
Farm

B1380

LOW LA

Stainton Beck

Stainton

TS8

Plum Tree
Farm

Upper
Farm

ROSEBERRY DR 1
MELDYKE PL 2
THE DRIVE 3
KELGATE TERR 4

PO

A19
B1380

14

47 A B 48 C

MALTBY RD

Thornton
Plantation

Thornton

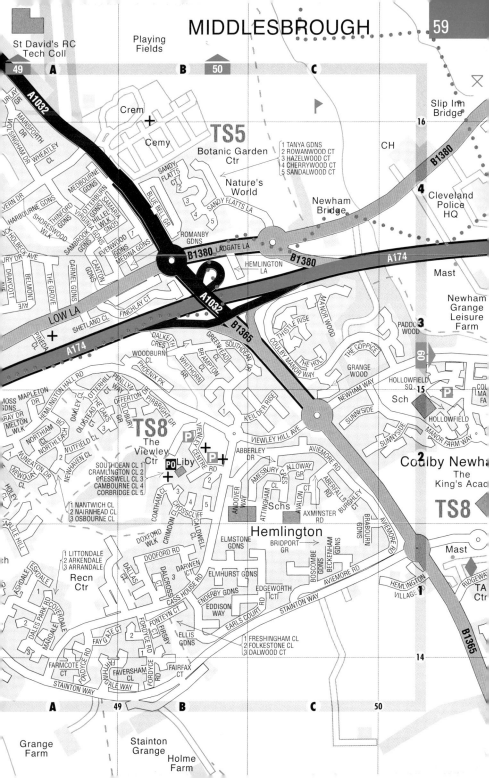

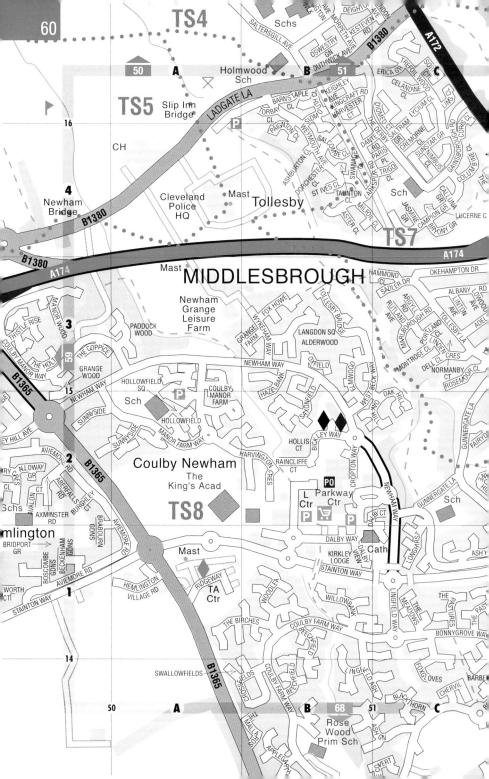

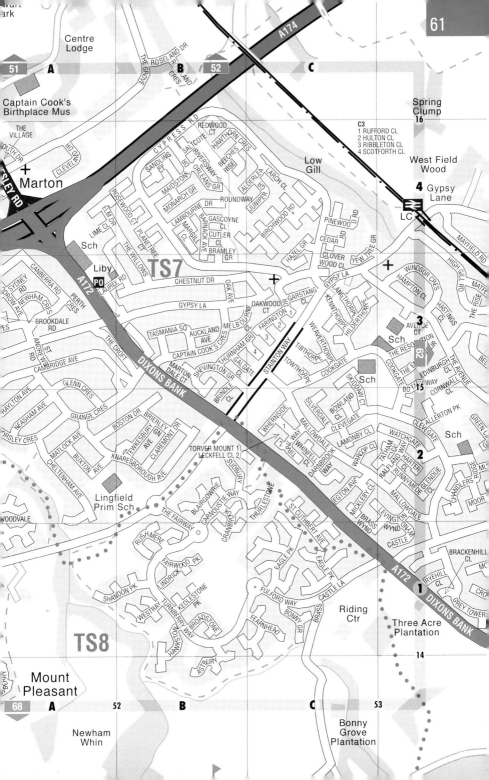

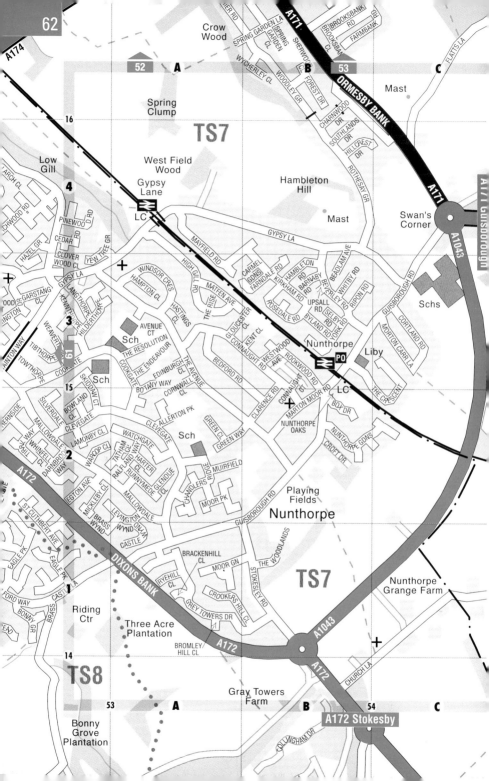

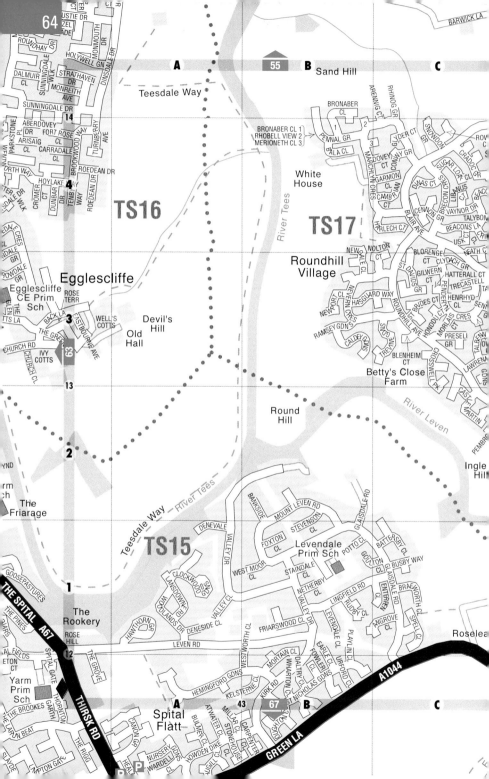

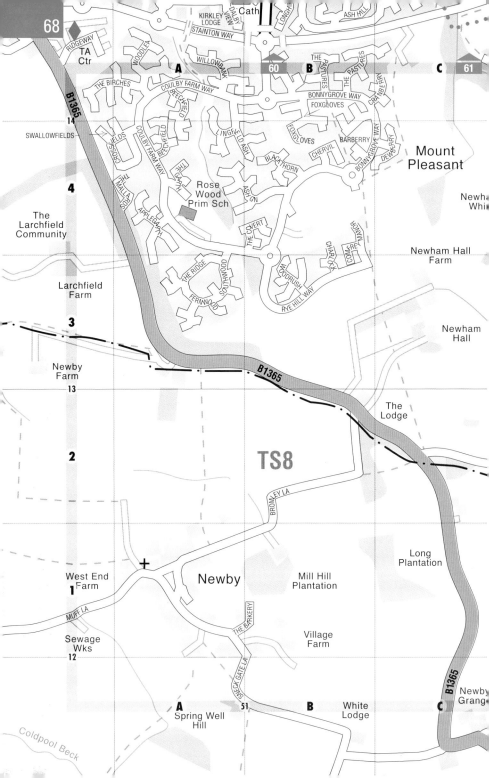

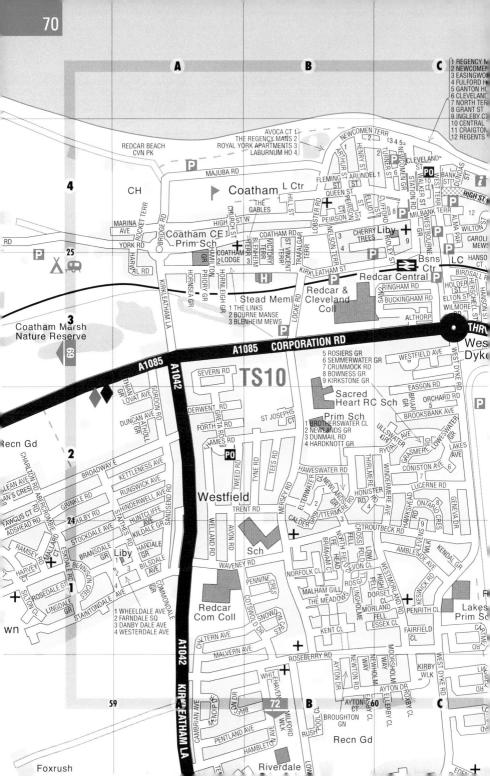

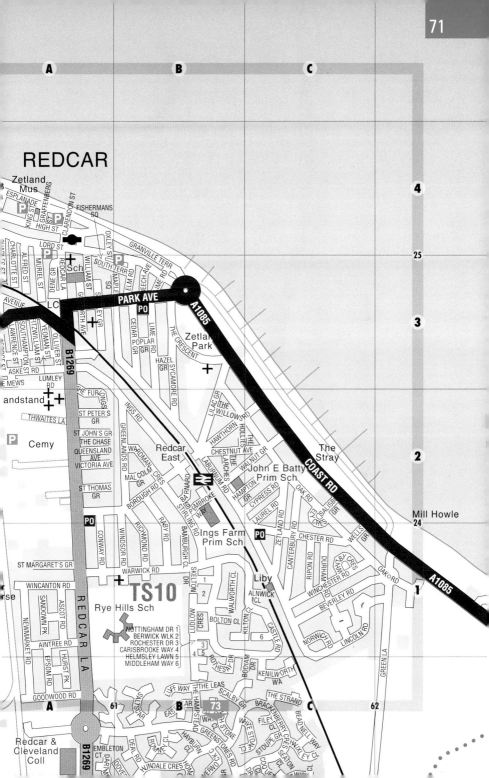

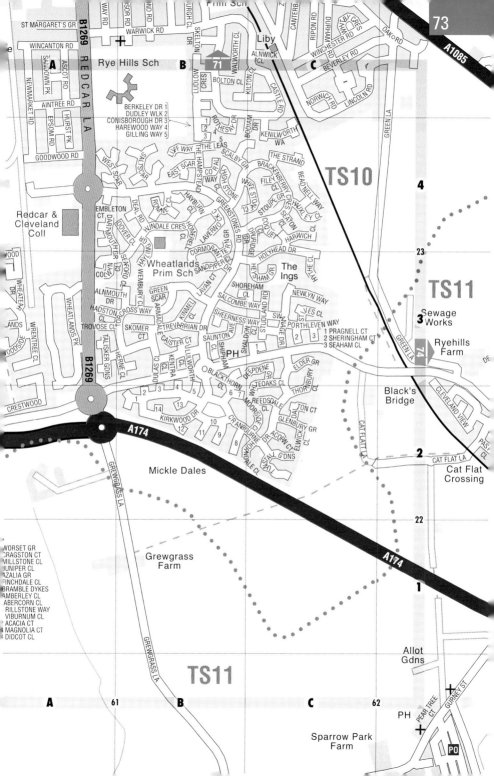

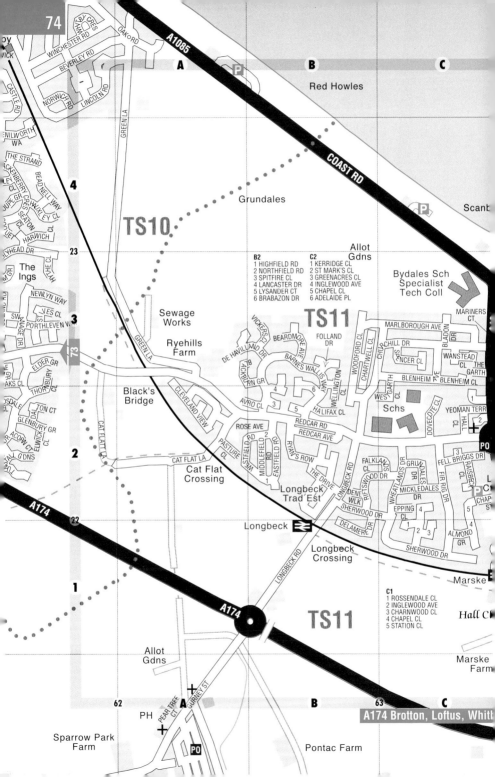

A1085

NORWICH RD
LINCOLN RD
BEVERLEY RD
WINCHESTER RD
ASHBY CRES
OAK RD
GREEN LA

P

A

B

C

Red Howles

COAST RD

P

Scant

Grundales

TS10

Allot
Gdns

B2
1 HIGHFIELD RD
2 NORTHFIELD RD
3 SPITFIRE CL
4 LANCASTER DR
5 LYSANDER CT
6 BRABAZON DR

C2
1 KERRIDGE CL
2 ST MARK'S CL
3 GREENACRES CL
4 INGLEWOOD AVE
5 CHAPEL CL
6 ADELAIDE PL

Bydales Sch
Specialist
Tech Coll

MARINERS
CT

CASTLE RD
KENILWORTH WA
THE STRAND
BEADNELL WAY
SEATON
HARWICH
REDHEAD DR
NEWLYN WAY
PORTHLEVEN WY
JVES CL

4

23

3

73

The
Ings

ELDER GR
THORNBURY
GLENBURY GR
ACORN CT

Sewage
Works

Ryehills
Farm

GREEN LA

Black's
Bridge

CLEVELAND VIEW

CAT FLAT LA

Cat Flat
Crossing

2

CAT FLAT

PASTURE CL

ROSE AVE

WESTFIELD
MIDDLEFIELD RD
EASTFIELD RD

VICKERS CL
DE HAVILLAND DR
ACORN GR
AVRO CL

BEARDMORE AV
BARNES WALLIS WAY

FOLLAND
DR

WELLINGTON WY

HALIFAX CL

REDCAR RD
REDCAR AVE

RYAN'S ROW

THE DRIVE

WOODFORD CL
CHARTWELL CL
CHURCHILL DR
SPENCER CL

MARLBOROUGH AVE

BLENHEIM CL
BLENHEIM

WEST
CL
GARTH

Schs

DOVECOTE CL

BLADON
DR

WANSTEAD
CL
THE
GARTH

YEOMAN TERR

HALL

PO

TS11

LONGBECK RD
DENE
WLK
SHERWOOD DR
DELAMERE DR
EPPING
CL

FALKLAN
RIFTSWOOD DR
WHEATLANDS DR
GRUNDALES DR
MICKLEDALES DR

FELL BRIGGS DR
FIR RIG DR
RAISBECK

ALMOND
GR

SHERWOOD DR

CHAP
ST

L

P

C

A174

22

1

A174

Longbeck
Trad Est

Longbeck

Longbeck
Crossing

Marske

C1
1 ROSSENDALE CL
2 INGLEWOOD AVE
3 CHARNWOOD CL
4 CHAPEL CL
5 STATION CL

Hall Cl

E

Marske
Farm

Allot
Gdns

TS11

62

A

B

63

C

PEAR TREE CT
GURNEY ST

PH

PO

Sparrow Park
Farm

Pontac Farm

A   B   C

4

23

MARSKE-
BY-THE-SEA

Marske Sands

Stone
Gap

3

Cemy

2

TS11

22

1

Windy Hil
Farm

ile

H. HEADLANDS
THE FIRLANDS
THE KIRKLANDS

ST GERMAIN'S LA

RYEHILLS DR

1 DUNSDALE CL
2 CORNGRAVE CL

RCH
4
NS LA

ST
GERMAIN'S
GR
Liby   Sch

CHURCH CL
VICARAGE DR
SCHOOL CL

KIRKLATHAM AVE
SCARBECK DR
PENNYMAN
WLK

2

TOFTS CL

CHURCH HOWLE CRES

HUMMERS HILL LA

PRIESTCROFTS
SKELTON DR
BYDALES DR

WARSETT RD

YEARBY CRES

HOWARD
DR

ST
FTON PL

MOUNT
PLEASANT
AVE
EAST
MDWS

SOUTHFIELD RD

RONALDSHAY TERR
ZETLAND
RD

3

WINDY HILL LA

MORDALES DR

DRAKE
CL

RALEIGH
CL

WINDY HILL LA

MEADOW RD

LAVENDER
CT

LIMES CRES

3
4
5
2
1

WETHERELL
CL
LORAINE
CL

HAMBLETON CRES

HAWKINS
CL

FENNER CL
SEYMOUR CL

GRENVILLE
CL
FROBISHER CL

HOWARD DR

DALE
GARTH

ROSEMARY
COTTS

B1
1 WHEATACRE CL
2 BARNABY CL
3 MORDALES DR
4 THRUSHWOOD CRES
5 ERRINGTON GARTH

A2
1 KING EDWARD TERR
2 THE CRESCENT
3 FITZWILLIAM CL

Tofts Farm

TS12

LC

A
G

76

MARTON
THE PARKWAY

A1085

A174

QUARRY LA

A   64

B   65

C

MARSKE RD

OX CLOSE
COTTS

Marske End
Farm

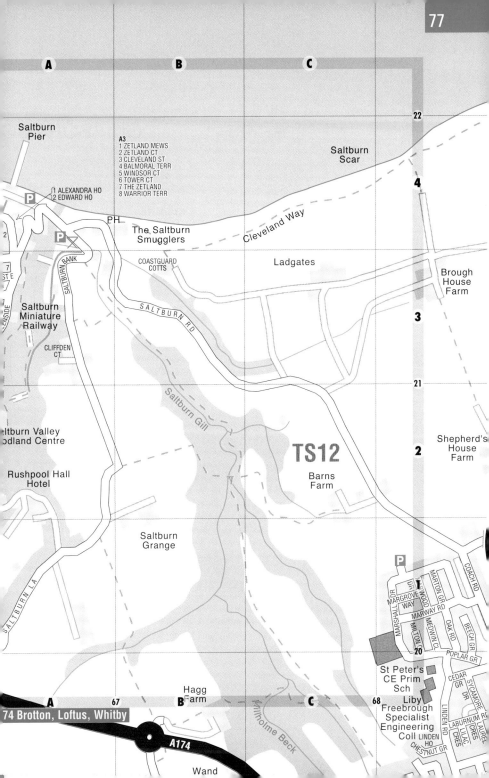

Saltburn
Pier

A3
1 ZETLAND MEWS
2 ZETLAND CT
3 CLEVELAND ST
4 BALMORAL TERR
5 WINDSOR CT
6 TOWER CT
7 THE ZETLAND
8 WARRIOR TERR

Saltburn
Scar

22

4

1 ALEXANDRA HO
2 EDWARD HO

PH

The Saltburn
Smugglers

Cleveland Way

Ladgates

COASTGUARD
COTTS

Brough
House
Farm

SALTBURN BANK

Saltburn
Miniature
Railway

SALTBURN RD

3

CLIFFDEN
CT

21

Saltburn Gill

ltburn Valley
odland Centre

TS12

2

Shepherd's
House
Farm

Rushpool Hall
Hotel

Barns
Farm

Saltburn
Grange

SALTBURN LA

P

MARGROVE WAY

MARSHALL DR

DI... WOOD

MARTON GR

COACH RD

MARWAY RD

MILTON CL

MEDWIN CL

OAK RD

BEECH GR

POPLAR GR

20

St Peter's
CE Prim
Sch

CEDAR GR

SYCAMORE DR

LABURNUM RD

LINDEN RD

Liby
Freebrough
Specialist
Engineering
Coll

LINDEN
HO

CHESTNUT GR

LILAC CRES

A

67

B

Hagg
Farm

C

68

Millholme Beck

A174

Wand

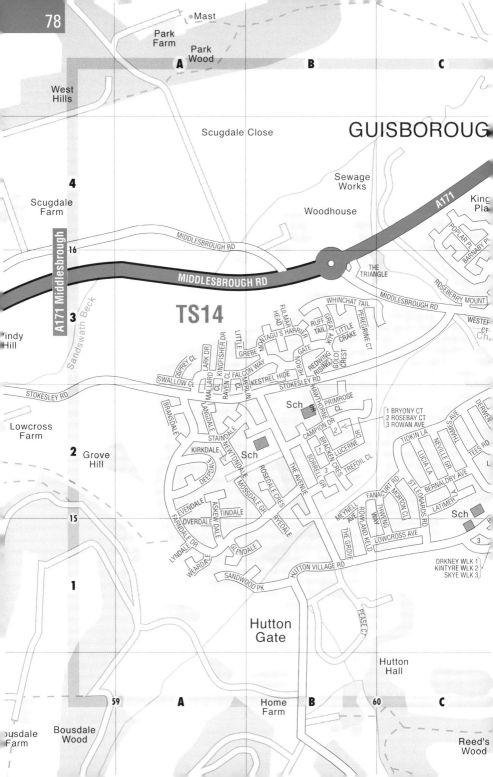

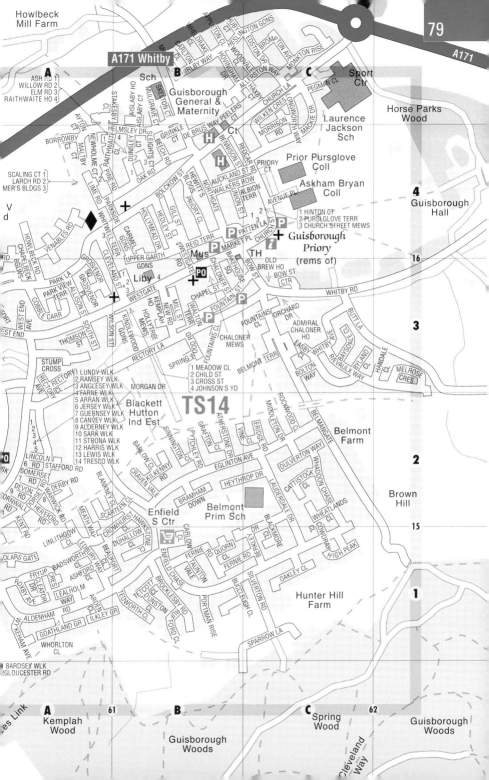

A171 Whitby

A171

Howlbeck
Mill Farm

A
ASH RD 1
WILLOW RD 2
ELM RD 3
RAITHWAITE HO 4

Sch

B

Guisborough
General &
Maternity

C

Sport
Ctr

Horse Parks
Wood

Laurence
Jackson
Sch

BORROWBY
CT

SCALING CT 1
LARCH RD 2
MER'S BLDGS 3

V
d

Prior Pursglove
Coll

Askham Bryan
Coll

1 HINTON CT
2 PURSLGLOVE TERR
3 CHURCH STREET MEWS

4
Guisborough
Hall

Guisborough
Priory
(rems of)

16

Liby

WHITBY RD

3

OLD
BREW HO
CTR

BOW ST

STUMP
CROSS

1 LUNDY WLK
2 RAMSEY WLK
3 ANGLESEY WLK
4 FARNE WLK
5 ARRAN WLK
6 JERSEY WLK
7 GUERNSEY WLK
8 CANVEY WLK
9 ALDERNEY WLK
10 SARK WLK
11 STRONA WLK
12 HARRIS WLK
13 LEWIS WLK
14 TRESCO WLK

1 MEADOW CL
2 CHILD ST
3 CROSS ST
4 JOHNSON'S YD

Blackett
Hutton
Ind Est

TS14

Belmont
Farm

LINCOLN
RD

SOMERSET
RD

Belmont
Prim Sch

Enfield
S Ctr

Brown
Hill

15

2

OLARS GATE

Hunter Hill
Farm

1

BARDSEY WLK
GLOUCESTER RD

A
61
Kemplah
Wood

B
Guisborough
Woods

C
62
Spring
Wood

Guisborough
Woods

Cleveland Way

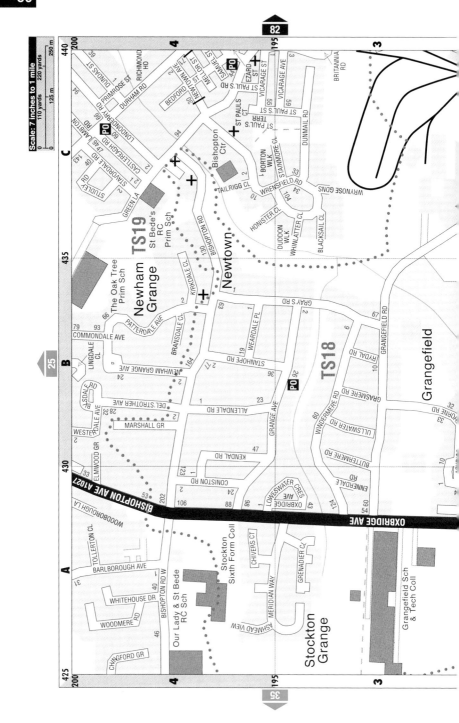

Scale: 7 inches to 1 mile

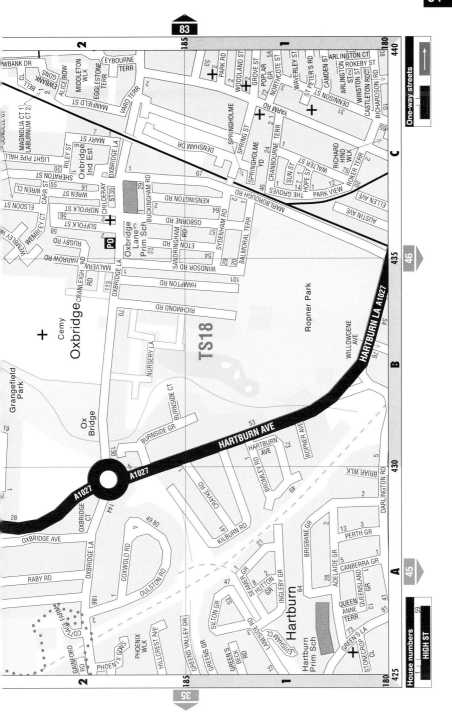

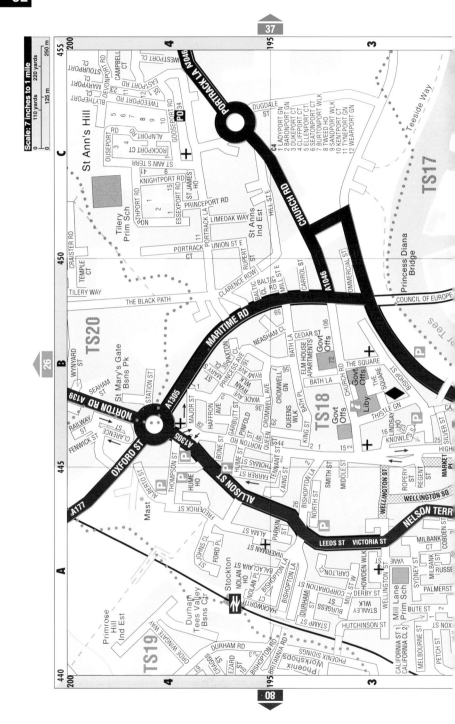

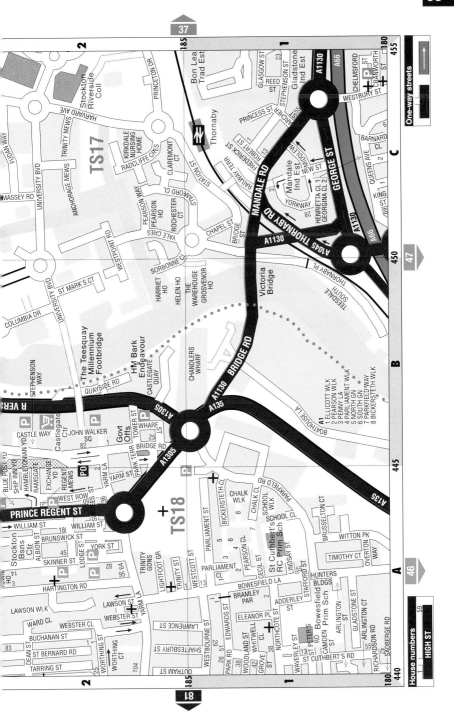

One-way streets

House numbers

59

HIGH ST

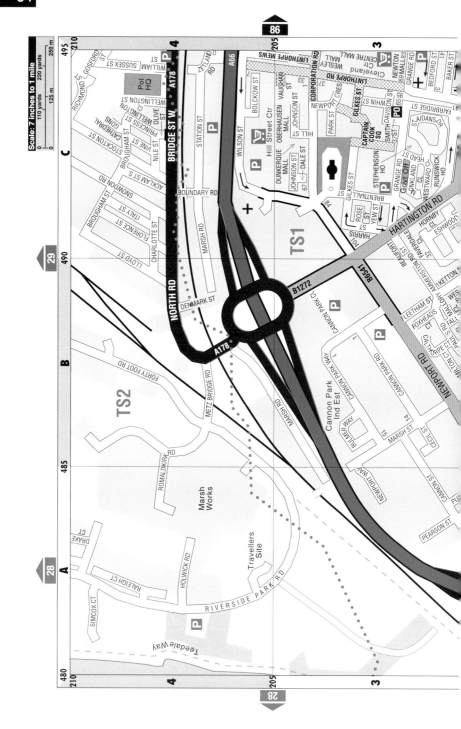

Scale: 7 inches to 1 mile

0   110 yards   220 yards
0   125 m   250 m

TS2

TS1

Marsh Works

Travellers Site

Cannon Park Ind Est

Pol HQ

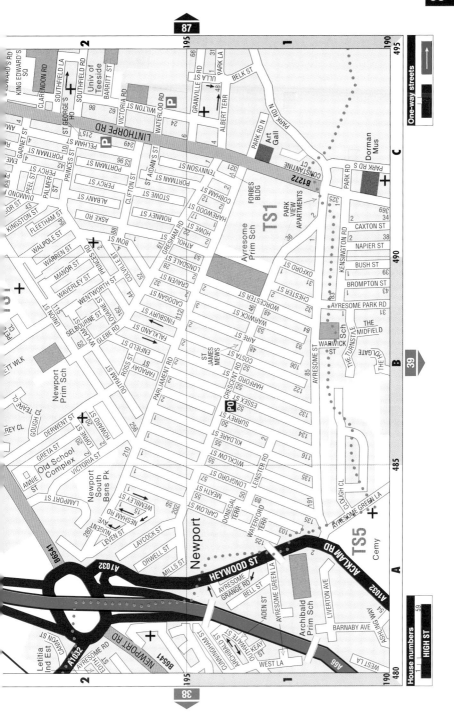

87
38
39

One-way streets

House numbers 59

HIGH ST

Scale: 7 inches to 1 mile

Dock Point

Riverside Stadium (Middlesbrough F.C.)

TS3

Teesdale Way

Middlesbrough Dock

THE HALYARD

SHEPHERDSON WAY

CARGO FLEET RD

THE LEEWAY

DOCKSIDE RD

LC

MARSH RD

A66

TS4

WINDWARD WAY

A66

CARGO FLEET RD

WOODSIDE ST

TATHUA CT

DORSETFIELD ST

STONE ST

CRAGGS ST

WHARF

NORTH ORMESP

PALIN CL

DINSDALE

HL

GRANGE RD

BRIGHT ST

RUSSELL ST

HAZEL CT

ELDER CT

CT

114

96

80

20

96

232

BEECH ST

OAK ST

ELLIOT ST

79

Cleveland Bsns Ctr

WATSON ST

ELM ST

FRY ST

PEACOCK ST

CORPORATION RD

Cts

RUSSELL ST

Central Gardens

GRANGE RD

MONTROSE ST

35

091

46

VULCAN ST

COMMERCIAL ST

TS2

GRAY ST

DOCK ST

SCOTT'S RD

LOWER EAST ST

LOWER FEVERSHAM ST

REDCAR ST

BROOK ST

LOWER GOSFORD ST

BRIDGE ST E

ST

SPRING ST

SCHOOL

CROFT

ZETLAND PL

EXCHANGE

Middlesbrough

WOOD ST

JACK HATFIELD SQ

KING HO

PARKINSON HO

PHILLIPS HO

RICKMAN HO

HODGES HO

FORSTER HO

WILSON ST

PINE ST

DUNNING ST

ALBERT MEWS

GURNEY ST

Council Offs

TH

ALBERT RD

Art Gall

Liby

DUNNING ST

Cts

CLEVELAND ST

A178

EAST ST

FEVERSHAM ST

GOSFORD ST

ALBERT ST

BRIDGE ST W

QUEEN'S SQ

QUEEN'S TERR

ZETLAND RD

BRUNSWICK ST

DUNDAS ST

DUNDAS MEWS

DUNDAS ARC

FLETCHER ST

CLEVELAND ST

9

31

33

81

127 SQ

210

495

500

505

510

210

205

205

29

30

30

A

B

C

4

A66

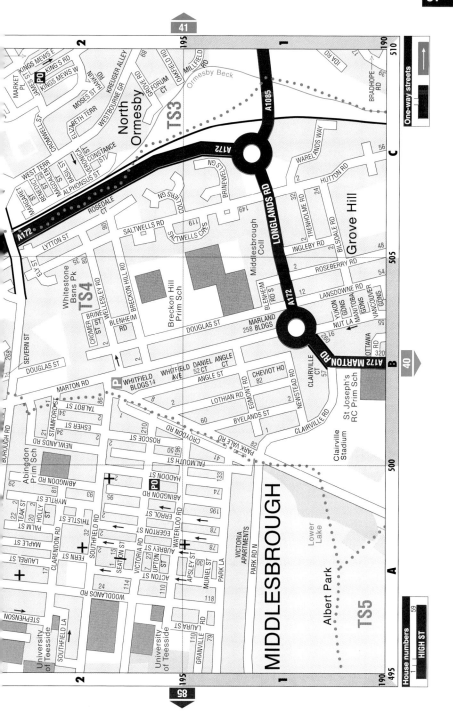

One-way streets

1
190
510

MARKET PL
KINGS MEWS E
KING'S RD
KINGS MEWS W
JAMES ST
HANN
MOSES ST
KREUGER ALLEY
FORUM CT
GROVE RD
OXFIELD RD
MILLFIELD
IDA RD
CROMWELL ST
ELIZ'BETH TERR
WESTBOURNE GR
Ormesby Beck
BRADHOPE RD
39
North
Ormesby
WEST TERR
BENEDICT ST
MAGDALEN ST
BASIL ST
JERNICA
CONSTANCE
ALPHONSUS ST
TS3
A1085
WARELANDS WAY
56
C
MARGARET
ROSEDALE CT
COLLIERS GN
BRIMEWELL'S GN
A172
HUTTON RD
A172
LYTTON ST
SALTWELLS RD
SALTWELLS CRES
119
LONGLANDS RD
TRENHOLME RD
24
INGLEBY RD
BILSDALE RD
Grove Hill
ELY ST
90
Middlesbrough Coll
48
505
Whitestone Bsns Pk
TS4
BRECKON HILL RD
WELLESLEY RD
Breckon Hill Prim Sch
BLENHEIM RD S
ROSEBERRY RD
LANSDOWNE RD
54
VANCOUVER GDNS
CROMER ST
BRINEL ST
BLENHEIM RD
DOUGLAS ST
BLENHEIM RD S
12
YUKON GDNS
MANITOBA
NUT LA
55
SEVERN ST
2
MARLAND BLDGS
258
OTTAWA RD
320
268
DOUGLAS ST
WHITFIELD BLDGS
WHITFIELD
DANIEL ANGLE CT
ANGLE ST
CLAIRVILLE CT
B
40
BOROUGH RD
MARTON RD
TALBOT ST
STAMFORD ST
ESHER ST
CROYDON RD
LOTHIAN RD
EGMONT RD
NEWSTEAD RD
CHEVIOT HO
82
St Joseph's RC Prim Sch
500
NEWLANDS RD
Abingdon Prim Sch
29
ROSCOE ST
BYELANDS ST
CLAIRVILLE RD
Clairville Stadium
MYRTLE ST
THISTLE ST
FALMOUTH ST
PARK VALE RD
PALM ST
TEAK ST
HOLLY ST
HADDON ST
ABINGDON RD
ABINGDON RD
ERROL ST
MAPLE ST
CLARENDON RD
FERN ST
SOUTHFIELD RD
EGERTON ST
AUBREY ST
WATERLOO RD
VICTORIA RD
VICTORIA APARTMENTS
PARK RD N
LAUREL ST
SEATON ST
UPTON ST
APSLEY ST
MURIEL ST
PARK LA
ACTON ST
WOODLANDS RD
LAURA ST
GRANVILLE RD
STEPHENSON
University of Teesside
SOUTHFIELD LA
University of Teesside
MIDDLESBROUGH
Albert Park
Lower Lake
TS5
A

House numbers 59
HIGH ST

Index

Street names are listed alphabetically and show the locality, the Postcode district, the page number and a reference to the square in which the name falls on the map page

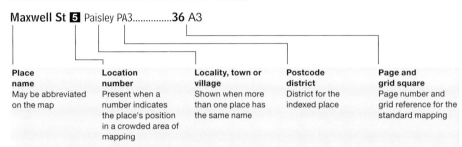

Maxwell St 5 Paisley PA3............36 A3

Place name	**Location number**	**Locality, town or village**	**Postcode district**	**Page and grid square**
May be abbreviated on the map	Present when a number indicates the place's position in a crowded area of mapping	Shown when more than one place has the same name	District for the indexed place	Page number and grid reference for the standard mapping

Towns and villages are listed in CAPITAL LETTERS
Public and commercial buildings are highlighted in **magenta. Places of interest** are highlighted in blue with a star*

Abbreviations used in the index

Acad	**Academy**	Ct	**Court**	Hts	**Heights**	Pl	**Place**
App	**Approach**	Ctr	**Centre**	Ind	**Industrial**	Prec	**Precinct**
Arc	**Arcade**	Ctry	**Country**	Inst	**Institute**	Prom	**Promenade**
Ave	**Avenue**	Cty	**County**	Int	**International**	Rd	**Road**
Bglw	**Bungalow**	Dr	**Drive**	Intc	**Interchange**	Recn	**Recreation**
Bldg	**Building**	Dro	**Drove**	Junc	**Junction**	Ret	**Retail**
Bsns, Bus	**Business**	Ed	**Education**	L	**Leisure**	Sh	**Shopping**
Bvd	**Boulevard**	Emb	**Embankment**	La	**Lane**	Sq	**Square**
Cath	**Cathedral**	Est	**Estate**	Liby	**Library**	St	**Street**
Cir	**Circus**	Ex	**Exhibition**	Mdw	**Meadow**	Sta	**Station**
Cl	**Close**	Gd	**Ground**	Meml	**Memorial**	Terr	**Terrace**
Cnr	**Corner**	Gdn	**Garden**	Mkt	**Market**	TH	**Town Hall**
Coll	**College**	Gn	**Green**	Mus	**Museum**	Univ	**University**
Com	**Community**	Gr	**Grove**	Orch	**Orchard**	Wk, Wlk	**Walk**
Comm	**Common**	H	**Hall**	Pal	**Palace**	Wr	**Water**
Cott	**Cottage**	Ho	**House**	Par	**Parade**	Yd	**Yard**
Cres	**Crescent**	Hospl	**Hospital**	Pas	**Passage**		
Cswy	**Causeway**	HQ	**Headquarters**	Pk	**Park**		

Index of towns, villages, streets, hospitals, industrial estates, railway stations, schools, shopping centres, universities and places of interest

Abb–Alb

A

Abberley Dr TS8 ..... 59 C2
Abberston Wlk TS4 .. 50 C3
Abbey Cl TS19 .... 34 A4
Abbey Ct TS6 .... 43 B2
Abbeyfield Dr TS16 .. 54 B1
Abbey Hill Sch & Tech
  Coll TS19 .... 25 A2
Abbey St TS24 ....7 B2
Abbotsford Ct TS17 .. 55 C2
Abbotsford Rd TS5... 49 A4
Abbots Way TS19 .... 34 A4
Abdale Ave TS5 ...... 49 A4
Abdeil Ho TS24 ...... 6 C1
Aberbran Cl TS17 .... 64 C3
Abercorn Cl 9 TS10 . 73 B2
Abercrombie Rd
  TS10 .... 69 C2
Aberdare Rd TS6..... 33 B1

Aberdeen Rd TS25 ... 12 B3
Aberdovey Dr TS16.. . 63 C4
Aberfalls Rd TS8..... 59 C2
Abigail Wlk 3 TS24... 6 A1
Abingdon Prim Sch
  TS1 .... 87 A2
Abingdon Rd TS1 .... 87 A2
Acacia Cl 12 TS10... 73 B2
Acacia Rd TS19 ..... 25 C1
Acclom St TS24....... 5 C1
Achilles Cl TS6 ..... 42 C4
ACKLAM 49 B3
ACKLAM BASE 49 C1
Acklam Ct TS5....... 49 B2
Acklam Grange Sch
  TS5 .... 49 A2
Acklam Rd
  Middlesbrough TS5... 49 B1
  Thornaby-on-T TS17 .. 48 A4
Acklam St N TS2..... 29 B3
Acklam St S TS2..... 84 C4
Acklam Whin Prim Sch
  TS5 .... 58 B4
Ackworth Gn TS3 .... 41 B3

Acorn Bank TS17 .... 65 B3
Acorn Ct TS10 ...... 73 C2
Acton St TS1 .... 87 A2
Adam Cl TS10........ 72 B3
Adam St TS18........ 46 C3
Adcott Rd TS5 ...... 49 B2
Adderley St TS18 .... 83 A1
Addington Dr TS3.... 41 B3
Addison Rd
  Hartlepool TS24 ...... 6 A1
  Middlesbrough TS5.... 39 B2
Adelaide Gr TS18 .... 81 A1
Adelaide Pl 6 TS11.. 74 C2
Adelaide Rd TS7 .... 60 C3
Aden St TS5 .... 85 A1
Admiral Chaloner Ho
  TS14 .... 79 C3
Admiral Ho TS24..... 10 B4
Admirals Ave TS3 ... 41 B3
Admiral Way TS24 ... 10 B4
Adshead Rd TS10 ... 69 C1
Adstock Ave TS4 .... 51 A3
Agecroft Gdns TS5.. 38 C1
Ainderby Gr TS18 ... 34 B1

Ainderby Way TS4 ... 50 C4
Ainderby Wlk TS24... 6 A3
Ainsdale Way TS4... 50 C3
Ainsford Way TS7 ... 53 A4
Ainsley St TS25 ..... 10 B2
Ainstable Rd TS7 ... 53 A3
Ainsworth Way TS7 .. 53 A4
Ainthorpe Pl 6 TS6.. 44 A3
Ainthorpe Rd TS6.... 44 A3
Aintree Oval
  Middlesbrough
  TS17 .... 38 B2
  Thornaby-on-T TS17 .. 38 A4
Aintree Rd
  Redcar TS10 .... 71 A1
  Stockton-on-T TS18... 27 C1
Airdrie Gr TS25 ..... 12 A3
Aireborough Cl TS19. 25 A1
Airedale Ho 6 TS5... 39 B1
Aire St
  Middlesbrough TS1... 85 B1
  South Bank TS6...... 36 A2
Aiskew Gr TS19 ..... 34 B2
Aislaby Ct TS14 ..... 79 B5

Aislaby Gr TS23 ..... 17 B3
Aislaby Ho TS14 ..... 79 B5
Aislaby Rd TS16...... 63 A3
Ajax Way TS6 .... 32 A1
Alan St 11 TS6 ...... 32 A2
Albany Ct 9 TS26.....9 B4
Albany Rd
  Marton TS7 .... 59 C2
  Stockton-on-T TS20... 26 C3
Albany St TS1........ 85 C2
Alberta Ho TS4 ..... 40 B2
Albert Ct 6 TS12 ... 76 C4
Albert Gate Apartments
  TS5 .... 39 C2
Albert Mews TS1 .... 86 A3
Alberto St TS18...... 82 A4
Albert Rd
  Eaglescliffe TS16 .... 54 C2
  Eston TS6 .... 43 B2
  Middlesbrough TS5.... 86 A3
  Stockton-on-T TS19... 34 C3
Albert St
  Hartlepool TS24 ..... 10 A3
  Middlesbrough TS2... 86 A4

Albert Terr TS1 . . . . . . 85 C1
Albion St TS18 . . . . . . 83 A2
Albion Terr
  Guisborough TS14 . . . . 79 C4
  Hartlepool TS24 . . . . 7 B2
  Saltburn-by-t-S TS12. . . 76 C3
Albourne Gn TS4 . . . 51 A2
Albury Way TS3. . . . . 42 A2
Alconbury Way TS3 . 42 A2
Aldbrough Cl TS19 . . 34 C3
Aldeburgh Cl TS25 . . 14 B4
Aldenham Rd TS14. . 79 A1
Aldergrove Dr TS4 . . 51 A3
Alderlea TS7 . . . . 61 C4
Alderney Wlk TS14. . 79 A2
Alder Rd TS19 . . . . . 25 C1
Alderson St [2] TS26. . . 9 B3
Alderwood TS8 . . . . . 60 B3
Alderwood Cl
  Hartlepool TS27 . . . . . . 2 B2
  Ormesby TS7. . . . . . . 53 A3
Aldridge Rd TS3 . . . 51 C4
Aldwark Cl TS5 . . . . 58 C3
Aldwych Cl TS6 . . . . 53 B3
Alexander Terr TS1. . 85 C1
Alexandra Ho TS12. . 77 A4
Alexandra Rd TS6. . . 33 A2
Alford Ct TS25 . . . . . 12 B3
Alford La TS19 . . . . . 25 A1
Alfred St
  Hartlepool TS24 . . . . . . 7 B3
  Redcar TS10 . . . . 71 A3
Alfriston Cl [3] TS17 . 65 B4
Alice Row TS18 . . . . 81 C2
Alice St TS20 . . . . . . 26 B4
Alison Pl TS24 . . . . . . 7 B3
Allendale Rd
  Billingham TS23 . . . . . 21 A3
  Ormesby TS7. . . . . . . 53 A3
  Stockton-on-T TS18. . . 80 B4
Allendale St TS25 . . . 13 C2
Allensway TS17 . . . . . 48 A1
Allens West Sta
  TS16 . . . . 54 A2
Allerford Cl TS17. . . . 65 B2
Allerston Way TS14 . 79 C5
Allerton Balk TS15 . . 66 A3
Allerton Cl TS24 . . . . . 6 A2
Allerton Pk TS7 . . . . 62 A2
Alliance St TS24 . . . . . 7 B3
Allington Dr TS23 . . 17 A2
Allington Wlk TS23 . 17 A2
Allinson St TS3 . . . . 41 A4
Allison St
  Guisborough TS14 . . . 79 A3
  Stockton-on-T TS18. . . 82 A4
Alloa Gr TS25 . . . . . . 12 B3
Alloway Gr TS8 . . . . . 59 C2
All Saints CE Sch
  TS17 . . . . 65 A4
Alma Par TS10 . . . . . 70 C4
Alma St
  Hartlepool TS26 . . . . . . 9 B4
  Stockton-on-T TS18. . . 82 A4
Almond Ct TS4 . . . . . 50 B4
Almond Gr
  Marske-by-t-S TS11 . . 74 C1
  Stockton-on-T TS19. . . 35 A3
Alness Gr TS25 . . . . . 12 B3
Alnmouth Dr TS10 . . 73 A3
Alnport Rd TS18 . . . 82 C4
Alnwick [7] TS4 . . . . 40 C1
Alnwick Cl
  Hartlepool TS27 . . . . . . 2 C1
  Redcar TS10 . . . . 71 C1
Alnwick Cr TS4 . . . . 40 B1
Alnwick Gr TS20 . . . 20 B1
Alpha Gr TS20 . . . . . 26 B2
Alphonsus St TS3 . . . 87 C2
Alpine Way TS20 . . . 25 C3
Alston Gn TS3 . . . . . 41 B3
Alston St TS26 . . . . . . 9 C2
Althorpe Cl TS3 . . . . 42 A1
Alton Rd TS5 . . . . . . 38 C2
Alva Gr TS25 . . . . . . 12 B3
Alverstone Ave [3]
  TS25 . . . . 9 C1

Alverton Cl TS3 . . . . . 42 A2
Alverton Gn TS3 . . . . 42 A2
Alvingham Terr [1]
  TS3 . . . . 52 B4
Alvis Cl TS23. . . . . . . 22 C4
Alvis Ct TS23 . . . . . . 22 C4
Alwent Rd TS1. . . . . . 84 C3
Alwin Cl TS17. . . . . . 65 B3
Alwinton Ct TS7 . . . . 52 C3
Amber Ct [7] TS12. . . 76 C4
Amberley Cl
  [8] Redcar TS10 . . . . . 73 B2
  Stockton-on-T TS18. . . 35 A1
Amberley Gn TS3 . . . 41 B3
Amberley Way TS16. . 54 A1
Amber St
  Middlesbrough TS1. . . 85 C2
  Saltburn-by-t-S TS12. . 77 A4
Amberton Rd TS24. . . . 6 A2
Amberwood Cl [2]
  TS27 . . . . 2 B2
Amberwood Wlk TS27. . 2 B2
Amble Cl TS26. . . . . . 8 B4
Ambleside Ave TS10 . 70 C1
Ambleside Gr TS5. . . 49 C3
Ambleside Rd
  Billingham TS23 . . . . . 21 C1
  Eston TS6 . . . . 43 B1
Amble View TS20 . . . 26 C3
Ambrose Rd TS6. . . . 43 C1
Amersham Rd TS3 . . 51 C4
Amesbury Cres TS8 . 59 C2
Ammerston Rd TS1 . 84 B3
Ampleforth Ave TS6. 43 B2
Ampleforth Rd
  Billingham TS23 . . . . . 17 C1
  Middlesbrough TS3. . . 41 A1
Amroth Gn TS3 . . . . 41 B3
Anchorage Mews
  TS17 . . . . 83 C2
Anchor Cl TS24 . . . . . 7 B2
Anchor Ho TS24 . . . . 10 B4
Anchor Ret Pk TS24 . . 6 B1
Ancroft Dr TS7. . . . . 53 A3
Ancroft Gdns TS20 . . 26 B3
Anderson Rd TS17 . . 37 B1
Andover Way TS8 . . . 59 B2
Andrew St [2] TS24. . 10 A3
Angle Ct TS4 . . . . . . 87 B1
Anglesey Ave [1] TS3 . 52 A4
Anglesey Gr TS26 . . . . 5 A2
Anglesey Wlk TS14. . 79 A2
Angrove Ct TS15 . . . 64 C1
Angus St TS24 . . . . . . 9 B4
Anlaby Cl TS23. . . . . 17 B4
Annan St TS25 . . . . . . 9 B2
Annandale Cres TS24 . 5 B4
Annan Rd TS23 . . . . 17 B2
Ann Crook Way TS24. . 7 B3
Annfield Cl TS23 . . . 17 A2
Annie St TS1. . . . . . . 85 A2
Ansdale Rd TS3 . . . . 42 B3
Anson Ho [2] TS17. . 47 C1
Anstey Ho [2] TS20 . 26 A4
Antrim Ave TS19 . . . 34 B4
Appleby Ave TS3 . . . 41 B3
Appleby Gr TS25 . . . . 6 A2
Appleby Ho [4] TS17. 47 C1
Appleby Rd TS23. . . 17 B1
Applegarth TS8 . . . . 68 A4
Appleton Cl TS14 . . . 79 B5
Appleton Rd
  Middlesbrough TS5. . . 49 A4
  Stockton-on-T TS19. . . 25 C1
Appletree Gdns TS7. . 53 A3
Applewood Cl TS27 . . 2 A2
Appley Cl TS16. . . . . 45 C1
Apsley St TS1. . . . . . 87 A1
Apsley Way TS17 . . . 55 C2
Arabella Cl TS24. . . . . 7 A3
Arabella St TS24 . . . . 7 A3
Arbroath Gr TS25 . . 12 A3
Arch Ct TS24. . . . . . . 6 B3
Archer St TS17. . . . . 83 C1

Archibald Prim Sch
  TS5 . . . . 85 A1
Archibald St TS5. . . . 85 A1
Arc (Theatre & Arts Ctr)
  TS18 . . . . 82 A3
Arden Cl TS14 . . . . . 79 A1
Arden Gr TS19 . . . . . 34 C2
Ardrossan Ct TS25 . . 12 B3
Ardrossan Rd TS25. . 12 B3
Arennig Ct TS17 . . . . 55 C1
Argory The TS17 . . . . 65 B4
Argyle Rd TS6 . . . . . 33 A2
Argyll Ct TS20 . . . . . 25 C3
Argyll Rd
  Hartlepool TS25 . . . . . 12 B3
  Marton TS7 . . . . 60 C3
  Stockton-on-T TS20. . . 25 C3
Arisaig Cl TS16 . . . . 63 C4
Arkendale TS8 . . . . . 59 A1
Arken Terr TS20 . . . . 26 B2
Arkgrove Ind Est
  TS18 . . . . 27 A1
Arkley Cres TS24. . . . . 5 C4
Ark Royal Cl
  Hartlepool TS25 . . . . . 13 C2
  Seaton Carew TS25 . . 13 B3
Arlington Ct TS18. . . 83 A1
Arlington Rd TS5 . . . 50 A4
Arlington St
  Stockton-on-T TS18. . . 81 C1
  Stockton-on-T TS18. . . 83 A1
Armadale TS10 . . . . . 73 B3
Armadale Ct TS19. . . 34 A4
Armadale Gr TS25 . . 12 A3
Armitage Rd TS10. . . 69 B1
Arncliffe Ave [2]
  TS18 . . . . 46 B4
Arncliffe Gdns TS26. . . 9 B3
Arncliffe Rd TS5 . . . 38 C3
Arnold Gr TS25 . . . . 11 C4
Arnside Ave TS3 . . . 41 B3
Arran Cl TS17. . . . . . 56 C4
Arrandale TS8 . . . . . 59 A1
Arran Gr TS25 . . . . . 12 B3
Arran Wlk TS14. . . . 79 A2
Arrathorne Rd TS18. . 34 B1
Arthur St TS10. . . . . 70 B4
Arundel Ct TS17 . . . 55 C2
Arundel Gn TS3 . . . . 41 B3
Arundel Rd
  Billingham TS23 . . . . . 17 A1
  Eston TS6 . . . . 43 C4
Arundel St TS10 . . . . 70 B4
Ascot Ave TS5 . . . . . 38 C1
Ascot Dr TS18 . . . . . 27 C1
Ascot Rd TS10 . . . . . 71 A1
Ashbourne Cl TS6. . . 44 A2
Ashbourne Rd TS19. . 26 A1
Ashbrooke Way TS5. . 38 C2
Ashburn St TS25 . . . 13 C2
Ashburton Cl TS8 . . 60 B4
Ashby Gr TS25 . . . . . 11 C1
Ashby Rd TS23. . . . . 17 A1
Ashcombe Cl TS22 . . 16 A2
Ashdale TS8 . . . . 59 A1
Ashdown Cl TS17 . . . 56 C4
Ashdown Way TS23 . 18 A2
Ashes The TS25 . . . . 13 C1
Ashfield Ave TS4 . . . 40 A1
Ashfield Cl TS25 . . . 14 B2
Ashford Ave TS5 . . . 48 C4
Ashford Cl TS14. . . . 79 A1
Ash Gn TS8 . . . . 68 B4
Ash Gr TS6 . . . . 32 B1
Ashgrove Ave TS25. . . 9 C1
Ash Hill TS8 . . . . . . 60 C1
Ashkirk Rd TS6 . . . . 43 A2
Ashley Gdns TS24. . . . 5 B1
Ashling Way TS5. . . . 85 A1
Ashmead View TS18. . 80 A4
Ash Rd TS14 . . . . . . 79 A1
Ashridge Cl TS17 . . . 56 C1
Ashton Rd TS20. . . . . 26 C3
Ash Trees Sch TS23 . 17 A2
Ash Vale Cvn Pk TS27. . 2 A2
Ashville Ave
  Eaglescliffe TS16 . . . . 55 A3

Ashville Ave continued
  Stockton-on-T TS20. . . 20 A1
Ashwood Cl
  Hartlepool TS27 . . . . . 2 B2
  [7] Ormesby TS7. . . . . 53 A3
Aske Rd
  Middlesbrough TS1. . . 85 C2
  Redcar TS10 . . . . 71 A3
Askern Dr TS5 . . . . . 50 A2
Askew Dale TS14 . . . 78 A2
Askham Bryan Coll
  TS14 . . . . 79 C4
Askham Cl TS4 . . . . 40 A1
Askrigg Rd TS18 . . . 80 B3
Askrigg Wlk [4] TS3 . 41 A1
Askwith Rd [1] TS5 . . 39 B1
Aspen Dr TS5. . . . . . 40 A1
Aspen Gdns TS19 . . . 24 B3
Aspen Rd TS16. . . . . 63 B4
Astbury
  Marton TS8 . . . . 61 B1
  Mount Pleasant TS8 . . 61 B1
Aster Cl TS7 . . . . 60 B4
Asterley Dr TS5. . . . . 48 C3
Astley Cl TS19 . . . . . 34 C3
Aston Ave TS3 . . . . . 41 C4
Astonbury Gn TS4 . . 51 A2
Aston Dr TS17 . . . . . 56 B4
Aston Rd TS22 . . . . . 16 B1
Atherstone Dr TS14 . 79 B2
Atherton Way TS15 . . 66 A3
Atholl Gr
  Hartlepool TS25 . . . . . 12 B3
  Redcar TS10 . . . . 70 A2
Athol St TS1 . . . . 85 C2
Atkinson Ct TS24 . . . . 3 C1
Atkinson Ind Est
  TS25 . . . . 10 A2
Atlas Wynd TS15. . . . 63 C2
Attingham Cl TS8 . . . 59 C2
Attlee Rd TS6. . . . . . 43 C4
Attlow Wlk TS3 . . . . 42 A2
Atwater Cl TS15 . . . . 67 A4
Atwick Cl TS23. . . . . 17 B4
Aubrey St TS1 . . . . . 87 A2
Auckland Ave TS7. . . 61 B3
Auckland Rd TS23 . . 18 A4
Auckland St TS14 . . . 79 B4
Auckland Way
  Hartlepool TS25 . . . . . 8 A3
  Stockton-on-T TS18. . . 34 C1
Audrey Gr TS18 . . . . 35 A1
Austen Ct TS23 . . . . 17 A4
Austin Ave TS18 . . . . 81 C1
Autumn Gr TS19 . . . 35 A3
Avalon Ct TS8. . . . . . 59 C2
Avebury Cl TS17 . . . 65 C4
Avens Way TS17 . . . . 56 B2
Avenue Ct TS7 . . . . . 62 A3
Avenue Pl TS14 . . . . 79 C4
Avenue Prim Sch The
  TS7 . . . . 62 A3
Avenue Rd TS24 . . . . 9 C4
Avenue The
  Eaglescliffe TS16 . . . . 54 C3
  Eston TS6 . . . . 43 A3
  Guisborough TS14 . . . 78 B2
  Middlesbrough TS5. . . 39 C1
  Nunthorpe TS7 . . . . . 62 A3
  Redcar TS10 . . . . 71 A3
  Stockton-on-T TS19. . . 34 C3
  Thornaby-on-T TS17 . . 47 C4
Aviemore Rd TS8 . . . 59 C2
Avill Gr TS17 . . . . . . 65 A2
Avoca Ct TS10 . . . . . 70 B4
Avon Cl TS17 . . . . . . 47 C2
Avondale Cl TS6 . . . . 43 B4
Avondale Gdns TS4 . . 5 C2
Avondene Flats [4]
  TS24 . . . . 10 A4
Avon Dr TS14 . . . . . 79 A2
Avon Gr TS22 . . . . . 16 A2
Avon Rd
  Redcar TS10 . . . . 70 A1
  Stockton-on-T TS20. . . 26 C3
Avon St TS12 . . . . . . 76 C2

Avro Cl
  Marske-by-t-S TS11 . . 74 B2
  Stockton-on-T TS16. . . 46 A2
Axbridge Ct TS23 . . . 17 A3
Axminster Rd TS8. . . 59 C2
Axton Cl TS17. . . . . . 56 B3
Aycliffe Cl TS19 . . . . 34 B3
Aycliffe Rd TS7 . . . . 61 A3
Aylsham Cl TS17 . . . 65 C4
Aylton Dr TS5. . . . . . 58 C3
Ayresome Grange Rd
  TS5 . . . . 85 A1
Ayresome Green La
  TS5 . . . . 39 B2
Ayresome Park Rd
  TS5 . . . . 39 B2
Ayresome Prim Sch
  TS1 . . . . 85 B1
Ayresome Rd TS5 . . . 38 C4
Ayresome St TS1. . . . 85 B1
Ayr Gr TS25. . . . . . . 12 B3
Aysgarth Rd
  Middlesbrough TS5. . . 39 A1
  Stockton-on-T TS18. . . 80 A3
Ayton Cres TS5 . . . . 43 C1
Ayton Ct
  Guisborough TS14 . . . 79 A5
  Redcar TS10 . . . . 72 B4
Ayton Dr TS10 . . . . . 72 C4
Ayton Rd TS10 . . . . . 72 B4
Ayton Pl TS20. . . . . . 26 B1
Ayton Rd TS17 . . . . . 47 B2
Azalia Gr [5] TS10 . . 73 B2
Azalia Rd TS19. . . . . 26 A1

B

Back La TS16 . . . . . . 63 C3
Back Throston St
  TS24 . . . . 7 B2
Bacon Wlk TS25 . . . 11 B4
Baden St TS26 . . . . . . 9 B2
Bader Prim Sch
  TS17 . . . . 56 C4
Badger La TS17 . . . . 56 C2
Badsworth Cl TS14. . 79 A1
Baffin Ct TS17 . . . . . 57 A4
Bailey St TS23 . . . . . 41 A3
Bainton Ct TS23. . . . 17 B4
Bakehouse Sq TS14 . . 79 B3
Baker Cl TS27 . . . . . . 2 C1
Baker St TS1. . . . . . . 84 C3
Bakery Dr TS19 . . . . 25 A1
Bakery Ho TS19 . . . . 25 A1
Bakery St TS18. . . . . 82 A3
Bala Cl TS17 . . . . . . 64 B4
Balaclava St TS18. . . 82 A4
Balcary Ct TS25. . . . . 12 A2
Balder Rd TS20 . . . . 26 A4
Baldoon Sands TS5 . . 58 B4
Balfour Terr TS5 . . . 49 A4
Ballater Gr TS25 . . . 12 B2
Balmoral Ave
  Billingham TS23 . . . . . 17 B1
  Thornaby-on-T TS17 . . 47 C4
Balmoral Ct TS25 . . . 12 B2
Balmoral Dr TS4 . . . 40 B1
Balmoral Rd
  Hartlepool TS25 . . . . . 12 A2
  Middlesbrough TS3. . . 52 B4
Balmoral Terr
  [4] Saltburn-by-t-S
  TS12 . . . . 77 A3
  Stockton-on-T TS18. . . 81 C1
Balmor Rd TS6 . . . . 43 A2
Baltic Cl TS18. . . . . . 82 B4
Baltic Rd TS18 . . . . . 82 B3
Baltic St TS25. . . . . . 10 A2
Bamborough [6] TS4 . 51 B1
Bamburgh Cl TS10. . 71 B1
Bamburgh Ct
  Hartlepool TS27 . . . . . 2 C1
  Ingleby Barwick TS17. . 55 C2

Bamburgh Dr TS7. . . . 52 C3
Bamburgh Rd TS27 . . . . 2 C1
Bamford Rd TS17 . . . . 47 B2
Banbury Gr TS5. . . . . 49 A2
Banff Gr TS5. . . . . . . 12 B2
Bangor Cl TS6 . . . . . 43 C4
Bangor St TS26 . . . . . . .9 B2
Bankfields St TS6. . . 53 C4
Bankfields Prim Sch
TS6 . . . . 43 C1
Bankfields Rd
Eston TS6 . . . . 43 C1
Normanby TS6 . . . . . . 53 C4
Bank Rd TS23. . . . . . . 21 B1
Bank Sands TS5 . . . . . 58 B3
Bankside TS15. . . . . . . 64 B2
Bankside Cl 6 TS6 . . 44 A1
Bank St TS10 . . . . . . 70 C4
Bankston Cl TS26 . . . . 4 B1
Bannockburn Way
TS23 . . . . 17 C3
Baptist St TS24 . . . . . . .7 B2
Barbara Mann Ct
TS26 . . . . 9 C4
Barberry TS8 . . . . 68 B4
Barberry Cl TS17. . . . 56 C2
Barden Rd TS3. . . . . . 41 A2
Bardsey Wlk TS14. . . . 79 A1
Bardsley Cl TS16. . . . 45 C1
Barford Cl
Hartlepool TS25 . . . . . 14 B4
Redcar TS10 . . . . 72 B3
Stockton-on-T TS20. . . . 19 C1
Barholm Cl TS3 . . . . . 42 A1
Barker Rd
Middlesbrough TS5. . . . 39 A1
Thornaby-on-T TS17 . . . 47 C4
Barkery The TS8 . . . . . 68 B1
Barkston Ave TS17 . . . 56 B3
Barkston Cl TS22 . . . . . 16 C2
Barlborough Ave
TS19 . . . . 80 A4
Barle Cl TS17 . . . . 65 B2
Barley Cl TS26 . . . . . . 5 A1
Barley Fields Prim Sch
TS17 . . . . 65 A4
Barley Hill Cl TS6 . . . 53 C4
Barlow Cl TS14 . . . . . . 79 B2
Barlow Ct TS23 . . . . . 17 B3
Barmoor Gr TS20 . . . . 20 B2
Barmouth Rd TS6. . . . 43 C3
Barmpton Rd TS23 . . . 17 B3
Barnaby Ave TS5. . . . . 85 A1
Barnaby Cl 2 TS11 . . 75 B1
Barnaby Cres TS6. . . . 44 A1
Barnaby Pl TS14 . . . . . 78 C4
Barnaby Rd TS7. . . . . 62 B3
Barnack Ave TS7. . . . . 61 B4
Barnard Ave TS19 . . . . 35 A2
Barnard Cl TS17 . . . . . 83 C1
Barnard Ct 4 TS4 . . . 40 B1
Barnard Gr
Hartlepool TS24 . . . . . 2 C2
Redcar TS10 . . . . 71 B2
Barnard Grove Prim
Sch TS24 . . . . 2 C2
Barnard Rd TS23. . . . . 21 C4
Barnes Ct TS24 . . . . . 3 A1
Barnes Wallis Way
TS11 . . . . 74 B3
Barnet Way TS23. . . . . 18 A3
Barnford Wlk 14 TS3 . 51 C4
Barnstaple Cl TS8. . . . 51 A1
Baronport Gn 2
TS18 . . . . 82 C4
Barra Gr TS25 . . . . . . 12 B2
Barras Gr TS3 . . . . . . 42 A3
Barras Way TS19. . . . . 24 A2
Barrhead Cl TS19 . . . . 34 A4
Barrington Ave TS19 . 35 A4
Barrington Cres TS3 . 42 A3
Barritt St TS1. . . . . . . 85 C2
Barrowburn Gn TS17 . 65 A3

Barsby Gn 4 TS3 . . . 41 A2
Barsford Rd TS3 . . . . 42 A3
Bartol Ct 5 TS6 . . . . 44 A1
Barton Ave TS25 . . . . . .9 B1
Barton Cl TS17. . . . . . 56 B3
Barton Cres TS22 . . . . 16 B1
Barton Rd TS2 . . . . . . 28 C3
Barwick Cl TS17 . . . . . 56 B2
Barwick Fields TS17 . 56 B1
Barwick La TS15,
TS17 . . . . 65 A3
Barwick View TS17. . . 56 B2
Barwick Way TS17 . . . 65 B3
Basildon Gn TS3 . . . . . 41 B3
Basil St TS3 . . . . 87 C2
Bassenthwaite TS5 . . 58 B4
Bassleton La TS17 . . . 56 B4
Bathgate Terr 1
TS24 . . . . 9 C2
Bath La TS18 . . . . 82 B3
Bath Pl TS18. . . . . . . 82 B3
Bath Rd TS6 . . . . 43 C2
Bath St
Redcar TS10 . . . . 70 C4
Saltburn-by-t-S TS12. . . 76 C3
Bath Terr TS24 . . . . . . 7 C2
Battersby Cl TS15. . . . 64 C1
Bayberry Mews TS5. . 49 C4
Baysdale Cl TS14 . . . . 79 C3
Baysdale Gr TS10 . . . . 69 C1
Baysdale Rd TS17. . . . 47 C2
Bayswale Wlk
Eston TS6 . . . . 44 B3
Middlesbrough TS5. . . . 50 A2
Beachfield Dr TS25 . . . .9 B1
Beaconsfield Rd
TS20 . . . . 20 C1
Beaconsfield Sq TS24 . .7 B3
Beaconsfield St TS24 . 7 B3
Beacons La TS17. . . . . 64 C4
Beacon St TS24 . . . . . . .7 B3
Beadlam Ave TS7 . . . . 62 B3
Beadnell Cl TS17. . . . . 56 C1
Beadnell Way TS10 . . . 73 C4
Beadon Gr TS5 . . . . . 38 C2
Beale Cl TS17. . . . . . . 56 C1
Beamish Rd TS23 . . . . 18 A2
Beardmore Ave TS11. . 74 B3
Beath Gr TS25 . . . . . . 12 B2
Beaufort Cl TS14. . . . . 79 B1
Beaufort St TS1. . . . . . 84 C3
Beauly Gr TS25 . . . . . 12 B2
Beaumaris Dr TS16 . . 63 C4
Beaumont Rd TS3. . . . 41 A4
Beaumont View
TS20 . . . . 26 C3
Beaver Cl TS17 . . . . . 56 C2
Beaver Ct TS6 . . . . . . 32 B1
Beccles Cl TS19. . . . . . 24 B1
Beckenham Gdns
TS8 . . . . 59 C1
Beckfields Ave TS17. . 65 B4
Beckfields Ctr TS17 . . 65 C4
Beckston Cl TS26 . . . . 8 A4
Beckwith Rd TS15 . . . 66 B3
Bedale Ave TS23 . . . . 21 C2
Bedale Gr TS19 . . . . . 34 B2
Bede Cl TS19 . . . . . . 25 A2
Bede Coll TS23 . . . . . . 17 B2
Bede Gr TS5 . . . . 9 A1
Bedford Rd TS7. . . . . 62 A3
Bedford St
Hartlepool TS24 . . . . . 7 B2
Middlesbrough TS1. . . . 84 C3
Stockton-on-T TS19. . . 80 C4
Bedford Terr TS23. . . 21 C2
Bedlington Wlk TS23. 17 A4
Beech Ave TS10. . . . . 71 B3
Beech Cl TS19 . . . . . . 24 C1
Beeches Rise TS7. . . . . 61 B4
Beeches The
Billingham TS23 . . . . . 21 A3
Eston TS6 . . . . 43 A3
Beechfield
Coulby Newham
TS8 . . . . 60 B1
Mount Pleasant TS8 . . . 68 A4

Beech Gr TS6. . . . . . . 42 C4
Beech Grove Prim Sch
TS6 . . . . 42 C4
Beech Grove Rd TS5 . . 50 A4
Beech Rd TS14 . . . . . . 79 B4
Beech St TS1. . . . . . . 86 A3
Beech Terr TS2 . . . . . 23 C1
Beechtree Ct TS15. . . . 63 B3
BEECHWOOD. 50 C3
Beechwood Ave
Middlesbrough TS4. . . . 50 C4
Saltburn-by-t-S TS12. . . 76 C2
Beechwood Prim Sch
TS4 . . . . 50 C4
Beechwood Rd
Eaglescliffe TS16 . . . . 54 C4
Thornaby-on-T TS17 . . . 47 B3
Beeford Cl TS23 . . . . . 17 B5
Beeford Dr TS5 . . . . . 50 A2
Belasis Ave TS23. . . . . 22 B2
Belasis Ct TS23 . . . . . 22 B3
Belasis Hall Tech Pk
TS23 . . . . 22 C3
Belford Cl TS19 . . . . . 35 A4
Belgrave Ct TS25 . . . . 13 C2
Belgrave Dr TS6 . . . . 53 B3
Belk Cl TS6 . . . . 33 A1
Belk St
Hartlepool TS24 . . . . . 6 A1
Middlesbrough TS1. . . . 85 C1
Bellamy Ct TS3 . . . . . 41 B3
Bellasis Gr TS27 . . . . . 2 C1
Bell Cl TS18 . . . . 81 C2
Bellerby Rd TS18 . . . . 34 C1
BELLEVUE. 10 A2
Belle Vue Ct TS20 . . . 26 B2
Belle Vue Gr TS4 . . . . 40 C1
Belle Vue Ho 11
TS20 . . . . 26 B2
Belle Vue Rd TS5. . . . 39 B2
Belle Vue Way TS25 . . 10 A1
Bell St TS5 . . . . 85 A1
Belmangate TS14 . . . . 79 C2
Belmont Ave
Billingham TS22 . . . . . 16 C1
Eston TS6 . . . . 42 C4
Middlesbrough TS5. . . . 59 A3
Stockton-on-T TS19. . . 25 C1
Belmont Gdns TS26 . . .9 B2
Belmont Prim Sch
TS14 . . . . 79 C2
Belmont St TS6 . . . . . 44 A2
Belmont Terr TS14 . . 79 C3
Belsay Cl TS19 . . . . . . 35 A4
Belton Dr TS5 . . . . . . 50 A2
Belvedere Rd
6 Middlesbrough
TS4 . . . . 40 B1
11 Thornaby-on-T
TS17 . . . . 47 C4
Benedict St TS3 . . . . . 87 C2
Beningborough Gdns
TS17 . . . . 56 B1
Benmore Rd TS25. . . . 12 B2
Bennett Rd TS25. . . . . .8 B1
Bennison Cres TS10. . 69 C1
Bennison St TS14 . . . . 79 B4
Benridge Cl TS5 . . . . . 49 A1
Benson St
4 Hartlepool TS26 . . . 9 B3
Middlesbrough TS5. . . . 39 C2
Stockton-on-T TS20. . . 26 B4
Bentick St TS26. . . . . . .9 B4
Bentinck Ave TS5 . . . . 50 A4
Bentinck Rd TS19 . . . . 34 C3
Bentley Ave TS23 . . . . 18 B1
Bentley St 5 TS26 . . . .9 B3
Bentley Wynd TS15 . . 63 B2
Benton Cl TS23 . . . . . 17 B4
Benton Rd TS5. . . . . . 50 A3
Benwell Cl TS19 . . . . . 35 A4
Berberis Gr TS19. . . . . 35 A3
Beresford Cres TS3 . . 42 A3
Berkeley Ave TS25 . . . 12 B1
Berkeley Cl TS23 . . . . 17 A1
Berkeley Dr TS10 . . . . 73 B4
Berkley Dr TS14 . . . . . 79 C1

Berkshire Ho TS6 . . . 43 C3
Berkshire Rd TS20 . . . 26 C3
Bernaldby Ave TS14. . 78 C2
Berner St TS5 . . . . . . 39 B2
Bernica Gr TS17 . . . . . 63 A3
Berrington Gdns 2
TS17 . . . . 65 B4
Bertha St TS26. . . . . . 10 A2
Berwick Gr TS20. . . . . 20 B1
BERWICK HILLS 41 A2
Berwick Hills Ave
TS3 . . . . 42 A3
Berwick Hills Prim Sch
TS3 . . . . 41 A2
Berwick St TS25 . . . . . 13 C2
Berwick Wlk TS10 . . . 71 B1
Bessemer Ct TS6 . . . . 33 A3
Bethune Rd TS5 . . . . . 38 C2
Betjeman Cl 1 TS23 . 17 B4
Bevan Cl TS19 . . . . . . 24 C2
Bevanlee Rd TS6. . . . . 32 B1
Beverley Rd
Billingham TS23 . . . . . 17 C4
Middlesbrough TS4. . . . 50 B3
Nunthorpe TS7 . . . . . . 62 B3
Redcar TS10 . . . . 71 C1
Beverley Sch TS4 . . . . 50 B3
Bewholme Cl TS23. . . 17 B5
Bewley Gr TS5. . . . . . 49 B2
Bewley Inf Sch TS23 . 18 A3
Bewley Jun Sch
TS23 . . . . 18 A3
Bexley Cl TS4. . . . . . . 51 A2
Bexley Dr
Hartlepool TS25 . . . . . 12 C4
Normanby TS6 . . . . . . 53 C3
Bickersteth Cl TS18 . . 83 A1
Bickersteth Wlk 8
TS18 . . . . 83 A1
Bickley Cl TS22 . . . . . 16 A1
Bickley Way TS8 . . . . 60 B2
Biddick Cl TS19. . . . . . 35 A4
Bielby Ave TS23. . . . . 17 B4
Biggin Cl TS5 . . . . . . 50 A2
BILLINGHAM 22 A1
Billingham Bank
TS23 . . . . 21 B1
Billingham Beck Valley
Country Pk★ TS23 . . 27 A4
Billingham Beck Valley
Ctry Pk & Visitor Ctr★
TS23 . . . . 21 A2
Billingham Campus Sch
TS23 . . . . 17 C3
Billingham Halt
TS23 . . . . 22 A4
Billingham Rd TS20 . . 21 A1
Billingham Reach Ind
Est TS23. . . . . 28 B3
Billingham South Com
Prim Sch TS23. . . . . 21 C2
Bilsdale Ave TS10 . . . . 70 A1
Bilsdale Rd
Hartlepool TS25 . . . . . 13 B1
Middlesbrough TS4. . . . 87 C1
Stockton-on-T TS19. . . 80 B4
Bingfield Ct TS23 . . . . 17 B4
Binks St TS5 . . . . 39 C2
Birches The TS8 . . . . . 60 A1
Birchfield Cl 1 TS16 . 54 B1
Birchfield Dr TS16 . . . 54 B1
Birchgate Rd TS5 . . . . 49 C4
Birch Gr TS19. . . . . . . 25 B3
Birchill Gdns TS26 . . . 5 A1
Birchington Ave TS6 . 44 A4
Birch Tree Cl 9 TS7 . . 53 A3
Birch Wlk TS24 . . . . . 5 C2
Birchwood Ave TS4 . . 40 B1
Birchwood Rd TS7 . . . 61 C4
Birdsall Brow TS20. . . 20 A1
Biretta Cl TS19. . . . . . 34 B4
Birkdale Cl 6 TS27 . . . 2 B2
Birkdale Dr TS6. . . . . . 43 C1
Birkdale Rd TS18 . . . . 34 C1
Birkhall Rd TS3 . . . . . 42 B2
Birkley Rd TS20. . . . . . 26 B2
Birtley Ave TS5 . . . . . 49 B1

Bisham Ave TS5 . . . . . 39 A1
BISHOPSGARTH 24 B2
Bishopsgarth Sch
TS19 . . . . 24 A2
Bishops Mill TS20. . . . 20 C1
Bishop St
Middlesbrough TS5. . . . 38 C3
Stockton-on-T TS18. . . . 82 B3
Bishops Way TS19 . . . 24 A1
Bishopton Ave TS19 . . 25 B1
Bishopton Ct TS19 . . . 34 C3
Bishopton Ctr TS19 . . 80 C4
Bishopton La TS18 . . . 82 A3
Bishopton Rd
Middlesbrough TS4. . . . 40 A1
Stockton-on-T TS18,
TS19 . . . . 80 C4
Bishopton Rd W
TS19 . . . . 34 C4
Blackburn Cl TS19 . . . 35 A3
Blackburn Gr TS11. . . 74 A3
Blackbush Wlk TS17 . 56 C3
Black Diamond Way
TS16 . . . . 54 B2
Blackett Ave TS20. . . . 26 B2
Blackett Hutton Ind Est
TS14 . . . . 79 B2
Blackfriars TS15. . . . . 63 C1
Blackhall Sands TS5 . 58 B3
Blackmore Cl TS14. . . 79 C1
Blackmore Wlk TS25 . 11 B4
Black Path The TS18,
TS20 . . . . 82 B4
Blacksail Cl TS19 . . . . 80 C3
Blacksmiths Cl TS6 . . 43 C2
Blackthorn TS8 . . . . . 68 B4
Blackthorn Cl TS10 . . 73 B3
Blackthorn Gr TS19 . . 35 A3
Blackton Rd TS26. . . . . 8 A4
Blackwell Cl TS23. . . . 18 A2
Blackwood Cl TS27 . . . .2 B2
Bladon Dr TS11 . . . . . 74 C3
Blair Ave TS17 . . . . . . 64 C4
Blairgowrie Cl TS8 . . . 61 B2
Blairgowrie Gr TS25 . 12 A2
Blairmore Gdns
TS16 . . . . 54 C1
Blaise Garden Village
TS26 . . . . .8 B4
Blake Cl TS23. . . . . . . 17 B4
Blakelock Rd TS25 . . . .9 B2
Blakelock Gdns TS25. .9 B2
Blake St TS26. . . . . . . 5 C1
Blakeston Ct TS19 . . . 19 B1
Blakeston La TS19,
TS21 . . . . 19 A2
Blakeston Rd TS23 . . . 17 C2
Blakeston Sch TS19. . 19 A1
Blake Wlk 2 TS26 . . . 5 C1
Blakey Cl TS10. . . . . . 72 C3
Blakey Wlk TS6 . . . . . 44 B3
Blanchland Rd TS3. . . 52 A4
Blanford Cl TS20. . . . . 20 C1
Blankney Cl TS14 . . . . 79 A2
Blantyre Rd TS6 . . . . . 43 A1
Blatchford Rd TS6 . . . 31 C1
Blayberry Cl TS10 . . . 72 C3
Blenavon Ct TS15. . . . 63 B2
Blenheim Ave TS11 . . 74 C3
Blenheim Cl TS11 . . . 74 C3
Blenheim Terr TS10 . . 70 B4
Bletchley Cl TS19 . . . . 35 A4
Blorenge Ct TS17 . . . . 64 C3
Bluebell Gr TS19 . . . . 35 A3
Blue Bell Gr TS5 . . . . 59 B4
Bluebell Way TS26 . . . 4 C4
Blue House Point Rd
TS18 . . . . 38 A4
Blue Post Yd TS18. . . . 83 A2
Blytheport Cl TS18. . . 82 C4
Boagey Wlk TS24 . . . . 5 C4
Boar La TS17 . . . . 56 C1

Boathouse La TS18 . . 83 B1
Bodiam Cl TS17 . . . . . . 56 A2
Bodiam Dr TS10 . . . . . 73 C4
Bodmin Gr TS26 . . . . . . 4 C2
Boeing Way TS18 . . . . . 46 B3
Bolam Gr TS23 . . . . 17 B3
Bolckow Rd TS6 . . . . . 33 A2
Bolckow St
  Eston TS6 . . . . 44 A1
  Guisborough TS14 . . . . 79 B4
  Middlesbrough TS1 . . . . 84 C4
Boldron Cl TS18 . . . . . . 34 B1
Bollington Rd TS4 . . . . 51 A2
Bolsover Rd TS20 . . . . . 26 B2
Boltby Cl TS5 . . . . 50 A2
Boltby Way TS16 . . . . . 54 B2
Bolton Cl TS10 . . . . . . 71 B1
Bolton Ct TS14 . . . . . . 40 A1
Bolton Gr TS25 . . . . . . 13 C2
Bolton Way TS14 . . . . . 79 C3
Bondene Gr TS19 . . . . . 24 A1
Bondfield Rd TS6 . . . . . 43 B3
Bond St TS24 . . . . .7 B2
Bone St TS18 . . . . 82 B4
Bonington Cres
  TS23 . . . . 17 A4
Bon Lea Trad Est
  TS17 . . . . 83 C1
Bonny Gr TS8 . . . . 61 C1
Bonnygrove Way
  Coulby Newham
  TS8 . . . . 60 C1
  Mount Pleasant TS8 . . 68 B4
Bonnyrigg Cl TS17 . . 65 B4
Bonnyrigg Wlk TS25 . 12 B2
Bordesley Gn TS3 . . . . 41 B3
Borough Rd
  Middlesbrough TS1 . . . 87 B2
  Redcar TS10 . . . . 71 B2
Borrowby Ct TS14 . . . 79 A4
Borrowdale Gr
  Eaglescliffe TS16 . . . . . 63 C3
  Middlesbrough TS5 . . . 49 B3
Borrowdale Rd TS6 . . . 8 C1
Borrowdale St TS25 . . . 9 C1
Borton Wlk TS19 . . . . 80 C4
Boscombe Gdns TS5 . . 59 C1
Boston Cl TS25 . . . . . . 12 A1
Boston Dr TS7 . . . . 61 B2
Boston Wlk TS20 . . . . 26 C3
Boswell Gr TS25 . . . . . 11 C4
Boswell St TS1 . . . . . . 86 A3
Bosworth Way TS23 . . 17 C2
Botany Way TS7 . . . . . . 62 A2
Bothal Dr TS19 . . . . . . 24 A1
Bothal Wlk TS19 . . . . . 24 A2
Boulby Rd TS10 . . . . . 69 C2
Boulby Wlk [T] TS6 . . 48 A2
Boundary Rd
  Middlesbrough TS1 . . . 84 C4
  Normanby TS6 . . . . . . 53 B4
Bourne Manse TS10 . . 70 A3
Bournemouth Ave
  TS3 . . . . 52 B4
Bournemouth Dr
  TS24 . . . . 2 C2
Bournemouth Rd
  TS3 . . . . 52 B4
Bourton Ct TS3 . . . . . . 51 C3
Bowesfield Cres
  TS18 . . . . 47 A3
Bowesfield Ind Est The
  TS18 . . . . 46 C3
Bowesfield La TS18 . . 46 C3
Bowesfield Prim Sch
  TS18 . . . . 83 A1
Bowes Gn TS24 . . . . 2 C2
Bowes Rd
  Billingham TS23 . . . . . 16 C2
  Middlesbrough TS2 . . . 29 A3
Bowfell Cl TS16 . . . . . . 54 B2
Bowfell Rd TS3 . . . . . . 41 A2
Bowhill Way TS25 . . . 18 A3
Bowland Cl TS7 . . . . . . 61 C2
Bowley Cl TS6 . . . . . . 42 C1
Bowley Wlk TS1 . . . . . 84 B3
Bowline Ho TS24 . . . . . .6 B1

Bowness Cl TS25 . . . . . 12 C4
Bowness Gr TS10 . . . . 70 C2
Bowood Cl TS17 . . . . . 56 A2
Bowron St TS20 . . . . . . 26 B1
Bow St Ctr TS14 . . . . . 79 C3
Bowser St TS24 . . . . . . 10 A3
Bow St
  Guisborough TS14 . . . 79 C3
  Middlesbrough TS1 . . . 85 C2
Box Dr TS7 . . . . 62 B2
Boxer Ct TS6 . . . . 32 A1
Boynton Rd TS4 . . . . . . 40 B2
Brabazon Dr [6] TS11 . 74 B2
Brabourn Gdns TS8 . . 59 C1
Brackenberry Cres
  TS10 . . . . 73 C4
Brackenberry Wlk [5]
  TS6 . . . . 44 A3
Bracken Cres TS14 . . . 78 B2
Brackenfield Ct TS6 . . 53 C4
Brackenhill Cl TS7 . . . 62 A1
Bracken Rd TS19 . . . . . 25 B3
Brackenthwaite TS5 . 58 B4
Bracknell Rd TS17 . . . 48 A3
Bradbury Rd TS20 . . . . 20 C1
Bradhope Rd TS3 . . . . 40 C2
Bradley Ct TS23 . . . . . 17 C2
Bradshaw Ct TS24 . . . . .5 B4
Brae Head TS16 . . . . . . 54 C1
Braemar Gr TS6 . . . . . . 42 C3
Braemar Rd
  Billingham TS23 . . . . . 17 A2
  Hartlepool TS25 . . . . . 12 B2
  Middlesbrough TS5 . . . 49 A4
Braeworth Cl TS15 . . . 64 C1
Brafferton Dr TS23 . . . 17 C4
Brafferton St [2] TS26 . 9 A4
Brafferton Wlk TS25 . . 12 B2
Braid Cres TS23 . . . . . . 21 B3
Braidwood Rd TS6 . . . 43 A1
Bramble Dykes [7]
  TS10 . . . . 73 B2
Bramble Rd TS19 . . . . . 25 B3
BRAMBLES FARM . . 42 A3
Brambles Prim Sch
  TS3 . . . . 41 C3
Brambling Cl TS20 . . . 20 A1
Bramcote Way TS17 . . 56 C3
Bramfield Way TS17 . . 56 A3
Bramham Down
  TS14 . . . . 79 B2
Bramley Ct TS25 . . . . . 12 B2
Bramley Gr TS7 . . . . . . 61 B4
Bramley Par TS18 . . . . 83 A1
Brampton Cl TS8 . . . . . 59 B3
Bramwith Ave TS3 . . . 51 C4
Brancepath Wlk TS24 . .3 B1
Brancepeth Ave TS3 . . 51 C4
Brancepeth Ct TS22 . . 16 C2
Brandon Cl
  Billingham TS23 . . . . . 17 A3
  Hartlepool TS25 . . . . . 14 A3
Brandon Rd TS3 . . . . . . 42 A2
Branklyn Gdns TS17 . . 65 B4
Branksome Ave TS5 . . 50 A3
Branksome Gr TS18 . . 45 B4
Bransdale TS14 . . . . . . 78 A2
Bransdale Cl TS19 . . . 80 B4
Bransdale Gr
  Hartlepool TS25 . . . . . 13 C2
  Redcar TS10 . . . . 69 C1
Bransdale Rd TS3 . . . . 41 A2
Brantingham Dr
  TS17 . . . . 55 B2
Brantwood Cl TS17 . . 65 C4
Brass Castle La TS8 . . 61 C1
Brass Wynd TS8 . . . . . . 61 C1
Breakwater Ho TS24 . 10 B4
Brechin Dr TS17 . . . . . 57 A3
Brechin Gr TS25 . . . . . 12 B2
Breckland Wlk [8]
  TS3 . . . . 41 B1
Breckon Hill Prim Sch
  TS4 . . . . 87 B2
Breckon Hill Rd TS4 . 87 B2
Brecon Cres TS17 . . . . 64 C4
Brecon Dr TS10 . . . . . . 72 A4

Brecon Gdns TS6 . . . . 43 B4
Brecongill Cl TS24 . . . . 6 A2
Brenda Rd TS25 . . . . . . 15 C4
Brendon Cres TS23 . . . 21 C4
Brendon Gr TS17 . . . . 65 B2
Brenkley Cl TS20 . . . . 19 C1
Brent Ct TS23 . . . . 21 A3
Brentford Rd TS20 . . . 26 B2
Brentnall St TS1 . . . . . 84 C3
Brereton Rd TS4 . . . . . 50 C3
Bretby Cl TS4 . . . . 50 C4
Brettenham Ave TS4 . 51 A2
Breward Wlk [4] TS24 . . 7 A1
Brewery St [7] TS24 . . . 9 C3
Brewsdale Rd TS3 . . . . 30 C1
Briardene Ave TS5 . . . 50 A3
Briardene Ct TS19 . . . 24 A3
Briardene Wlk TS19 . . 24 A3
Briargate TS6 . . . . 44 A2
Briar Gr TS10 . . . . 70 C2
Briarhill Gdns TS26 . . . 5 A1
Briar Rd TS17 . . . . 47 B2
Briarvale Ave TS5 . . . . 49 C4
Briar Wlk
  Hartlepool TS26 . . . . . . 9 B4
  Stockton-on-T TS18 . . 81 A1
Brickton Rd TS5 . . . . . 38 C2
Bridge Ct
  Eston TS6 . . . . 43 A1
  Yarm TS15 . . . . 63 B3
Bridgend Cl TS6 . . . . . 33 B1
Bridgepool Cl TS24 . . . .6 B1
Bridge Rd
  Redcar TS10 . . . . 70 A4
  Stockton-on-T TS18 . . 83 B1
Bridge St E TS2 . . . . . . 86 A4
Bridge St W TS2 . . . . . 84 C4
Bridge St
  Hartlepool TS24 . . . . . 10 B3
  Thornaby-on-T TS17 . . 83 C1
  Yarm TS15 . . . . 63 B3
Bridnor Rd TS3 . . . . . . 51 B4
Bridport Cl TS18 . . . . . 37 A4
Bridport Gr TS8 . . . . . . 59 C1
Brierley Gn TS7 . . . . . . 61 B2
Brierton Com Sch
  TS25 . . . . 11 C3
Brierton La TS25 . . . . . 11 A3
Brierville Rd TS19 . . . 25 C1
Brigandine Cl TS25 . . 13 B2
Briggs Ave TS6 . . . . . . 32 A1
Brigham Rd TS3 . . . . . 41 A1
Brighouse Bsns Village
  TS2 . . . . 28 C4
Brighton Cl TS17 . . . . 56 B4
Bright St
  Hartlepool TS26 . . . . . . 9 A4
  Middlesbrough TS1 . . . 86 B3
  Stockton-on-T TS18 . . 82 A3
Brignall Rd TS18 . . . . . 81 A4
Brignell Rd TS2 . . . . . . 29 A3
Brig Open TS24 . . . . . . .7 B2
Brimham Cl TS17 . . . . 56 C1
Brimham Ct TS10 . . . . 70 B1
Brimston Cl TS26 . . . . . 4 C1
Brindle Cl TS7 . . . . 61 B2
Brine St TS4 . . . . 87 C1
Brinewells Gn TS4 . . . 87 C1
Brinkburn Ct TS25 . . . . 9 A2
Brinkburn Rd
  Hartlepool TS25 . . . . . . 9 A2
  Stockton-on-T TS20 . . 26 A2
Brisbane Cres TS17 . . 47 B1
Brisbane Gr TS18 . . . . 81 A1
Briscoe Way TS8 . . . . . 58 C1
Bristol Ave TS12 . . . . . 76 C3
Bristol Wlk TS26 . . . . . . 5 A4
Bristow Rd TS4 . . . . . . 40 C1
Bristow St TS5 . . . . . . 31 A4
Britain Ave TS5 . . . . . . 49 B3
Britannia Cl [7] TS24 . 10 A3
Britannia Ho TS24 . . . . 6 C1
Britannia Pl TS10 . . . . 69 B3
Britannia Rd TS20 . . . 80 C3
Broad Cl TS8 . . . . 58 B1
Broad Field Rd TS24 . . 7 B3
Broadgate Gdns TS5 . . .7 B4

Broadgate Rd TS5 . . . 49 B4
Broadhaven Cl TS6 . . . 43 C3
Broadlands TS17 . . . . . 56 A2
Broadstone TS8 . . . . . . 61 B1
Broadway TS6 . . . . 33 B1
Broadway E TS10 . . . . 69 C2
Broadway W TS10 . . . 69 B1
Broadwell Rd TS4 . . . . 51 A2
Brocklesby Rd TS14 . . 79 B1
Brockrigg Ct TS14 . . . 79 A5
Brodie Cl TS17 . . . . . . 55 C2
Brogden Gn TS3 . . . . . 41 A1
Bromley Cl TS17 . . . . 62 A1
Bromley La TS8 . . . . . . 68 B2
Bromley Rd TS18 . . . . 81 A1
Brompton Gr TS18 . . . 45 B4
Brompton Rd TS5 . . . . 39 B2
Brompton St TS5 . . . . . 39 B2
Brompton Wlk TS25 . . 13 B1
Bronaber Cl TS17 . . . . 64 B4
Bronte Way TS23 . . . . 17 A3
Brookdale Rd TS7 . . . . 61 A3
Brookes The TS15 . . . . 66 C4
BROOKFIELD 58 B3
Brookfield Rd TS19 . . 34 B3
Brooklime Ave TS18 . . 46 C1
Brooklime Cl TS26 . . . . 4 C4
Brooksbank Ave
  TS10 . . . . 70 C2
Brooksbank Cl TS7 . . . 53 A1
Brooksbank Rd TS7 . . 53 A1
Brookside Ave [8]
  TS4 . . . . 50 B4
Brook St
  [3] Hartlepool TS26 . . . 9 B4
  Middlesbrough TS2 . . . 86 A4
Brookwood Way
  TS16 . . . . 63 C4
Broomfield Ave [2]
  TS16 . . . . 54 B1
Broom Hill Ave TS17 . 56 A2
Broomhill Gdns TS26 . . 5 A1
Broomlee Cl TS17 . . . . 65 A3
Brotherswater Cl
  TS10 . . . . 70 B2
Brotton Rd TS17 . . . . . 47 C3
Brougham Cl TS17 . . . 55 C3
Brougham Ent Ctr
  TS24 . . . . 6 A1
Brougham Ho [2]
  TS24 . . . . 6 A1
Brougham Prim Sch
  TS24 . . . . 6 A1
Brougham St TS2 . . . . 84 C4
Brougham Terr TS24 . 6 A1
Brough Cl TS17 . . . . . 48 A1
Brough Ct
  Hartlepool TS27 . . . . . . 2 C1
  [1] Middlesbrough
  TS4 . . . . 40 B1
Brough Field Cl
  TS17 . . . . 56 A2
Brough Rd TS23 . . . . . . 17 B1
Broughton Ave TS4 . . 51 A2
Broughton Gn TS10 . . 72 B4
Broughton Rd TS22 . . 16 B1
Browning Ave TS25 . . . 9 A1
Brownsea Ct TS17 . . . 65 B4
Broxa Cl TS10 . . . . 72 B3
Bruce Ave TS5 . . . . . . 38 C1
Bruce Cres TS24 . . . . . . 3 C1
Brundall Cl TS19 . . . . . 24 B1
Brunel Cl TS24 . . . . .6 B3
Brunel Ct TS24 . . . . . . 31 C1
Brunel Rd TS6 . . . . 63 B2
Brunner [6] TS23 . . . . 41 B1
Brunner Rd TS23 . . . . . 27 B4
Brunswick Ave TS6 . . 42 C4
Brunswick St
  [1] Hartlepool TS24 . . 10 A3
  Middlesbrough TS1 . . . 86 A4
  Stockton-on-T TS18 . . 83 A2
Bruntoft Ave TS24 . . . .3 B1
Bruntons Manor Ct
  TS3 . . . . 41 C2
Brus Cnr TS24 . . . . 3 C1

Brus Ho [5] TS17 . . . . 47 C1
Brusselton Cl TS5 . . . . 49 B1
Brusselton Ct TS18 . . 83 A1
Brylston Rd TS3 . . . . . 42 A3
Bryony Ct TS17 . . . . . . 78 B2
Bryony Gr TS7 . . . . 60 C4
Buccleugh Cl TS14 . . . 79 B1
Buchanan St TS18 . . . 83 A2
Buckie Gr TS25 . . . . . . 12 B2
Buckingham Dr TS6 . . 53 C3
Buckingham Rd
  TS18 . . . . 81 C2
Buckland Cl TS17 . . . . 65 C4
Buck St TS2 . . . . 29 B3
Budworth Cl TS23 . . . 17 B4
Bulmer Ct TS15 . . . . . . 67 A4
Bulmer Ct TS6 . . . . 43 B1
Bulmer Pl TS24 . . . . . . .5 B4
Bulmer's Bldgs TS14 . 79 A4
Bulmer Way TS11 . . . . 84 B3
Bungalows The TS6 . . 33 B1
Bunting Cl
  Hartlepool TS26 . . . . . . 5 A3
  Ingleby Barwick TS17 . 56 B1
Burbank Ct [1] TS24 . . 10 A3
Burbank St TS24 . . . . . 10 A3
Burdale Cl TS16 . . . . . . 54 A2
Burdon Cl TS19 . . . . . . 35 A4
Burdon Garth TS17 . . 54 A2
Burdon View TS16 . . . 63 B3
Burford Ave TS18 . . . . 46 A4
Burgess St TS18 . . . . . 82 A3
Burghley Ct TS8 . . . . . 59 C2
Burghley Dr TS17 . . . . 56 C2
Burlam Rd TS5 . . . . . . 39 A2
Burnaby Cl TS25 . . . . . 12 C4
Burneston Gr TS18 . . . 34 B1
Burnet Cl TS17 . . . . . . 56 B2
Burnholme Ave TS3 . . 41 C3
Burnhope Rd TS26 . . . . 8 A4
Burniston Dr
  Billingham TS22 . . . . . 16 B1
  Thornaby-on-T TS17 . . 56 B3
Burnmoor Cl TS10 . . . 72 C3
Burnmoor Dr TS16 . . . 54 B2
Burn Rd TS25 . . . . 10 A2
Burnsall Rd TS3 . . . . . 40 C2
Burns Ave TS25 . . . . 8 C1
Burnside Ct TS18 . . . . 81 B2
Burnside Gr TS18 . . . . 81 B2
Burns Rd TS6 . . . . 43 A3
Burnston Cl TS26 . . . . . 4 C1
Burnsville Rd TS6 . . . 33 A1
Burns Wlk TS6 . . . . . . 43 A3
Burn Valley Gr TS25 . . .9 B2
Burn Valley Rd TS26 . .9 B2
Burringham Rd TS20 . 25 C4
Burtonport Wlk [7]
  TS18 . . . . 82 C4
Burwell Dr TS19 . . . . . 34 B4
Burwell Rd TS3 . . . . . . 42 A1
Burwell Wlk TS25 . . . 14 B4
Burythorpe Cl TS4 . . . 40 B2
Busby Way TS15 . . . . . 64 C1
Bushmead Terr [3]
  TS3 . . . . 52 A4
Bush St TS5 . . . . 39 B2
Bushston Cl TS26 . . . . . 4 C1
Business Ctr The
  TS23 . . . . 22 C3
Bute Ave TS25 . . . . .9 B1
Bute Cl TS17 . . . . 56 C4
Bute St TS18 . . . . 82 A3
Butler St TS20 . . . . 26 B2
Butsfield Way [7]
  TS23 . . . . 17 B3
Buttercup Cl TS19 . . . 24 C2
Butterfield Cl [3]
  TS16 . . . . 63 B4
Butterfield Dr TS16 . . 54 B1
Butterfield Gr [2]
  TS16 . . . . 63 B4
Butterfly World ✷
  TS16 . . . . 55 A4

Buttermere Ave TS5 . . 49 B3
Buttermere Rd
  Eston TS6 . . . . 44 A4
  Redcar TS10 . . . . 70 B2
  Stockton-on-T TS18. . . . 80 B3
Butterwick Rd TS24 . . . 3 A1
Butterworth Ho 🟦
  TS17 . . . . 47 C1
Butt La TS14 . . . . 79 D3
Butts La TS16 . . . . 63 C3
Buxton Ave TS7 . . . . . . 61 A2
Buxton Gdns TS22 . . . 16 C1
Bydales Dr TS11 . . . . . 75 B2
Bydales Sch Specialist
  Tech Coll TS11 . . . . . 74 C3
Byelands St TS4 . . . . . 87 B1
Byfleet Ave TS3 . . . . . 41 B3
Byland Cl
  Guisborough TS14 . . . 79 C3
  Redcar TS10 . . . . 72 B4
Byland Gr TS25 . . . . . 13 C2
Byland Rd TS7 . . . . . . 62 B3
Bylands Gr TS19 . . . . 34 C2
Bylands Rd TS6 . . . . . 43 B2
Byland Way TS23 . . . 22 B3
By Pass Rd TS23 . . . . 21 B1
Byrneside Ave TS4 . . . 40 A1
Byron Cl TS23. . . . . . . 17 B4
Byron St TS26 . . . . 9 A4
Bywell Gr TS7 . . . . . . 52 C3

C

Cabot Ct TS17 . . . . . . 57 A4
Cadogan St
  Middlesbrough, North
  Ormesby TS3. . . . . 41 A4
  Middlesbrough TS1. . . . 85 B2
Cadwell Cl TS3 . . . . . 42 B1
Caedmon Prim Sch
  TS6 . . . . 43 C4
Caernarvon Cl TS6. . . 43 C4
Caernarvon Gr TS26 . . 4 C2
Cairn Ct TS2. . . . . 29 A4
Cairn Rd TS25 . . . . . . 1 B2
Cairnston Rd TS26 . . . . 4 B1
Caister Ct TS10 . . . . . 73 B3
Caistor Dr TS25. . . . . 14 C4
Caithness Rd
  Eston TS6 . . . . 42 C3
  Hartlepool TS25 . . . . . 12 A1
Calcott Cl TS19 . . . . . 35 A4
Calder Cl TS22. . . . . . 16 A2
Calder Gr
  Hartlepool TS25 . . . . . 12 A2
  Middlesbrough TS4. . . . 51 A2
  Redcar TS10 . . . . 70 B1
Caldey Gdns TS17. . . 64 B3
Caldicot Cl TS6 . . . . . 44 A4
Caldicotes Prim Sch
  TS3 . . . . 42 B3
Caldwell Cl TS8. . . . . 59 B2
Caledonian Rd TS25 . . 9 B1
Calf Fallow La TS20 . . 20 A2
CALIFORNIA 44 A2
California Cl TS18. . . 82 A3
California Rd TS6 . . . . 44 A2
California St TS18. . . 82 A3
Callander Rd TS25 . . 12 A2
Calluna Gr TS7 . . . . . 60 C4
Calthorpe Ct TS1 . . . 84 B3
Calverley Rd TS3. . . . 42 A2
Calvert Cl TS3 . . . . . . 87 C2
Calvert's La TS18 . . . 82 B3
Camborne Ho TS3 . . . 41 B3
Cambourne Cl TS8. . . 59 B2
Cambrian Ave TS10 . . 72 A4
Cambrian Ct TS17. . . 64 C4
Cambrian Rd TS23 . . 16 C1
Cambridge Ave
  Marton TS7. . . . . 61 A3
  Middlesbrough TS5. . . . 49 B4

Cambridge Rd
  Middlesbrough, Cargo
  Fleet TS3 . . . . 30 C1
  Middlesbrough TS5. . . . 49 B4
  Thornaby-on-T TS17 . . . 47 B4
Cambridge Sq TS5 . . 49 C4
Cambridge St 🟦
  TS12 . . . . 76 C3
Cambridge Terr TS2. . 23 C1
Camden St
  Middlesbrough TS1. . . . 87 B2
  Stockton-on-T TS18. . . . 81 C1
Camellia Cres TS20 . . 25 C3
Camelon St 🟨 TS17. . 47 C4
Cameron Rd TS24. . . . . 6 A1
Cameron St 🟦 TS26. . 10 A4
Campbell Ct TS18. . . . 82 C4
Campbell Rd TS25 . . 12 A2
Campion Cl TS17 . . . 56 B2
Campion Dr TS14 . . . 78 B2
Campion Gr TS7 . . . . 60 C4
Campion St 🟨 TS26. . . 9 B3
Camsell Ct TS5 . . . . . 39 B2
Canberra Gr TS18. . . 81 A1
Canberra Rd TS7 . . . 61 A3
Canewood TS3 . . . . . . 42 A2
Cannock Rd TS3 . . . . 41 A1
Cannon Park Cl TS1. . 84 B3
Cannon Park Ind Est
  TS1 . . . . 84 B3
Cannon Park Rd TS1. . 84 B3
Cannon Park Way
  TS1 . . . . 84 B3
Cannon St
  Middlesbrough TS1. . . . 84 A3
  Middlesbrough TS1. . . . 85 A2
Canon Gr TS15. . . . . . 67 A4
Canterbury Gr TS5 . . 39 C2
Canterbury Rd TS10. . 71 C1
Canton Gdns TS5 . . . 59 A3
Canvey Wlk TS14. . . . 79 A2
Capstan Ho TS24. . . . 10 B4
Captain Cook Prim Sch
  TS7 . . . . 61 A4
Captain Cook's
  Birthplace Mus ★
  TS7 . . . . 51 C1
Captain Cook's Cres
  TS7 . . . . 61 B3
Captain Cook Sq
  TS1 . . . . 84 C3
Captains Wlk TS24. . . 10 B4
Carburt Rd TS19 . . . . 24 B3
Carcut Rd TS3 . . . . . . 30 C1
Cardigan Cl TS6 . . . . 43 C4
Cardigan Gr TS26 . . . . 5 A3
Cardinal Gr TS19. . . . 34 A4
Cardwell Wlk 🟦
  TS17 . . . . 47 B4
Carew Cl TS15 . . . . . 66 A3
Carey Cl TS1. . . . . . . 85 B2
CARGO FLEET 31 A1
Cargo Fleet La TS3. . 41 C3
Cargo Fleet Rd
  Middlesbrough TS1. . . . 86 B3
  Middlesbrough TS3. . . . 86 C3
Carisbrooke Ave TS3. . 42 A2
Carisbrooke Rd TS26. . 8 B3
Carisbrooke Way
  TS10 . . . . 73 B4
Carlbury Ave TS5 . . . 58 C4
Carleton Terr TS15 . . 63 B2
Carlile Hill TS8 . . . . . 59 A1
Carlile Wlk 🟦 TS20 . . 26 B1
Carlisle St TS25 . . . . 13 C2
Carlow Cl TS14 . . . . . 79 B1
Carlow St TS1 . . . . . . 85 A1
Carlton Ave TS22 . . . 16 C2
Carlton Cl
  Guisborough TS14 . . . 79 B5
  Stockton-on-T TS18. . . . 82 A3
Carlton Dr TS17. . . . . 56 B4
Carlton St TS26 . . . . . . 9 B3
Carlyle Rd TS6. . . . . . 43 B3
Carmarthen Rd TS3 . . 52 A4
Carmel Gdns
  Guisborough TS14 . . . . 79 B4

Carmel Gdns continued
  Middlesbrough TS5. . . . 59 A3
  Nunthorpe TS7 . . . . . . 62 B3
  Stockton-on-T TS20. . . . 26 C3
Carnaby Wlk TS5 . . . 50 A3
Carnoustie Dr TS16 . . 54 C1
Carnoustie Gr TS27 . . . 2 B2
Carnoustie Way TS8 . 61 B2
Caroline Mews TS10 . . 71 A3
Caroline St TS26 . . . . . 9 C2
Carpenter Cl TS15 . . . 67 B4
Carradale Cl TS16. . . 63 C4
Carr Bridge Cl TS16. . 63 A3
Carriage Wlk TS16 . . 54 B2
Carrick Ct TS2 . . . . . . 29 A4
Carrick St TS24 . . . . . . 5 B4
Carroll Wlk TS25. . . . 11 B4
Carrol St TS18 . . . . . . 82 B3
Carron Gr TS6 . . . . . . 43 A1
Carr St
  🟦 Hartlepool TS26 . . . . . 5 C1
  Stockton-on-T TS18. . . . 81 C2
Carter Bequest Hospl
  TS5 . . . . 49 C4
Carthorpe Dr TS23 . . 17 B2
Cartmel Rd TS10 . . . 70 C1
Carville Ct 🟦 TS19 . . 24 B2
Casebourne Rd TS25. 10 A1
Casper Ct TS16 . . . . . 54 C2
Cass House Rd TS8 . . 59 B1
Casson Ct TS23 . . . . . 17 A2
Casson Way TS23 . . . 17 A2
Cassop Gr TS5 . . . . . . 49 A1
Cassop Wlk 🟦 TS19 . . 24 B2
Castle Cl TS19 . . . . . . 35 A4
Castle Dyke Wynd
  TS15 . . . . 63 C2
Castlegate Ctr TS18. . 83 B2
Castlegate Quay
  TS18 . . . . 83 B2
Castle Howard Cl
  TS27 . . . . 2 C1
Castlemartin TS17 . . . 64 C2
Castle Rd TS10 . . . . . 71 C1
Castlereagh Rd TS19. 80 C4
Castleton Ave TS5 . . . 49 A4
Castleton Dr TS22. . . 16 B1
Castleton Rd
  Eston TS6 . . . . 44 A3
  Hartlepool TS25 . . . . . 13 C1
  Stockton-on-T TS18. . . . 81 B3
Castleton Wlk TS17 . . 56 C4
Castle Way
  Middlesbrough TS4. . . . 40 B1
  Stockton-on-T TS18. . . . 83 B2
Castlewood TS3 . . . . . 42 A1
Castle Wynd TS7. . . . 62 A1
Catcote Rd TS25 . . . . 11 C4
Catcote Sch TS25. . . . 11 C4
Caterton Cl TS15. . . . 67 B4
Cat Flat La TS11 . . . . 74 A2
Cathedral Dr TS19 . . 24 A1
Cathedral Gdns TS2. . 84 C4
Catherine Rd TS24. . . 10 B3
Catherine St TS24. . . . 7 C2
Catterall Ho TS3 . . . . 41 B3
Cattistock Cl TS14 . . 79 C2
Caudwell Cl TS19 . . . 24 A3
Causeway The TS23 . . 21 B4
Cavendish Rd TS4 . . . 50 C4
Caversham Rd TS4. . . 51 A3
Cawood Dr TS5 . . . . . 50 A2
Cawthorn Cl TS8. . . . 58 C2
Caxton Gr TS25 . . . . . 81 C1
Caxton St TS5 . . . . . . 85 C1
Cayton Cl TS10 . . . . . 72 B3
Cayton Dr
  Billingham TS22 . . . . . 16 B1
  Middlesbrough TS5. . . . 50 A3
  Thornaby-on-T TS17 . . . 56 B3
Cecil St
  Middlesbrough TS1. . . . 84 B3
  Stockton-on-T TS18. . . . 83 A1
Cedar Cl TS6 . . . . 43 B2
Cedar Cres TS16 . . . . 55 A4
Cedar Ct TS17 . . . . . . 47 B3

Cedar Gr
  Redcar TS10 . . . . 71 B3
  Thornaby-on-T TS17 . . . 47 B3
Cedar Ho TS19. . . . . . 24 C1
Cedar Rd
  Marton TS7 . . . . 61 C4
  Ormesby TS7. . . . . 53 A2
Cedar St TS18 . . . . . . 82 B3
Cedar Terr TS2. . . . . . 29 C4
Cedar Wlk 🟦 TS24. . . 5 C2
Cedarwood Glade
  TS8 . . . . 58 C1
Celandine Cl TS7 . . . 51 B1
Celandine Way TS19 . 24 C1
Cennon Gr TS17 . . . . 64 C4
Centenary Cres TS20. 26 A3
Central Ave
  Billingham TS23 . . . . . 21 B2
  Middlesbrough TS5. . . . 38 C2
Central Bldgs 🟦
  TS24 . . . . 10 A4
Central St TS15 . . . . . 63 B2
Central Terr TS10 . . . 70 C4
Centre Ct TS5. . . . . . . 58 C3
Centre Mall TS1 . . . . 84 C3
Chadburn Gn TS4. . . . 50 B3
Chadburn Rd TS20. . . 26 A2
Chadderton Dr TS17 . 48 B2
Chadwell Ave 🟦 TS3. 51 C4
Chaffinch Cl TS26. . . . 5 A3
Chalcot Wlk TS3 . . . . 41 B3
Chaldron Way TS16 . . 54 A1
Chalfield Cl 🟦 TS17. . 56 C1
Chalford Oaks TS5 . . 49 A3
Chalk Cl TS18. . . . . . . 83 A1
Chalk Wlk TS18. . . . . 83 A1
Challacombe Cres
  TS17 . . . . 65 A2
Challoner Rd
  Hartlepool TS24 . . . . . . 5 C2
  Yarm TS15. . . . . 66 B4
Challoner Sq 🟦 TS24 . 5 C2
Chaloner Mews TS14. 79 B4
Chaloner Prim Sch
  TS14 . . . . 79 B5
Chaloner St TS14 . . . 79 B3
Chamomile Dr TS19. . 24 C2
Chancel Way TS6 . . . 43 C2
Chancery Rise TS17. . 56 B4
Chandlers Cl TS24 . . 10 B4
Chandlers Ridge
  TS7 . . . . 62 A2
Chandlers Ridge Prim
  Sch TS7 . . . . 62 A2
Chandlers Wharf
  TS18 . . . . 83 B1
Chantry Cl
  Middlesbrough TS3. . . . 51 B4
  Stockton-on-T TS20. . . . 26 A4
Chapelbeck Bglws
  TS14 . . . . 79 A3
Chapel Cl
  🟦 Marske-by-t-S
  TS11 . . . . 74 C1
  Middlesbrough TS3. . . . 52 B4
Chapel Ct TS23 . . . . . 21 B1
Chapelgarth TS8. . . . 58 C1
Chapel Rd TS23 . . . . 21 B1
Chapel St
  Guisborough TS14 . . . 79 B3
  Marske-by-t-S TS11 . . . 74 C2
  Thornaby-on-T TS17 . . . 83 C1
Chapman Ct TS3. . . . 41 C2
Chapman St 🟦 TS20 . 26 B3
Chard Wlk TS3. . . . . . 51 B4
Charlbury Rd TS3 . . . 41 B3
Charles St
  Hartlepool TS24 . . . . . 10 A3
  Redcar TS10 . . . . 71 A3
  Seaton Carew TS25 . . . 13 C2
  Thornaby-on-T TS17 . . . 47 B4
Charlock TS8 . . . . 68 B3
Charlotte St
  Middlesbrough TS3. . . . 84 C4
  Redcar TS10 . . . . 71 A3
Charlton Rd TS10 . . . 69 C2
Charnley Gn TS4. . . . 51 A2

Charnwood Cl 🟦
  TS11 . . . . 74 C1
Charnwood Dr TS7. . . 53 A1
Charrington Ave
  TS17 . . . . 56 B4
Charterhouse St TS25. . 9 B1
Chart Ho TS24 . . . . . . 10 B4
Chartwell Cl
  Ingleby Barwick
  TS17 . . . . 65 C4
  Marske-by-t-S TS11 . . . 74 B3
Charwood TS3. . . . . . 42 A2
Chase The
  Redcar TS10 . . . . 71 A2
  Stockton-on-T TS19. . . . 34 C3
Chatham Gdns TS24 . . 5 C2
Chatham Rd TS24. . . . 5 C2
Chatham Sq 🟦 TS25 . . 5 C2
Chathill Wlk TS7. . . . 52 C3
Chatsworth Ct TS19 . 25 A1
Chatsworth Gdns
  TS22 . . . . 16 C1
Chatsworth Ho TS3 . . 41 B3
Chatton Cl 🟨 TS11 . . 51 C4
Chaucer Ave TS25. . . . 9 A1
Chaucer Cl TS23 . . . . 17 A3
Chaytor Lee TS15 . . . 63 C1
Cheadle Wlk 🟦 TS1. . 51 C4
Cheam Ave TS3 . . . . . 41 B3
Cheddar Cl TS6 . . . . . 43 C4
Chedworth Ct TS17 . . 55 C3
Cheetham St TS6 . . . 33 A2
Chelker Cl TS25 . . . . . 8 A4
Chelmsford Ave
  TS18 . . . . 35 A2
Chelmsford Rd TS5 . . 39 C2
Chelmsford St TS17 . . 83 C1
Chelmsford Wlk TS5 . 39 C1
Chelsea Gdns TS20 . . 19 C1
Chelston Cl TS26. . . . . 4 B1
Cheltenham Ave
  Marton TS7. . . . . 61 A2
  🟦 Thornaby-on-T
  TS17 . . . . 47 C4
Cheltenham Cl TS5 . . 40 A2
Cheltenham Rd TS18. 27 C1
Chepstow Cl TS23. . . 17 A1
Chepstow Wlk TS26. . . 5 A2
Cheriton Gn TS3 . . . . 41 B3
Cherry Ct TS19. . . . . . 26 A1
Cherry Garth TS17 . . 56 A2
Cherry Tree Cl 🟦
  TS7 . . . . 53 A3
Cherry Tree Gdns
  TS20 . . . . 26 C3
Cherry Trees TS10. . . 70 B4
Cherrywood Ct TS5 . . 59 B4
Chertsey Ave TS3 . . . 41 B3
Chervil TS8. . . . . 68 B4
Cherwell Terr TS3. . . 41 C4
Chesham Cl TS20 . . . 26 C4
Chesham Gr TS20. . . 26 C4
Chesham Rd TS20. . . 26 C4
Chesham St TS5 . . . . 39 C2
Cheshire Rd TS20 . . . 26 C4
Chesneywood TS3 . . 42 A2
Chester Rd
  Hartlepool TS26 . . . . . . 5 B1
  Redcar TS10 . . . . 71 C1
Chester St TS1. . . . . . 85 B1
Chesterton Ave TS17. 56 B4
Chesterton Ct 🟦
  TS20 . . . . 26 B3
Chesterton Rd TS25. . 8 C1
Chesterwood TS3. . . 42 A2
Chestnut Ave TS10 . . 71 B2
Chestnut Cl TS12 . . . 76 B2
Chestnut Dr TS7 . . . . 61 B3
Chestnut Gr TS17 . . . 47 B3
Chestnut Rd TS16. . . 55 A4
Chestnut Sq TS19 . . . 25 C1
Chetwode Terr 🟦
  TS3 . . . . 51 C4
Chetwynd Ct TS19 . . 34 C4
Chevin Wlk TS3. . . . . 41 A1
Cheviot Cres TS23 . . 21 B3
Cheviot Ho TS4 . . . . . 87 B4

Chez Nous Ave TS25 . . 9 C1
Chichester Cl TS25. . 14 C4
Chilcroft Cl TS22. . . . . 16 A1
Childeray St TS18 . . . 81 C2
Child St TS14 . . . . 79 B3
Chillingham Ct TS23 . 17 B3
Chiltern Ave TS10. . . . 70 A1
Chilton Cl
 Middlesbrough TS5. . . . 49 B2
 Stockton-on-T TS19. . . 24 A3
Chiltons Ave TS23. . . 21 C1
Chine The TS12 . . . . . 76 B3
Chingford Ave TS3 . . 42 A4
Chingford Gr TS19 . . 80 A4
Chipchase Rd TS5 . . . 39 B2
Chippenham Rd TS4 . 50 C2
Chivers Ct TS18. . . . . 80 A4
Chopwell Cl TS19 . . . 24 B3
Christ Church Art Gal★
 TS24 . . . . 10 A4
Christchurch Dr
 TS18 . . . . 34 C1
Christopher Ho TS20. 20 C1
Christopher St
 4 Hartlepool TS26 . . . 9 B4
 5 Stockton-on-T
 TS20 . . . . 26 B1
Christ the King RC Prim
 Sch TS17 . . . . 57 B4
Church Cl
 Egglescliffe TS16 . . . . 63 C3
 Hartlepool TS24 . . . . . 7 B3
 Marske-by-t-S TS11 . . 75 A2
 Ormesby TS7. . . . . 52 C3
 Stainton TS8 . . . . 58 C1
 Thornaby-on-T TS17 . . 47 A4
Churchend Cl TS23 . . 21 B1
Church Field Way
 TS17 . . . . 56 A2
Church Howle Cres
 TS11 . . . . 75 B2
Churchill Cl TS6 . . . . 43 C3
Churchill Dr TS11. . . 74 C3
Churchill Rd TS6. . . . 43 C2
Church La
 Eston TS6 . . . . 43 B4
 Marske-by-t-S TS11 . . 75 A3
 Middlesbrough TS5. . . 49 B2
 Nunthorpe TS7. . . . . . 62 C1
 Ormesby TS7. . . . . 52 C2
 Ormesby TS7. . . . . 52 C2
Church Mount TS6. . . 43 C2
Church Rd
 Billingham TS23 . . . . . 21 B1
 Egglescliffe TS16 . . . . 63 C3
 Stockton-on-T TS18. . . 82 C3
Church Row
 Hartlepool TS24 . . . . . 9 C2
 Wolviston TS22 . . . . . 16 C4
Church Sq 1 TS24. . . 10 A4
Church St
 Guisborough TS14 . . . 79 C4
 Hartlepool TS24 . . . . . 10 A4
 Marske-by-t-S TS11 . . 75 A3
 Redcar TS10 . . . . 70 A4
 Seaton Carew TS25 . . . 13 D2
Church Street Mews
 TS14 . . . . 79 C4
Church Wlk
 Hartlepool TS24 . . . . . 7 B2
 Middlesbrough TS3. . . 42 A3
Cinderwood TS3. . . . . 42 A2
Cinnabar Rd TS19. . . 24 B1
Claire Ho 7 TS12. . . 76 C3
Clairville Ct TS4 . . . . 87 B1
Clairville Rd TS4 . . . . 87 B1
Clairville Stad TS4 . . 87 B1
Clapham Gn TS3. . . . . 40 C2
Clapham Rd TS15. . . . 66 B4
Claremont Ct TS17. . . 83 C2
Claremont Dr
 Hartlepool TS26 . . . . . 9 A3
 Marton TS7 . . . . 61 B2
Claremont Gdns
 TS19 . . . . 34 C3
Claremont Pk TS26 . . . 9 A2

Clarence Rd
 Eaglescliffe TS16 . . . . 54 C2
 Hartlepool TS24 . . . . . 9 C4
 Middlesbrough TS2. . . 23 C1
 Nunthorpe TS7 . . . . . . 62 B2
Clarence Row TS18 . . 82 B4
Clarence St
 Billingham TS23 . . . . . 23 C2
 Hartlepool TS24 . . . . . 7 B3
 Stockton-on-T TS18. . . 82 B4
Clarendon Rd
 Middlesbrough TS1. . . 85 C2
 Middlesbrough TS5. . . 87 A2
 Stockton-on-T TS20. . . 26 A2
 Thornaby-on-T TS17 . . 47 C2
Clarendon St TS10 . . 71 A4
Clarkson Ct TS25 . . . 12 A3
Clark St TS24 . . . . . . 10 A4
Claude Ave TS5 . . . . . 50 A4
Clavering Prim Sch
 TS24 . . . . 2 B1
Clavering Rd TS27 . . . 2 C1
Claxton Cl TS19 . . . . 24 A3
Claydon Gr TS17 . . . . 65 B4
Claygate TS17 . . . . . . 17 A3
Clay Lane Commercial
 Pk TS6 . . . . 32 B3
Claymond Ct TS20 . . 26 A4
Claymore Rd TS25 . . . 12 A1
Clayton Ct TS18. . . . . 46 C3
Cleadon Ave TS23. . . 17 B3
Cleadon Wlk 3
 TS19 . . . . 24 B2
Clearpool Cl TS24. . . .6 B3
Cleasby Way TS16. . . 54 B3
Cleatlam Cl TS19 . . . 24 B3
Cleator Dr TS14. . . . . 79 A1
Clee Terr TS23 . . . . . 21 C4
Clements Rise TS20. . 25 C4
Clepstone Ave TS5. . . 49 B4
Clevegate TS7 . . . . . . 62 A2
Cleveland Ave
 Middlesbrough TS5. . . 49 C4
 Stockton-on-T TS20. . . 26 B3
Cleveland Bsns Ctr
 TS1 . . . . 86 A3
Cleveland Cl TS7. . . . 52 C2
Cleveland Coll of Art &
 Design TS5 . . . . 49 C4
Cleveland Ct TS6 . . . 32 B2
Cleveland Ctr TS1 . . 84 C3
Cleveland Dr TS7 . . . 61 A4
Cleveland Gdns 5
 TS16 . . . . 54 B1
Cleveland Nuffield
 Hospl The TS26 . . . . . 19 C1
Cleveland Rd TS24. . . .6 B3
Cleveland Ret Pk
 TS6 . . . . 42 B4
Cleveland St
 Eston, California
 TS6 . . . . 44 A2
 Guisborough TS14 . . . 79 A3
 Hartlepool TS24 . . . . . 7 B3
 Middlesbrough TS2. . . 86 A4
 Normanby TS6 . . . . . . 43 B1
 Redcar TS10 . . . . 70 C4
Cleveland View
 Marske-by-t-S TS11 . . 74 A2
 Middlesbrough TS3. . . 41 C2
Cliff Cotts TS5 . . . . . 39 A1
Cliffden Ct TS12 . . . . 77 A3
Cliffe Ct TS25. . . . . . 13 C3
Cliff Ho TS11 . . . . . . 75 A3
Clifford Ct TS24. . . . . .5 B4
Clifford St TS10. . . . . 70 C4
Cliffport Ct 4 TS18 . 82 C4
Cliff Terr
 Hartlepool TS24 . . . . . 7 C2
 Marske-by-t-S TS11 . . 75 A3
Cliff The
 Hartlepool TS25 . . . . 13 D2
 Seaton Carew TS25 . . 13 D3
Cliffwood Cl TS6. . . . 44 A1

Clifton Ave
 Billingham TS22 . . . . . 16 B2
 Eaglescliffe TS16 . . . . 55 A3
 Hartlepool TS26 . . . . . 9 B3
 Stockton-on-T TS18. . . 46 B4
Clifton Gdns TS16. . . 55 A3
Clifton Pl TS6. . . . . . 43 B1
Clifton St TS2 . . . . . . 85 C2
Clive Cres TS20 . . . . 26 A3
Clive Rd
 Eston TS6 . . . . 43 B1
 Middlesbrough TS5. . . 39 B2
Clockwood Gdns
 TS15 . . . . 64 A1
Cloisters The TS19 . . 34 B4
Close The TS4 . . . . . . 40 B1
Clough Cl TS1 . . . . . . 85 A1
Clove Hitch Ho TS24 . . 6 B1
Clover Ct TS19. . . . . . 24 B1
Clover Dr TS26. . . . . . . 5 A1
Clover Wood Cl TS7. . 61 C3
Clydach Gr TS17 . . . . 64 C3
Clyde Gdns TS22. . . . 16 B2
Clyde Gr TS18 . . . . . . 46 B4
Clynes Rd TS6 . . . . . . 43 C4
Coach House Mews
 TS6 . . . . 53 B4
Coal La TS22. . . . . . . 16 C4
Coastguard Cotts
 TS12 . . . . 77 B3
Coast Rd
 Marske-by-t-S TS11 . . 74 B4
 Redcar TS10 . . . . 71 C2
Coate Cl TS8. . . . . . . 59 A2
COATHAM 70 B4
Coatham CE Prim Sch
 TS10 . . . . 70 B4
Coatham Cl TS8 . . . . 59 B2
Coatham Dr TS26 . . . .8 B3
Coatham Gr TS23 . . . 17 B3
Coatham Lo TS10 . . . 70 B4
Coatham Marsh Nature
 Reserve★ TS10 . . . . 69 C3
Coatham Rd
 Redcar TS10 . . . . 70 B4
 Stockton-on-T TS19. . . 24 B2
Coatham Vale TS16. . 63 A4
Coatsay Cl TS19. . . . . 24 B2
Cobble Carr TS14 . . . 79 A3
Cobblewood TS3 . . . . 42 A2
Cobb Wlk TS24 . . . . . .7 A3
Cobden St
 Hartlepool TS26 . . . . . 9 A4
 Stockton-on-T TS18. . . 82 A3
 Thornaby-on-T TS17 . . 47 C4
Cobham St TS1 . . . . . 85 C1
Cobwood TS3 . . . . . . 42 A2
Cocken Rd TS19 . . . . 24 B2
Cockerton Wlk TS19 . 24 B2
Cockfield Ave TS23 . . 17 C3
Cohen Ct TS20. . . . . . 25 C4
Colburn Wlk 4 TS6. . 44 A2
Colchester Rd TS20. . 26 B4
Coleby Ave TS4 . . . . 50 C2
Coledale Rd TS3 . . . . 41 A1
Colenso St TS26 . . . . .9 B2
Coleridge Ave TS25 . . 12 A1
Coleridge Rd TS23 . . 17 B4
Coleshill Cl TS23. . . . 17 B1
Coleton Gdns TS17. . 65 B4
College Rd TS3 . . . . . 42 A3
Colley Wlk 7 TS3 . . 41 B1
Colliers Gn TS4 . . . . 87 C2
Collin Ave TS4 . . . . . 50 B2
Collingwood St TS2. . 28 C4
Collingwood Rd
 Billingham TS23 . . . . . 27 A4
 Hartlepool TS26 . . . . . 9 B4
Collingwood Wlk 1
 TS26 . . . . 9 A4
Collins Ave TS20 . . . 26 C3
Collinson Ave TS5 . . . 48 C4
Colmans Nook TS23. . 22 C3
Colmore Ave TS3 . . . 42 A4
Colpitt Cl 6 TS20. . . 26 A4
Colsterdale Cl TS23. . 17 B2
Coltman St TS3 . . . . . 41 A4

Coltsfoot Dr TS18. . . . 46 C1
Columbia Dr TS17 . . . 83 B2
Columbine Cl TS7. . . . 60 C4
Colville St TS1. . . . . . 85 B2
Colwyn Cl TS10 . . . . . 73 A3
Colwyn Rd
 Hartlepool TS26 . . . . . 9 B2
 Stockton-on-T TS20. . . 26 C4
Comfrey Manor TS8. . 68 B4
Commerce Way TS6 . 42 B4
Commercial St
 TS24 . . . . 6 C1
 Hartlepool TS24 . . . . . 7 B3
 Middlesbrough TS2. . . 29 C3
 Stockton-on-T TS18. . . 82 B3
Commondale Ave
 TS19 . . . . 25 B1
Commondale Dr
 TS25 . . . . 13 B1
Commondale Gr
 TS10 . . . . 70 A1
Compass Ho TS24. . . 10 B4
Compton Cl 2 TS20 . 26 B1
Compton Ho TS3 . . . . 41 B3
Compton Rd TS25. . . 11 B4
Comrie Rd TS25 . . . . 12 A1
Concorde Way TS18. . 46 B2
Condercum Ct TS7 . . 55 C3
Coney Cl TS7 . . . . 56 C1
Conifer Cl TS7 . . . . . . 53 A3
Conifer Cres TS23. . . 21 A3
Conifer Dr TS19. . . . . 25 B2
Conifer Gr TS23. . . . . 21 A3
Coningsby Cl TS25 . . 14 B4
Conisborough Dr
 TS10 . . . . 73 B4
Coniscliffe Ct TS26. . . .8 B4
Coniscliffe Rd
 Hartlepool TS26 . . . . . 8 A3
 Stockton-on-T TS19. . . 24 B2
Coniston Ave TS10 . . 70 C2
Coniston Gr TS5 . . . . 49 B3
Coniston Rd
 Eston TS6 . . . . 44 A4
 Hartlepool TS25 . . . . . 10 A1
 Stockton-on-T TS18. . . 80 A4
Connaught Ct TS7 . . 62 B3
Connaught Rd
 Middlesbrough TS5. . . 38 C3
 Nunthorpe TS7 . . . . . . 62 B3
Conrad Wlk TS25 . . . 11 B4
Consett Cl TS19 . . . . 24 B2
Consett Dryden Cl
 TS6 . . . . 43 B1
Consort Cl TS19 . . . . 35 A3
Constable Gr TS23 . . 17 A3
Constance St TS3 . . . 87 C2
Constantine Ct TS1,
 TS2 . . . . 85 C1
Convalescent St 2
 TS12 . . . . 76 C4
Conway Ave TS23 . . . 17 B1
Conway Rd TS10 . . . . 71 A1
Conway Wlk TS26. . . . .5 A2
Conwy Gr TS17 . . . . . 64 C4
Conyers Cl TS15 . . . . 66 B4
Conyers Sch TS15 . . . 66 C3
Cook Cres TS20 . . . . 26 A3
Cookgate TS7 . . . . . . 61 C3
Cook's Ct TS7 . . . . . . 53 A3
Coombe Way TS18. . . 34 B1
Cooper Ct TS6. . . . . . 43 C2
Copeland TS7 . . . . . . 52 A4
Copgrove Cl TS3. . . . 40 C2
Copley Cl TS19. . . . . . 24 B2
Copley Wlk 5 TS3 . . 51 C4
Copnor Wlk 3 TS3 . . 51 C4
Copperwood TS3 . . . . 42 A1
Copperwood Cl 1
 TS27 . . . . .2 B2
Coppice Rd TS4. . . . . 40 B1
Coppice The TS8. . . . 59 A2
Copse Cl TS17 . . . . . . 56 B2
Copse La TS17 . . . . . . 56 B1
Copse The TS24. . . . . . 5 C2

Coquet Cl
 Ingleby Barwick
 TS17 . . . . 65 B3
 Redcar TS10 . . . . 73 C4
Coral Ho TS12 . . . . . . 76 C3
Coral St
 Middlesbrough TS1. . . 85 C2
 Saltburn-by-t-S TS12. . 76 C4
Coral Way TS10. . . . . 73 B4
Corbridge Ct TS8 . . . 59 B2
Corbridge Ct 5
 TS19 . . . . 24 B2
Corby 5 TS4 . . . . . . 40 C1
Corby Ave TS5 . . . . . 48 C3
Corby Lo TS20 . . . . . 20 A1
Corder Rd TS5 . . . . . 38 C3
Corfe Cres TS23 . . . . 17 A1
Coris Cl TS7 . . . . 60 C4
Cormland Cl TS20. . . 26 C3
Cormorant Dr TS10 . . 73 B3
Corncroft Mews TS6. . 33 B2
Cornfield Rd
 Middlesbrough TS5. . . 39 C1
 Stockton-on-T TS19. . . 34 B3
 Thornaby-on-T TS17 . . 47 A4
Cornfields Ho TS6 . . . 53 C4
Cornflower Cl TS26 . . 4 C4
Cornforth Ave TS3 . . 51 C4
Cornforth Cl TS19. . . 24 B2
Cornforth Gr TS23 . . 17 C3
Corngrave Cl TS11 . . 75 B2
Cornhill Wlk TS7. . . . 52 C3
Cornriggs Wlk 4
 TS19 . . . . 24 B3
Cornsay Cl
 Middlesbrough TS5. . . 49 A2
 Stockton-on-T TS19. . . 24 B2
Cornwall Cl TS7 . . . . 62 A3
Cornwall Cres TS23 . . 22 A3
Cornwall Gr TS20 . . . 26 C3
Cornwall Rd TS14. . . 79 A2
Cornwall St TS25 . . . .9 B1
Coronation Cres
 TS15 . . . . 66 A4
Coronation Ct 1
 TS6 . . . . 43 B1
Coronation Dr TS25. . 10 B1
Coronation Gn TS3. . 52 B4
Coronation St TS3 . . 41 A4
Corporation Rd
 Hartlepool TS24 . . . . . 7 A3
 Middlesbrough TS1. . . 86 A3
 Redcar TS10 . . . . 70 B3
Corporation St TS18 . 82 A3
Corpus Christi RC Prim
 Sch TS3 . . . . 41 C3
Corsham Wlk 4 TS3 . 51 C4
Cortland Rd TS7 . . . . 62 C3
Coryton Wlk 3 TS3 . . 51 C4
Costain Gr TS20 . . . . 21 A1
Costa St
 Middlesbrough TS1. . . 85 B1
 South Bank TS6. . . . . . 32 A2
Cotgarth Way TS19 . . 24 A2
Cotherstone Dr TS5. . 58 C4
Cotherstone Rd
 TS18 . . . . 46 B4
Cotswold Ave TS3. . . 41 A2
Cotswold Cres TS23. . 21 B3
Cotswold Dr TS10. . . 70 B1
Cottage Farm TS19 . . 81 A2
Cottersloe Rd TS20 . . 20 C1
Cottingham Dr TS3 . . 41 B3
Cottonwood TS3. . . . 42 A2
Coulby Farm Way
 Coulby Newham
 TS8 . . . . 60 B1
 Mount Pleasant TS8 . . 60 A4
Coulby Manor Farm
 TS8 . . . . 60 A2
Coulby Manor Way
 TS8 . . . . 59 C3
COULBY NEWHAM . 60 A2
Coulson Cl TS15 . . . . 66 B3

Coulthard Ct **9** TS6.. . 32 A2
Coulton Gr TS22 . . . . . 16 A1
Council Of Europe Bvd
TS17 . . . . 82 B3
Coundon Gn **2** TS19 . . 24 B2
Countisbury Rd TS20. 19 C2
Courageous Cl TS25 . . 13 B3
Courtney Wlk TS3. . . . 41 C3
Court Rd TS4 . . . . 40 B1
Covent Cl TS6 . . . . 53 B3
Coverdale TS8 . . . . 59 A1
Coverdale Rd TS19. . . 35 A2
Covert The TS8 . . . . . . 68 B4
Cowdray Cl TS14. . . . . 79 C1
Cowley Cl
Eaglescliffe TS16 . . . . . 45 C1
Seaton Carew TS25 . . . 13 C4
Cowley Rd TS5. . . . . . . 49 C2
Cowpen Bewley Rd
TS23 . . . . 23 A4
Cowpen Bewley
Woodland Ctry Pk &
Visitor Ctr ★ TS23. . 18 C3
Cowpen Cres TS19 . . . 24 B2
Cowpen Ind Est
TS23 . . . . 22 C4
Cowpen La TS23 . . . . . 18 A1
Cowper Gr TS25 . . . . . 11 B4
Cowper Rd TS20 . . . . . 26 C1
Cowshill Gn **7** TS19 . . 24 B2
Cowton Way TS16. . . . 54 B3
Coxgreen Cl TS19 . . . . 24 B2
Coxhoe Rd TS23 . . . . . 17 C1
Coxwold Cl TS5. . . . . . 50 A2
Coxwold Rd TS18 . . . . 81 A2
Coxwold Way TS23. . . 22 C3
Cradley Dr TS5 . . . . . . 58 C3
Cradoc Gr TS17 . . . . . . 64 C4
Cragdale Rd TS3. . . . . 41 A2
Craggs St
Middlesbrough TS4. . . . 86 B3
Stockton-on-T TS19. . . 82 A4
Cragside Ct TS17 . . . . 56 B1
Cragston Cl TS26 . . . . 4 C1
Cragston Ct **2** TS10 . . 73 B2
Craigearn Rd TS6. . . . 43 A2
Craigton Ho TS10 . . . . 70 C4
Craigweil Cres TS19 . . 25 C1
Crail Wlk TS25. . . . . . . 12 A2
Craister Rd TS20. . . . . 82 A4
Cramlington Cl TS8 . . 59 B2
Cranage Cl TS5 . . . . . . 49 A4
Cranberry Rd TS3 . . . . 61 A1
Cranbourne Dr TS10 . 73 C2
Cranbourne Terr
TS18 . . . . 81 C1
Cranbrook TS8 . . . . . . 61 B4
Cranfield Ave TS3. . . . 42 A4
Cranford Ave TS6 . . . . 42 C4
Cranford Cl TS6. . . . . . 42 C4
Cranford Gdns TS5. . . 49 A3
Cranleigh Rd TS18. . . 81 B2
Cranmore Rd TS3 . . . . 41 B3
Cranstock Cl TS22 . . . 11 B4
Cranswick Cl TS23 . . . 17 C4
Cranswick Dr TS5. . . . 50 A2
Cranwell Gr TS17 . . . . 57 A3
Cranwell Rd TS25 . . . . 11 C1
Cranworth Gn TS17 . . 37 B1
Cranworth St TS17. . . 83 C1
Crathorne Cres TS5 . . 38 C2
Crathorne Pk
Eston TS6 . . . . 43 A1
Normanby TS6 . . . . 53 B4
Crathorne Rd TS20. . . 26 B4
Craven St TS1 . . . . 85 B2
Craven Vale TS14 . . . . 79 B2
Crawcrook Wlk TS19 . 24 B2
Crawford St TS25 . . . . 13 C2
Crawley Rd TS17. . . . . 48 A3
Crayke Rd TS18. . . . . . 81 A1
Creekwood TS3. . . . . . 42 A2
Cremorne Cl TS7 . . . . 60 C4
Crescent Ave TS23 . . . 21 C1

Crescent Lo **8** TS5 . . . 39 B1
Crescent Rd TS1 . . . . . 85 B1
Crescent The
Egglescliffe TS16 . . . . . 63 B4
Hartlepool TS26 . . . . . . 9 A4
2 Marske-by-t-S
TS11 . . . . 75 A2
Middlesbrough TS5. . . . 39 B1
Nunthorpe TS7 . . . . . . 62 C2
Ormesby TS7. . . . . 52 B3
Redcar TS10 . . . . 71 B3
Saltburn-by-t-S TS12. . 76 C2
Thornaby-on-T TS17. . . 47 B3
Cresswell Cl TS8. . . . . 59 B2
Cresswell Ct TS26 . . . . 8 A4
Cresswell Dr TS26 . . . 8 C4
Cresswell Rd
Eston TS6 . . . . 33 B2
Hartlepool TS26 . . . . . . 8 C4
Crest The TS26. . . . . . . 8 B4
Crestwood
Middlesbrough TS3. . . . 42 A2
Redcar TS10 . . . . 73 A2
Cribyn Cl TS17. . . . . . . 64 C4
Cricket La TS6. . . . . . . 53 B4
Crieff Wlk TS25 . . . . . . 12 A2
Crimdon Cl TS18. . . . . 59 B2
Crimdon Wlk TS19 . . . 24 A3
Crinklewood TS3 . . . . 42 A1
Croft Ave TS5. . . . . 49 A3
Croft Dr TS7 . . . . 62 B2
Crofton Ave **2** TS4. . . 40 A1
Crofton Ct TS18 . . . . . 37 B4
Crofton Rd TS18 . . . . . 37 B4
Croft Rd TS16. . . . . . . 63 B4
Croft Terr TS24. . . . . . .7 B2
Croft The TS7 . . . . 61 B3
Cromer Cl TS16. . . . . . 63 C4
Cromer St TS14. . . . . . 87 B2
Cromer Wlk TS25 . . . . 11 C1
Cromore Cl TS17. . . . . 56 C4
Cromwell Ave TS18 . . 82 B4
Cromwell Gn TS18 . . . 82 B3
Cromwell Rd TS6 . . . . 32 A1
Cromwell Road Prim
Sch TS6 . . . . 32 A1
Cromwell St
Hartlepool TS26 . . . . . . 10 A2
Middlesbrough TS3. . . . 87 C2
Cromwell Terr TS17 . . 47 B4
Crookers Hill Cl TS7. . 62 A1
Crookhall Wlk **6**
TS19 . . . . 24 B2
Crooks Barn La TS20. 20 C2
Crooksbarn Prim Sch
TS20 . . . . 20 B2
Crook St TS20 . . . . 20 B1
Cropton Cl TS10 . . . . . 72 B3
Cropton Way TS8 . . . . 60 B2
Crosby Ct TS16 . . . . . . 55 A1
Crosby Ho TS3. . . . . . . 41 B3
Crosby Wlk **8** TS17. . 47 B4
Crossbeck Terr **4**
TS6 . . . . 43 B1
Crossbeck Way TS7 . . 53 A3
Crosscliff TS8 . . . . 59 B2
Cross Fell TS10 . . . . . . 70 B1
Crossfell Rd TS3 . . . . . 41 A1
Crossfields TS8 . . . . . . 68 A4
Cross St
4 Eston TS6 . . . . 44 A2
Guisborough TS14 . . . . 79 B3
Stockton-on-T TS20. . . 26 B4
Crosswell Pk TS17 . . . 64 C3
Crosthwaite Ave **1**
TS4 . . . . 50 B4
Crowhurst Cl TS14 . . . 79 B2
Crow La TS6. . . . . 44 C3
Crowland Ave TS3 . . . 42 B1
Crowland Rd TS25 . . . 14 B4
Croxdale Gr TS19 . . . . 34 C2
Croxdale Rd TS23 . . . . 17 B1
Croxden Gr **7** TS3 . . . 52 A4
Croxton Ave TS25 . . . . 14 C4
Croxton Cl TS19. . . . . . 34 A3
Croydon Rd TS1 . . . . . 87 B1

Crummackdale TS17. . 65 B2
Crummock Rd TS10. . . 70 C2
Culgaith Ave TS3 . . . . 41 A2
Cullen Rd TS25 . . . . . . 12 A2
Culloden Way TS23 . . 18 A2
Culross Gr TS19. . . . . . 34 A3
Cumberland Cres
TS23 . . . . 21 B2
Cumberland Gr TS20. 20 A1
Cumberland Rd TS5. . 39 C2
Cumbernauld Rd
TS17 . . . . 48 A3
Cumbria Wlk **11** TS5 . 9 C2
Cumnor Wlk TS3. . . . . 41 B3
Cundall Rd TS26 . . . . . 9 A4
Cunningham Dr
TS17 . . . . 57 A3
Cunningham St TS5. . 85 A1
Curlew La TS20 . . . . . . 20 B2
Curran Ave TS5 . . . . . . 38 C1
Curson St **1** TS6 . . . . 44 A1
Curthwaite TS5. . . . . . 58 B4
Cuthbert Cl TS17. . . . . 47 B4
Cutler Cl TS7 . . . . 61 B4
Cygnet Dr TS18 . . . . . . 46 C2
Cypress Rd
Marton TS7 . . . . 61 B4
Redcar TS10 . . . . 71 C2

D

Dacre Cl TS17 . . . . 47 B2
Daimler Dr TS23 . . . . . 18 B1
Daisy Cl TS19. . . . . 24 C1
Daisy La TS7. . . . . 53 A3
Dalby Cl
Billingham TS22 . . . . . . 16 A1
Redcar TS10 . . . . 72 C3
Dalby Ct TS8. . . . . 60 C2
Dalby View TS8 . . . . . . 60 B1
Dalby Way TS8. . . . . . . 60 B1
Dalcross Ct TS8. . . . . . 59 B1
Dale Cl TS19. . . . . 24 A2
Dale Garth TS11 . . . . . 75 A1
Dale Gr TS19 . . . . 34 C2
Dales Park Rd TS8 . . . 59 A1
Dale St TS1. . . . . 84 C3
Daleston Ave TS5 . . . . 49 C4
Daleston Cl TS26. . . . . .4 B1
Daleville Cl TS4. . . . . . 50 C4
Dalkeith Cres TS8. . . . 59 B3
Dalkeith Rd TS25 . . . . 11 C3
Dallas Ct TS8 . . . . 59 B1
Dallas Rd TS25. . . . . . . 11 C3
Dalmuir Cl TS16 . . . . . 54 C1
Dalry Gr TS25. . . . . 11 C2
Dalston Ct **12** TS7 . . . . 53 A3
Dalton Ct TS10. . . . . . . 73 C2
Dalton Gr
Billingham TS23 . . . . . . 17 B3
Stockton-on-T TS20. . . 26 A2
Dalton St TS26. . . . . . . .9 B3
Daltry Cl TS15 . . . . 67 B4
Dalwood Ct TS8 . . . . . 59 B1
Danby Ct **1** TS20 . . . . 26 B1
Danby Dale Ave
TS10 . . . . 70 A1
Danby Gr
Hartlepool TS25 . . . . . . 13 C2
Thornaby-on-T TS17 . . . 47 C3
Danby Rd
Eston TS6 . . . . 44 A3
Stockton-on-T TS20. . . 26 B1
Danby Wlk TS23 . . . . . 16 C1
Danby Wynd TS15. . . . 63 B2
Danesbrook Cl TS17 . 65 B2
Danesfort Ave TS14 . . 79 A3
Daniel Ct TS4 . . . . 50 B4
Dante Rd TS7 . . . . 60 B4
Daphne Rd TS19 . . . . . 26 A1
Darcy Cl TS15. . . . . 66 B2
Darenth Cres TS3 . . . . 41 B1
Darlington La
Stockton-on-T,
Bishopsgarth TS19 . . . 25 A2
Stockton-on-T TS20. . . 25 C3
Darlington Rd TS18 . . 45 B4

Darlington St TS24. . . .7 B2
Darnbrook Way TS7. . 61 C2
Darnell Gn TS4 . . . . . . 51 A2
Darnton Dr TS4 . . . . . . 51 A2
Darras Wlk TS3 . . . . . . 41 B3
Dartmouth Gr TS10 . . 73 A4
Darvel Rd TS25 . . . . . . 11 C3
Darwen Ct TS8 . . . . . . 59 B1
Darwin Cl TS19 . . . . . . 24 B3
Darwin Gr TS25 . . . . . . .8 B1
Dauntless Cl TS25. . . . 13 C3
Davenport Rd TS15 . . 66 B3
Daventry Ave TS19 . . . 25 B2
David Rd TS20 . . . . 26 C2
Davison Dr TS24 . . . . . .5 B4
Davison St TS1 . . . . . . 84 C3
Davy Rd TS6. . . . . 31 C1
Dawdon Cl TS19 . . . . . 24 B3
Dawley Cl TS17 . . . . . . 48 A3
Dawlish Dr TS25 . . . . . 12 B1
Dawlish Gn TS4. . . . . . 51 A2
Dawn Cl TS20. . . . . 20 B2
Dawson Ho TS3. . . . . . 21 B4
Dawson Sq TS5. . . . . . 38 C2
Dawsons Wharf Ind Est
TS5 . . . . 29 B3
Daylight Rd TS19 . . . . 25 B1
Deacon Gdns TS25. . . 13 C1
Deacon St TS3. . . . . . . 41 A4
Deal Cl TS19. . . . . 25 B2
Deal Ct TS4 . . . . 40 B1
Deal Rd
Billingham TS23 . . . . . . 17 A2
Redcar TS10 . . . . 73 B4
Deansgate TS6 . . . . . . 44 B2
Dean St TS18 . . . . 83 A2
De Brus Ct **4** TS12. . . 76 C4
Debruse Ave TS15 . . . 66 A4
De Brus Way TS14 . . . 79 B4
Deepdale TS14 . . . . . . 78 A2
Deepdale Ave
Eston TS6 . . . . 44 A4
Middlesbrough,
Beechwood TS4. . . . . . 50 C4
Middlesbrough TS4. . . . 40 A1
Deepdene Cl TS10 . . . 73 C3
Deepgrove Wlk **3**
TS6 . . . . 44 A3
Dee Rd TS6. . . . . 43 B3
Deerpool Cl TS24 . . . . .6 B3
De Havilland Dr
TS11 . . . . 74 B3
Deighton Gr TS23. . . . 17 A2
Deighton Rd TS4. . . . . 51 A1
De La Mare Dr TS23 . . 17 B4
Delamere Dr TS11 . . . 74 B1
Delamere Rd TS13 . . . 51 C4
Delarden Rd TS3. . . . . 41 B3
Delaval Rd TS23 . . . . . 17 C1
Dell Cl TS7 . . . . 60 C3
Dellfield Cl TS3. . . . . . 51 C4
Del'strother Ave
TS19 . . . . 80 B4
Denbigh Rd TS23 . . . . 17 B2
Dene Cl TS17 . . . . 48 A3
Dene Gr TS10 . . . . 71 A3
Dene Rd TS4. . . . . 40 B2
Deneside Cl TS15. . . . 64 A1
Denevale TS15 . . . . . . 64 A1
Dene Wlk TS11 . . . . . . 74 B2
Denham Gn TS3 . . . . . 41 B3
Denholme Rd TS18. . . 46 A4
Denmark St TS2 . . . . . 84 B4
Dennison St TS13 . . . . 81 C1
Densham Dr TS18. . . . 81 C1
Denshaw Ct TS19 . . . . 34 B3
Dentdale Cl TS15 . . . . 66 C3
Denton Cl
Middlesbrough TS5. . . . 58 B4
Stockton-on-T TS19. . . 24 B3
Dent St TS26. . . . . .9 C4
Depot Rd TS2. . . . . . . 29 B3
Derby Ave TS5 . . . . . . 48 C4
Derby Cl **3** TS17. . . . . 47 C4
Derby Rd TS14. . . . . . . 79 A2
Derby St
Hartlepool TS25 . . . . . . .9 C1

Derby St continued
Stockton-on-T TS18. . . 82 A3
Derby Terr TS17. . . . . . 37 B1
Derby The TS7 . . . . . . 60 C4
Derwent Ave TS14 . . . 78 C2
Derwent Grange TS24..6 B3
Derwent Ho TS3. . . . . 18 A3
Derwent Rd
Redcar TS10 . . . . 70 A2
Thornaby-on-T TS17. . . 47 C2
Derwent St
Hartlepool TS26 . . . . . . 9 C4
Middlesbrough, North
Ormesby TS3. . . . . 41 A4
Middlesbrough TS1. . . . 85 B2
Stockton-on-T TS20. . . 26 A2
Derwentwater Ave
TS5 . . . . 49 B3
Derwentwater Rd
TS6 . . . . 44 A4
Desford Gn TS3. . . . . . 41 B3
Deva Cl TS4 . . . . 40 C1
Devon Cl TS10 . . . . . . 70 B1
Devon Cres TS23. . . . . 22 A3
Devonport Rd
Middlesbrough TS5. . . . 40 A1
Stockton-on-T TS18. . . 82 C4
Devon Rd
Eston TS6 . . . . 43 C4
Guisborough TS14 . . . . 79 A2
Devonshire Rd TS5. . . 39 B2
Devonshire St TS18 . . 46 B4
Devon St TS25 . . . . . . 9 C1
Dewberry TS8 . . . . 68 C4
Dewberry Cl TS26. . . . 4 C4
Dew La TS7. . . . . 52 C2
Diamond Ct TS18 . . . . 46 B2
Diamond Rd
Middlesbrough TS1. . . . 85 C2
Thornaby-on-T TS17 . . . 47 C3
Diamond St TS12 . . . . 76 C4
Dickens Ct TS23 . . . . . 17 A3
Dickens Gr TS25 . . . . . 9 A1
Dickens St TS24 . . . . . .3 B1
Didcot Cl **14** TS10 . . . 73 B2
Diligence Way TS16. . 54 B2
Dillside TS19 . . . . 24 C1
Dinas Ct TS17. . . . . . . 64 C4
Dingleside TS19 . . . . . 35 A4
Dinsdale Ave TS5 . . . . 49 B1
Dinsdale Cres TS23. . . 17 C2
Dinsdale Dr TS16 . . . . 54 C1
Dinsdale Rd TS19 . . . . 24 B3
Diomed Ct TS7 . . . . . . 51 B1
Dionysia Rd TS3 . . . . . 41 A3
Dipton Gn TS4 . . . . . . 51 A2
Dipton Rd TS19 . . . . . . 24 B4
Dishforth Cl TS17 . . . . 57 A3
Dixon Gr TS3 . . . . 41 A3
Dixons Bank
Marton TS7 . . . . 61 B3
Nunthorpe TS7 . . . . . . 62 A1
Dixon St TS18. . . . . . . 82 A3
Dobson Pl TS24. . . . . . 3 A1
Dockside Rd
Middlesbrough TS3. . . . 31 B2
South Bank TS6. . . . . . 32 C2
Dockside Road Ind Est
TS3 . . . . 30 C2
Dock St TS2 . . . . 86 B4
Dodford Rd TS8. . . . . . 59 B1
Dodsworth Wlk TS27. . 2 C1
Doncaster Cres TS19 . 25 C3
Donegal Terr TS1 . . . . 85 A1
Donington Gn TS3 . . . 42 B1
Dorchester Cl
Middlesbrough TS8. . . . 60 B4
Stockton-on-T TS19. . . 25 C2
Dorchester Dr TS24 . . 2 C2
Dorlcote Pl **11** TS20. . 26 B2
Dorman Gdns TS5 . . . 39 B1
Dorman Mus ★ TS5 . . 85 C1
Dorman Rd TS6. . . . . . 44 A4
Dorman's Cres TS10 . 69 C2
DORMANSTOWN 69 B1
Dormanstown Ind Est
TS10 . . . . 69 B1

Dormanstown Prim Sch
TS10 . . . . 69 B1
Dormer Parkhurst's
Hospl Almshouses
TS25 . . . . 14 B2
Dormer Way TS6. . . . . 31 C1
Dornoch Sands TS5 . . 58 B3
Dorothy St TS3 . . . . . 41 A4
Dorothy Terr 9
TS17 . . . . 47 B4
Dorrien Cres TS3 . . . 41 A3
Dorset Cl
Middlesbrough TS5. . . . 39 B2
Redcar TS10 . . . . 70 C1
Dorset Cres TS23 . . . 22 A4
Dorset Rd
Guisborough TS14 . . . . 79 A2
Stockton-on-T TS20. . . 26 C3
Dorset St TS25. . . . . 9 C1
Douglas Cl TS18 . . . . 46 B2
Douglas St TS4 . . . . . 87 B1
Douglas Terr TS6 . . . 43 B1
Douglas Wlk 8 TS20. 26 B1
Dovecote Cl TS11. . . . 74 C2
Dovecot St TS18 . . . . 83 A2
Dovedale Ave TS6. . . 44 A4
Dovedale Cl TS20 . . . 26 C4
Dovedale Rd TS20 . . . 26 C3
Dove La TS20 . . . . . . 20 B1
Dover Cl
Billingham TS23 . . . . . 16 C2
Redcar TS10 . . . . 73 B4
Dover Rd TS19. . . . . . 25 C2
Dover St TS4 . . . . . . 10 A4
Dovey Ct TS17 . . . . . . 64 C4
Downham Ave TS3 . . 51 C4
Downham Gr TS25 . . . 11 C1
Downholme Gr TS18 . 45 B4
Downside Rd TS5 . . . 48 C4
Dowson Rd TS24. . . . . . . 3 B1
Doxford Wlk TS8 . . . 59 B1
Doyle Ct TS18 . . . . . . 11 B4
Doyle Wlk TS25 . . . . 11 B4
Dragon Ct 9 TS20. . 26 B4
Drake Cl TS11 . . . . . . 75 B2
Drake Ct TS2 . . . . . . 28 C3
Drake Rd TS20. . . . . . 26 B3
Draycott Ave TS5 . . . 59 A3
Draycott Cl
Redcar TS10 . . . . 72 B3
Stockton-on-T TS20. . . 25 B4
Drayton Rd TS25. . . . 11 B4
Dresser La 3 TS5. . . 39 B1
Driffield Way TS23 . . 17 C4
Driftwell Dr TS19 . . . 34 B4
Drive The
Greatham TS25. . . . . . 14 B2
Marske-by-t-S TS11 . . 74 B2
Stainton TS8 . . . . 58 C1
Thornaby-on-T TS17 . . 56 C4
Droitwich Ave TS19 . . 25 B2
Druridge Gr TS10 . . . 73 C4
Dryburn Rd TS19. . . . 24 A4
Dryden Cl 2 TS23 . . 17 B4
Dryden Rd TS25. . . . . 11 C4
Duchy Rd TS26 . . . . . . 8 A3
Duddon Sands TS5. . . 58 B3
Duddon Wlk TS19. . . . 80 C3
Dudley Rd TS23 . . . . 17 A2
Dudley Wlk TS10. . . . 73 B4
Dufton Rd TS5. . . . . . 39 A1
Dugdale St TS18 . . . . 82 C4
Duhallow Cl TS14. . . . 79 B1
Dukeport Ct 3 TS18 . 82 C4
Dukes Ct TS17 . . . . . 57 A1
Duke St TS10. . . . . 9 A4
Dukesway TS17 . . . . 57 A1
Dulas Ct TS10. . . . . . 73 B3
Dulverton Cl TS17. . . 65 B2
Dulverton Way TS14 . 79 C2
Dumbarton Ave
TS19 . . . . 25 C2
Dumfries Rd TS25. . . 12 A2
Dunbar Ave TS4 . . . . 51 A2
Dunbar Dr TS16. . . . . 63 C4
Dunbar Rd
Billingham TS23 . . . . . 17 A1

Dunbar Rd continued
Hartlepool TS25 . . . . . 12 A3
Duncan Ave TS10 . . . 70 A2
Duncan Rd TS25 . . . . 11 C3
Duncombe Rd TS4 . . . 86 B3
Dundas Arc TS1. . . . . 86 A3
Dundas Mews TS1 . . 86 A3
Dundas St E TS12 . . . 77 A3
Dundas St W TS12 . . . 76 C3
Dundas St
Middlesbrough TS1. . . 86 A4
Redcar TS10 . . . . 70 C4
Stockton-on-T TS18 . . 82 C4
Dundee Rd TS25. . . . . 12 A2
Dunedin Ave TS18 . . . 35 A1
Dunelm Rd TS19 . . . . 24 C1
Duneside TS19 . . . . . . 24 C1
Dunford Cl 3 TS19 . . 24 B3
Dunholm Ave TS3 . . . 52 C4
Dunkeld Cl TS19 . . . . 24 B4
Dunkerque Mall TS1 . 84 C3
Dunkery Cl TS17 . . . . 65 A2
Dunlane Cl TS5. . . . . 38 C3
Dunlin Cl TS20. . . . . . 20 C2
Dunlin Ho TS24. . . . . 10 B4
Dunlin Rd TS26 . . . . . . 5 A3
Dunmail Rd
Redcar TS10 . . . . 70 B2
Stockton-on-T TS19 . . 80 C3
Dunmoor Gr TS17. . . . 65 A3
Dunmow Rd 2 TS3 . 52 A4
Dunnet Cl TS10 . . . . . 72 C2
Dunning Rd TS1. . . . . 86 A3
Dunning St TS1. . . . . 86 A3
Dunoon Cl TS19 . . . . 25 C2
Dunoon Rd TS25 . . . . 11 C2
Dunottar Ave TS16. . . 54 C3
Dunsdale Cl
Eston TS6 . . . . 43 C1
Marske-by-t-S TS11 . . 75 B2
Dunsley Cl TS3 . . . . . 40 C2
Dunsley Ct TS14 . . . . 79 B4
Dunsley Dr TS23 . . . . 17 B2
Dunsop Ave TS4 . . . . 51 A2
Dunstable Cl TS19 . . . 25 B2
Dunstable Rd TS5. . . 38 C3
Dunster Ho 4 TS3 . . 41 B1
Dunster Rd TS23 . . . . 17 B2
Dunston Cl TS14 . . . . 79 B1
Dunston Rd
Hartlepool TS26 . . . . . . 4 C1
Stockton-on-T TS19. . . 24 B3
Durham 4 TS4 . . . . . 40 C1
Durham Lane Ind Pk
TS16 . . . . 54 C1
Durham Lane Prim Sch
TS16 . . . . 54 A1
Durham Rd
Eston TS6 . . . . 44 A2
Redcar TS10 . . . . 71 C1
Stockton-on-T TS19. . . 25 A3
Wolviston TS22 . . . . . . 16 C4
Durham St
Hartlepool TS24 . . . . . 7 B3
Middlesbrough TS2 . . . 29 C3
Stockton-on-T TS18. . . 82 A3
Durham Tees Valley
Bsns Ctr TS19. . . . . . 82 A4
Durness Gr TS25. . . . 11 C2
Durnford Rd TS3. . . . 42 A1
Dyke House Comp Sch
TS24 . . . . 5 C2

E

Eagle Ct TS18. . . . . . . 46 B2
Eagle Pk TS8 . . . . 61 C1
EAGLESCLIFFE 54 B2
Eaglescliffe Ind Est
TS16 . . . . 54 C2
Eaglescliffe Sta
TS16 . . . . 54 C3
Eaglesfield Rd TS5. . . 11 B3
Eamont Gdns TS26. . . . 9 B3
Eamont Rd TS20 . . . . 26 A3
Eamont Terr TS25 . . . . 9 B2
Earle Cl TS15 . . . . . . 67 B4

Earleston Wlk TS25 . . 11 B3
Earls Court Rd TS8. . . 59 B1
Earls Ct TS20 . . . . . . 26 B3
Earlsdon Ave TS5 . . . 58 C4
Earlsferry Rd TS25 . . 11 B3
Earls Nook TS23 . . . . 22 B3
Earl St TS24 . . . . 6 C4
Earlsway TS17 . . . . . . 57 B1
Earn Wlk TS25 . . . . . 11 B3
Earsdon Cl TS20 . . . . 25 B4
Easby Ave TS5 . . . . . 50 A4
Easby Cl
Eston TS6 . . . . 44 B3
Guisborough TS14 . . . 79 C3
Redcar TS10 . . . . 72 B4
Easby Gr
Eston TS6 . . . . 43 B2
Thornaby-on-T TS17 . . 47 C3
Easby Rd TS23. . . . . . 21 C4
Easdale Cl TS17 . . . . 48 A2
Easdale Wlk TS5 . . . . 50 A4
Easington Rd
Hartlepool TS24,
TS27 . . . . 2 C2
Stockton-on-T TS23. . . 17 C4
Easingwold Ho TS10 . 70 C4
Easson St TS4 . . . . . 40 B2
East Ave TS23. . . . . . 21 B1
Eastbank Rd TS7. . . . 53 A2
Eastbourne Ave
TS16 . . . . 63 C3
Eastbourne Gdns
TS3 . . . . 52 B4
Eastbourne Rd
Middlesbrough TS5. . . 39 C1
Stockton-on-T TS19. . . 26 A1
Eastbury Cl TS17. . . . 65 C4
East Cres TS5 . . . . . . 38 C1
Eastcroft 2 TS3 . . . . 41 A2
Eastcroft Rd TS6. . . . 33 B2
East Dr TS17 . . . . . . 37 B2
Easter Pk TS17 . . . . . 57 A2
EASTERSIDE 50 C2
Easterside Prim Sch
TS4 . . . . 51 A1
Easterside Rd TS4 . . . 51 A2
East Farm Cl TS6 . . . 53 C4
Eastfield Rd TS11 . . . 74 B2
Eastgate Rd TS5 . . . . 49 C4
Eastham Sands TS5. . 58 B3
Eastland Ave TS26 . . . 9 A2
Eastland View TS3 . . 41 A2
Eastleigh TS17. . . . . . 48 A1
East Lodge Gdns
TS10 . . . . 72 C2
Eastlowthian St TS2. . 29 C4
East Mdws TS11 . . . . 75 A2
East Middlesbrough Ind
Est TS3 . . . . 31 B1
Easton St TS17. . . . . 47 C4
East Par TS24. . . . . 6 C4
Eastport Rd TS18 . . . 82 C4
East Prec TS23 . . . . . 21 B4
East Row
3 Eston TS6 . . . . . . 44 A2
Middlesbrough TS5. . . 38 C1
East St
Marske-by-t-S TS11 . . 75 A2
Middlesbrough TS2. . . 29 C3
East View Terr
Middlesbrough TS4. . . 40 B2
Seaton Carew TS25 . . 13 C3
Eastwood Rd TS3 . . . 42 B1
Ebchester Cl TS19 . . . 24 B4
Eccleston Wlk TS4 . . . 51 A2
Eckert Ave TS5 . . . . . 38 B1
Eckford Wlk TS25. . . 11 B3
Eddison Way TS8 . . . 59 B1
Eddleston Wlk TS25. . 11 B3
Edenhall Gr TS10 . . . 72 C4
Eden Ho TS23. . . . . . . 21 B1
Eden Rd TS4. . . . . . . 40 A2
Eden St
Hartlepool TS25 . . . . . 7 B4
Saltburn-by-t-S TS12. . 76 C3
Eden Way TS22 . . . . . 16 A2

Eder Rd TS20 . . . . . . 26 B2
Edgar St
Hartlepool TS25 . . . . . 10 A1
6 Stockton-on-T
TS20 . . . . 26 B2
Edgehill Way TS23 . . 18 A2
Edgeworth Ct TS8 . . . 59 C1
Edgley Rd TS18 . . . . 34 C1
Edinburgh Ave TS5. . 49 C4
Edinburgh Cl TS7 . . . 62 A3
Edinburgh Gr TS25. . 12 C2
Edith St TS5 . . . . 38 C4
Edmondbyers Rd
TS19 . . . . 24 B4
Edmondsley Wlk 2
TS19 . . . . 24 C4
Edmundsbury Rd
TS5 . . . . 40 A2
Ednam Gr TS25 . . . . 11 C3
Edridge Gn TS3 . . . . 41 C3
Edston Dr TS14 . . . . 79 C5
Edward Ho TS12 . . . . 77 A4
Edwards St
Eston TS6 . . . . 44 A1
Stockton-on-T TS18 . . 83 A1
Edward St
Middlesbrough TS3. . . 41 A4
South Bank TS6. . . . . 32 A1
Edzell Wlk TS25. . . . . 11 B3
Egerton Cl TS20 . . . . 19 C1
Egerton Rd TS26. . . . . 8 B3
Egerton St TS1 . . . . . 87 A2
Egerton Terr TS25. . . 14 B2
EGGLESCLIFFE 63 C3
Egglescliffe CE Prim
Sch TS16 . . . . 63 C3
Egglescliffe Cl 1
TS19 . . . . 24 C4
Egglescliffe Cl TS16 . 63 C3
Egglescliffe Sch
TS16 . . . . 63 A4
Eggleston Ct TS2 . . . 28 C3
Eggleston Ct TS23 . . 17 B1
Eggleston Dr TS16. . . 54 A1
Eggleston Terr
TS18 . . . . 81 C2
Eggleston Rd TS10. . . 72 C2
Eglington Rd TS6 . . . 33 B2
Eglinton Ave TS14 . . 79 B2
Egmont Rd TS4 . . . . . 87 B1
Egton Ave TS7 . . . . . 61 C2
Egton Cl TS10 . . . . . 72 C3
Egton Dr TS25 . . . . . 13 B1
Egton Rd TS20 . . . . . 26 B2
Eider Cl
Hartlepool TS26 . . . . . 4 C2
Ingleby Barwick TS17. . 56 B1
Elcho St TS6. . . . . 9 B4
Elcoat Rd TS20 . . . . . 20 C1
Elder Cl TS1 . . . . 86 A3
Elder Gr
Redcar TS10 . . . . 73 C3
Stockton-on-T TS19. . . 25 B3
Elderslie Wlk TS25 . . 11 B3
Elderwood Ct 5 TS4. 50 B4
Eldon Gr TS26 . . . . . . 9 A2
Eldon Grove Prim Sch
TS26 . . . . 9 A2
Eldon St TS17 . . . . . . 47 B4
Eldon Wlk 1 TS17 . . 47 C4
Eleanor Pl TS18 . . . . 83 A1
Elemere St TS23 . . . . 17 B2
Elgin Ave
Eston TS6 . . . . 33 A2
Middlesbrough TS3. . . 51 C4
Elgin Rd
Hartlepool TS25 . . . . . 11 C3
Thornaby-on-T TS17 . . 47 A3
Eliot Ct TS23. . . . . . . 17 A3
Elishaw Gn 4 TS17 . . 65 A3
Elizabeth St 2 TS17 . 47 C4
Elizabeth Terr TS3 . . 87 C2
Elkington Cl 9 TS17 . 47 C1
Elkington Wlk TS3 . . 52 A4
Elland Ave TS4 . . . . . 51 A2
Ellary Wlk TS25 . . . . 11 B3

Ellen Ave TS18. . . . . . 81 C1
Ellenport Ct 5 TS18 . 82 C4
Ellerbeck Way TS7 . . 53 A4
Ellerburne St 7
TS17 . . . . 47 C4
Ellerby Cl TS10 . . . . . 72 C4
Ellerby Gn TS3. . . . . . 41 A2
Ellerby Rd TS6. . . . . . 44 A3
Ellerton Cl TS5 . . . . . 50 A2
Ellerton Rd TS18. . . . 45 A4
Ellesmere Wlk TS3. . . 41 C3
Ellett Ct TS24 . . . . 5 B4
Ellicott Wlk 1 TS18. . 83 A1
Elliot St
Middlesbrough TS1. . . 86 A3
Redcar TS10 . . . . 70 B4
Elliott St TS26 . . . . . . 9 C4
Ellis Gdns TS8 . . . . . 59 B1
Ellison St TS26. . . . . . . 9 B2
Elm Cl
Eston TS6 . . . . 43 A3
Saltburn-by-t-S TS12. . 76 A3
Elm Dr TS7 . . . . 61 A4
Elmfield Gdns TS25 . . 12 A3
Elm Gr
Hartlepool TS26 . . . . . 9 A4
Thornaby-on-T TS17 . . 47 B3
Elm House Apartments
TS18 . . . . 82 B3
Elmhurst Gdns TS8 . . 59 B1
Elm Rd
Guisborough TS14 . . . 79 B4
Redcar TS10 . . . . 71 B3
Elm St
Middlesbrough TS1. . . 86 A3
South Bank TS6. . . . . 32 A2
Elmstone Gdns TS8 . . 59 B1
ELM TREE 24 C1
Elm Tree Ave TS19 . . 34 C4
Elm Tree Ctr TS19 . . 35 A4
Elmwood TS8. . . . . . . 60 B3
Elmwood Ct TS19 . . . 24 B1
Elmwood Gr TS19 . . . 80 A4
Elmwood Pl TS26 . . . . 5 A1
Elmwood Rd
Eaglescliffe TS16 . . . . 54 C4
Hartlepool TS26 . . . . . . 5 A1
Elphin Wlk TS25 . . . . 11 B3
Elsdon Gdns TS17. . . 65 A3
Elsdon St TS18. . . . . . 81 C2
Elstob Cl TS19 . . . . . 24 B4
Elstone Rd TS4 . . . . . 87 B2
Elterwater Cl TS10. . . 70 B3
Eltham Cres TS17 . . . 57 B2
Eltisley Gn TS3 . . . . . 41 C3
Elton Cl TS19 . . . . . . 24 C4
Elton Gr TS19 . . . . . . 34 B2
Elton La TS16 . . . . . . 63 B4
Elton Rd TS22 . . . . . . 16 B2
Eltringham Rd TS26. . . 9 B3
Elvan Gr TS25. . . . . . 11 C3
Elvington TS13 . . . . . 17 C5
Elvington Sch TS3 . . . 41 C2
Elwick Ave TS5 . . . . . 49 B2
Elwick Cl
Redcar TS10 . . . . 73 C2
Stockton-on-T TS19. . . 24 B4
Elwick Ct 3 TS26 . . . 9 B2
Elwick Gdns TS19 . . . 24 B4
Elwick Grange 1
TS26 . . . . 9 B2
Elwick Rd TS26 . . . . . . 8 B3
Ely Cres TS10 . . . . . . 71 C2
Ely St TS4 . . . . 87 B2
Embleton Ave TS5 . . . 49 B2
Embleton Cl TS19 . . . 24 B4
Embleton Ct TS10. . . . 73 A4
Embleton Rd TS22 . . . 16 B2
Embleton Wlk TS19 . . 24 B4
Embsay Cl
Ingleby Barwick
TS17 . . . . 65 B3
Middlesbrough TS4. . . 50 C4

Emerald St
Middlesbrough TS1.... **85** C2
Saltburn-by-t-S TS12.. **76** C4
Emerson Ave TS5 ..... **50** A4
Emerson Ct TS24 ...... **5** B4
Emily St TS1 .... **86** A3
Emma Simpson Ct
TS18 .... **45** B4
Emmerson St TS5.... **39** C2
Emmetts Gdn TS17... **65** B4
Emsworth Dr TS16 ... **54** A1
Endeavour Cl TS25... **13** C3
Endeavour Dr TS7 ... **53** C2
Endeavour The TS7 .. **62** A3
Enderby Gdns TS8 ... **59** B1
Endeston Rd TS3 .... **52** A4
Endrick Rd TS25 ..... **11** B3
Endsleigh Dr TS5 .... **48** C4
Enfield Chase TS14 .. **79** B1
Enfield Gn TS6 ...... **53** B3
Enfield S Ctr TS14 ... **79** B1
Enfield St TS1 .... **85** B2
English Martyrs Sch &
Sixth Form Coll The
TS25 .... **8** C1
Ennerdale Ave TS5... **49** B3
Ennerdale Rd TS18... **80** A3
Ennis Rd TS10 .... **69** B2
Ennis Sq TS10 .... **69** B2
Ensign Ct TS24 ...... **10** B4
Enterpen Cl TS15 .... **64** C1
Enterprise Ct TS6.... **32** A3
Enterprise Ho TS25 .. **10** A1
Epping Ave TS3 ..... **51** C4
Epping Cl
Marske-by-t-S TS11 .. **74** C2
Thornaby-on-T TS17... **56** C4
Epsom Ave TS4 ...... **51** A2
Epsom Rd TS10 ...... **73** A4
Epworth Gn TS3 ..... **41** C2
Erica Gr TS7 .... **51** B1
Eric Ave TS17 .... **47** C4
Eridge Rd TS14 ..... **79** C2
Eriskay Wlk TS25 .... **11** B3
Erith Gr TS4 .... **51** A1
Ernest St TS26 .... **5** C1
Ernest Wlk ☐ TS26 ... **5** C1
Errington Garth ☐
TS11 .... **75** B1
Errington Prim Sch
TS11 .... **75** A2
Errol St
Hartlepool TS24 ...... **9** C4
Middlesbrough TS1.... **87** A2
Erskine Rd TS25 ..... **11** C3
Escomb ☐ TS4 ...... **40** C1
Escomb Cl TS19 ..... **24** B4
Escombe Rd TS23 .... **24** B4
Escombe Ave TS4.... **51** A2
Esha Ness Ct TS25 ... **11** B3
Esher Ave TS6 ...... **53** B3
Esher St TS1 .... **87** B2
Eshwood Sq TS1 ..... **84** C2
Esk Cl TS14 .... **79** A2
Eskdale TS8 .... **59** A1
Eskdale Cl TS15...... **66** B3
Eskdale Ct TS25 ..... **11** B3
Eskdale Rd
Hartlepool TS25 ...... **11** B3
Redcar TS10 .... **69** C1
Esk Gn TS16 .... **63** B4
Esk Gr TS25......... **11** C3
Esk Rd TS20 .... **26** B3
Esk St TS3 .... **41** A4
Esplanade TS10...... **71** A4
Essex Ave TS6 ...... **33** A1
Essex Cl TS10....... **70** C1
Essex Cres TS23 ..... **22** A3
Essexport Rd TS18 ... **82** C4
Essex St TS1......... **85** B1
ESTON **43** B2
Eston Park Sch TS6... **43** B3
Eston Rd TS6 .... **32** C2

Eston View TS3 ...... **41** B1
Etherley Cl TS19 ..... **24** B4
Etherley Wlk TS19 ... **24** B4
Eton Rd
Middlesbrough TS5.... **39** A1
Stockton-on-T TS18... **81** C2
Eton St TS25.......... **9** B1
Ettersgill Cl TS16 .... **54** A1
Ettington Ave TS3 ... **51** C4
Etton Rd TS23 ...... **17** B5
Ettrick Wlk TS25 .... **11** B3
Evans Bsns Ctr TS6 .. **42** B4
Evans St TS6......... **33** A1
Evendale TS14 ...... **78** A2
Evenwood Cl TS19 ... **24** B4
Evenwood Gdns TS5 . **59** A4
Everett St TS26 ...... **5** C1
Evergreen Wlk ☐
TS4 .... **50** B4
Everingham Rd TS15 . **66** B3
Eversham Rd TS6 .... **33** B2
Eversley Wlk TS3 .... **51** C4
Evesham Rd TS3 ..... **51** C3
Evesham Way TS18 .. **18** A3
Ewbank Dr TS18 ..... **81** C2
Ewbank Gdns TS18... **81** C2
Exchange Pl TS1...... **86** A4
Exchange Sq TS1 .... **86** A4
Exchange Yd TS18 ... **83** A2
Exeter Rd
Eston TS6 .... **43** C2
Middlesbrough TS5.... **40** A2
Exeter St
Hartlepool TS24 ...... **10** A4
Saltburn-by-t-S TS12... **76** C3
Exford Cl TS17 ...... **65** B2
Exmoor Gr TS26 ...... **5** A2
Eyebright Cl TS26..... **4** C4
Ezard St TS19........ **82** A4

F

Fabian Ct TS6 .... **43** C3
Fabian Rd TS6....... **43** C3
Faceby Pl TS20 ...... **26** B1
Faceby Wlk TS3 ..... **41** A1
Fagg St TS18 .... **83** A2
Fairbridge St TS1 .... **84** C3
Fairburn Cl TS19 .... **34** B4
Fairdene Ave TS19 ... **34** B3
Fairfax Ct
Thornton TS8 .... **59** B1
Yarm TS15............ **63** B2
FAIRFIELD **35** A4
Fairfield Ave
Middlesbrough TS5.... **49** A4
Ormesby TS7.......... **52** C1
Fairfield Cl
Redcar TS10 .... **70** C1
Stockton-on-T TS19... **34** C3
Fairfield Prim Sch
TS19 .... **34** B3
Fairfield Rd
Middlesbrough TS4.... **40** A1
Stockton-on-T TS19... **34** C3
Fairmead
Redcar TS10 .... **72** A3
Yarm TS15............ **66** A4
Fairstone Ave TS19 .. **34** B4
Fairthorn Ave TS19 .. **34** B3
Fairville Rd TS19...... **34** B3
Fairway The
Eaglescliffe TS16 ..... **54** C1
Marton TS8 .... **61** B2
Saltburn-by-t-S TS12... **76** B1
Fairwell Rd TS19 ..... **24** B1
Fairwood Pk TS8 ..... **61** B1
Fairy Cove Wlk TS24 .. **7** B3
Fairydell TS7 .... **60** C2
Fakenham Ave TS5... **49** A4
Falconberg Way
TS15 .... **66** A3
Falcon Cl TS18 ...... **46** B2
Falcon La TS20 ...... **20** B2
Falcon Rd
Hartlepool TS26 .... **4** C1
Middlesbrough TS3.... **41** C4

Falcon Way TS14..... **78** A3
Falkirk Rd TS25 ..... **11** C2
Falkirk St TS17 ...... **47** C4
Falklands Cl TS11 .... **74** C2
Falkland St TS1...... **85** B2
Fallow Cl TS17....... **56** B1
Fallows Ct TS1....... **84** B3
Fall Way TS6......... **53** B3
Falmouth Gr TS26..... **5** A2
Falmouth St TS1..... **87** B1
Falston Cl TS23 ..... **16** C2
Fanacurt Rd TS14.... **78** C2
Fane Cl TS19 .... **34** C3
Fane Gr TS5 .... **49** B2
Faraday Dr TS19 .... **24** B3
Faraday St TS1 ..... **85** B2
Faray Gn TS17 ...... **48** A3
Fareham Cl TS25..... **14** C4
Farington Dr TS7 .... **61** C3
Farleigh Cl TS23 .... **17** B2
Farley Dr TS5 .... **48** C2
Farmbank Rd TS7.... **53** B1
Farmcote Ct TS8..... **59** A1
Farm La TS17 .... **56** B1
Farnborough Ave
TS5 .... **49** B4
Farndale Cres TS4 ... **40** B1
Farndale Ct TS4 .... **40** B1
Farndale Dr TS14 ... **78** A1
Farndale Gn TS19 ... **25** B1
Farndale Rd
Hartlepool TS25 ...... **13** C2
Middlesbrough TS4.... **40** B1
Nunthorpe TS7 .... **62** B3
Farndale Sq TS10.... **70** A1
Farndale Wlk ☐ TS6 . **44** A3
Farne Ct TS17 ...... **65** B4
Farnell Gr TS25 ..... **11** C3
Farne Wlk TS14 ..... **79** A2
Farnham Cl TS16 .... **54** A1
Farnham Wlk TS3.... **51** B4
Farrer St TS18 ...... **82** A4
Farrier Cl TS17 ...... **56** B1
Farr Wlk ☐ TS25..... **11** C2
Farthingale Way TS8. **59** A1
Fastnet Gr ☐ TS24... **10** A3
Faulder Wlk TS25 ... **12** C4
Faverdale Ave TS5 ... **58** B4
Faverdale Cl
Middlesbrough TS1.... **84** C3
Stockton-on-T TS19... **24** C1
Faversham Cl TS18 .. **59** B1
Fawcett Ave TS8 .... **58** C1
Fawcett Rd TS17..... **47** C1
Fawcett Way ☐
TS17 .... **47** C1
Fawcus Ct TS10...... **69** C1
Faygate Ct TS8 ..... **59** A1
Fearby Rd TS18 ..... **34** B1
Fearnhead TS8 ...... **61** C1
Felbrigg La TS17..... **65** B4
Felby Ave TS3 ...... **51** C3
Felixstowe Cl TS25... **14** B4
Fell Bridge Dr TS11 .. **74** C2
Fellston Cl TS26 ...... **4** C1
Felton La TS19....... **24** A1
Fencote Gdns TS19 .. **34** C3
Fenham Ct TS7 ..... **52** C3
Fenmoor Cl TS8 ..... **58** C2
Fenner Cl TS11 ...... **75** C1
Fens Cres TS25 ...... **12** A1
Fens Ct TS25 .... **12** A1
Fens Prim Sch TS25 . **14** C4
Fens The TS27 .... **2** A1
Fenton Cl
Ingleby Barwick
TS17 .... **65** B4
☐ South Bank TS6.... **32** A2
Fenton Rd TS15 ..... **11** A1
Fenwick St TS18..... **82** B4
Ferndale TS19 ...... **24** C1
Ferndale Ave TS3.... **41** C4
Ferndale Ct TS3 .... **42** A3
Fernhill Rd TS6 ..... **44** A1
Fernie Rd
Guisborough TS14 .... **79** B1
Stockton-on-T TS20... **20** C1

Fern St TS1.......... **87** A2
Fernwood
Mount Pleasant
TS8 .... **68** A3
Redcar TS10 .... **73** A3
Fernwood Ave TS25.... **9** B1
Ferry Rd
Hartlepool TS24 .... **7** A2
Middlesbrough TS2.... **29** C3
Fescue Cl TS18 ..... **46** C1
Feversham St TS2 ... **86** A4
Fewston Cl
Hartlepool TS26 ...... **8** A4
Middlesbrough TS3.... **41** A2
Field Cl TS17 .... **48** A3
Fieldfare La
Stockton-on-T, Norton
TS20 .... **20** C1
Stockton-on-T TS20... **20** C2
Fieldfare Rd TS26..... **5** A2
Field Head TS10 ..... **70** B1
Fielding Ct TS23 .... **17** A3
Fieldview Cl TS2 .... **23** C1
Fife Gr TS25 .... **11** B2
Fife Rd TS20 .... **20** B1
Fife St TS1 .... **86** B3
Filey Cl TS10 .... **73** C4
Finchale Ave
Billingham TS23 ...... **17** A1
Middlesbrough TS3.... **52** A4
Fincham Cl TS20..... **25** B4
Finchdale Cl ☐ TS10 . **73** B2
Finchfield Cl TS16 ... **54** B1
Finchlay Cl TS5 ..... **59** B3
Finchley Rd TS20 ... **20** C1
Findlay Gr TS25..... **11** C2
Finkle St TS18 ...... **83** B2
Finsbury St TS1..... **85** B2
Firbeck Wlk TS17 ... **56** C3
Firby Cl
Hartlepool TS25 ...... **14** B2
Stockton-on-T TS20... **19** C1
Fir Gr
Redcar TS10 .... **72** A3
Thornaby-on-T TS17 .. **47** B3
Firlands The TS11 ... **75** A3
Fir Rigg Dr TS11 .... **74** C2
Firsby Ct TS8 .... **59** B1
Firsby Wlk ☐ TS3.... **41** B2
Firtree Ave TS6 ..... **53** C4
Firtree Dr TS6 ...... **53** B4
Firtree Rd TS19 ..... **25** B1
Fishbourne Gr TS17.. **55** B3
Fishermans Sq TS10 . **71** A3
Fiske Ct TS5 .... **58** C3
Fitzwilliam Cl ☐
TS11 .... **75** C1
Fitzwilliam St TS10 .. **71** A3
Flamborough ☐ TS4. **40** C1
Flatts La
Eston TS6 .... **43** B1
Ormesby TS7.......... **52** C1
Flatts Lane Dr TS6 .. **53** C3
Flaxton Ct ☐ TS26 .... **9** B2
Flaxton St TS26 ...... **9** B2
Fleck Way TS17 ..... **57** B1
Fleet Ave TS24 ...... **10** B4
Fleet Bridge Rd TS18,
TS20 .... **27** A2
Fleetham Gr TS18.... **34** C1
Fleetham St
Middlesbrough TS1.... **84** B3
Middlesbrough TS1.... **85** C2
Fleet Ho
Hartlepool TS24 ...... **10** B4
Middlesbrough TS3.... **42** A2
Fleet Rd TS18, TS20.. **26** C4
Fleet The
Redcar TS10 .... **69** B1
Thornaby-on-T TS17.. **48** B3
Fleming Cl TS19 ..... **24** C2
Fleming Rd TS6...... **42** B4
Fleming St TS10 .... **70** B4
Fletcher St TS1 ..... **86** A3
Fletcher Wlk TS25 ... **11** B4
Flexley Ave TS3 ..... **52** B4
Flint Wlk TS26 .... **4** C2

Flixton Gr TS22 ..... **16** B1
Flodden Way TS23 ... **18** A3
Flora St TS6 .... **43** C2
Florence Ct ☐ TS17.. **65** B4
Florence St TS2...... **84** C4
Florida Gdns TS5 .... **49** C3
Flottila Ho TS24 ..... **10** B4
Flounders Ho TS16... **63** B3
Flounders Rd TS15... **66** A4
FOGGY FURZE **13** A4
Folkestone Cl TS8 ... **59** B1
Folland Dr TS11 ..... **74** B3
Fonteyn Ct TS8 ..... **59** B1
Fontwell Cl TS19..... **24** A1
Forber Rd TS4....... **50** B3
Forbes Ave TS5...... **38** C1
Forbes Bldg TS1 .... **85** C1
Forcett Cl TS5 ...... **58** C4
Fordon Pl TS4....... **50** C3
Ford Pl TS18........ **82** A4
Fordwell Rd TS19 ... **34** B4
Fordyce Rd
Hartlepool TS25 ...... **11** C2
Hemlington TS8....... **59** A1
Hemlington TS8....... **59** B1
Fordy Gr TS17 ...... **47** B2
Foreland Point TS17 . **65** A2
Forest Dr TS7....... **53** A1
Forest Cres TS5 ..... **13** B3
Forest Mews TS17 ... **57** A4
Forfar Ave TS4 ..... **51** A1
Forfar Rd TS25 ..... **11** B2
Forget Me Not Gr
TS19 .... **25** A1
Formby Cl TS27 ...... **2** C2
Formby Gn TS4 ..... **50** C3
Formby Wlk TS16 ... **54** C2
Forres Wlk ☐ TS25 .. **11** B2
Forster Ho TS1...... **86** A3
Forth Gr TS25....... **11** C2
Forth Rd TS10 ...... **70** A2
Fort Rose Cl TS16.... **63** C4
Forty Foot Rd TS2.... **29** A3
Forum Ct TS3........ **87** C2
Fosdyke Gn TS3...... **42** B1
Fossfeld TS19 .... **24** A1
Foston Cl TS20....... **20** A1
Founders Ct TS25.... **14** B2
Fountains Ave TS17.. **56** C1
Fountains Cl
Guisborough TS14 .... **79** B3
Guisborough TS14 .... **79** C3
Fountains Cres TS6 .. **43** B2
Fountains Dr TS5 .... **50** A3
Fountain St TS14 ... **79** B3
Four Winds Ct TS26.... **8** B4
Fowler Cl TS15 ...... **67** B4
Fox Almshouses ☐
TS20 .... **26** B4
Foxberry Ave TS5 ... **58** B4
Fox Cl TS17......... **56** C2
Foxglove Cl
Hartlepool TS26 .... **4** C3
Stockton-on-T TS19... **24** C1
Foxgloves
Coulby Newham
TS8 .... **60** C1
Mount Pleasant TS8 .. **68** B3
Foxheads Ct TS1..... **84** B3
Fox Howe TS8 ...... **60** B3
Foxrush Cl TS10 ..... **72** C3
Fox St TS20......... **26** B3
Foxton Cl TS15...... **64** B1
Foxton Dr TS23 ..... **17** B4
Foxwood Dr TS19 ... **24** C1
Frampton Gn TS3.... **51** C2
France St TS10 ..... **71** A4
Francis Wlk ☐ TS17 . **47** B4
Franklin Cl TS18 .... **34** C1
Franklin Ct TS17..... **57** A4
Fransham Rd TS3.... **41** B2
Fraser Ct TS25....... **11** B2
Fraser Gr TS25....... **11** B2
Fraser Rd TS18 ..... **45** C4
Frederick Nattrass Prim
Sch TS20 .... **26** A4

Frederick St
Middlesbrough TS3.... **41** A4
Stockton-on-T TS18.... **82** A4
Thornaby-on-T TS17 . . . **83** C1
Frederic St TS24...... **7** A3
Fredric Terr TS23 .... **23** B2
Freemantle Gr TS25.. **12** C2
Fremantle Cres TS4.. **50** C4
Fremington Wlk TS4. **51** A1
Frensham Dr TS3...... **41** A4
Freshingham Cl TS8 . **59** B1
Freville St TS24...... **10** A3
Friarage Gdns TS24 . . .**7** B2
Friar St TS24 ....**7** B2
Friarswood Cl TS15 .. **64** B1
Friar Terr TS24........**7** B2
Friendship La TS24 . . .**7** B2
Frimley Ave TS3 ..... **41** B2
Frobisher Cl TS11.... **75** C1
Frobisher Rd TS17 .... **57** A4
Frome Ho **11** TS4.... **50** B4
Frome Rd TS20 ...... **26** B2
Front St TS25........ **14** B2
Front The TS25....... **13** D2
Frosterley Gr TS23 .. **17** C3
Fry St TS1 .... **86** A3
Fryup Cres TS14 ..... **79** A1
Fuchsia Rd TS19..... **35** A3
Fudan Way TS17 ..... **83** C2
Fulbeck Cl TS25...... **12** A3
Fulbeck Ct TS23 ..... **22** A4
Fulbeck Ho TS3...... **42** B1
Fulbeck Rd TS3...... **52** C4
Fulford Ho TS10 ..... **70** C4
Fulford Way TS8 ..... **61** C1
Fulmar Cres TS20 .... **25** C4
Fullerton Way TS17 . . **47** C1
Fulmar Head TS14 ... **78** B3
Fulmar Ho TS24 ..... **10** B4
Fulmar Rd TS20...... **20** B2
Fulmerton Cres
  TS10 .... **72** C2
Fulthorp Ave TS24 ... **3** A1
Fulthorpe Rd TS20.... **25** C4
Fulwood Ave TS4 .... **50** C4
Furlongs The TS19 ... **71** A2
Furness St TS24 ...... **6** A1

G

Gables The
  Marton TS7 .... **61** A3
  Redcar TS10 ...... **70** B4
  8 Saltburn-by-t-S
    TS12 .... **76** C3
Gainford Ave TS5.... **50** A4
Gainford Ho **6** TS24 .. **9** C3
Gainford Rd
  Billingham TS23 ..... **17** C1
  Stockton-on-T TS19... **35** A2
Gainford St **4** TS24... **9** C3
Gainsborough Cl
  TS6................ **53** C3
Gainsborough Cres
  TS23 .... **17** A3
Gainsborough Rd
  TS7................ **60** C4
Gaisgill Cl TS7....... **53** A3
Gala Cl TS25......... **13** C4
Galgate Cl TS7....... **61** B3
Galley Hill Prim Sch
  TS14 .... **78** B2
Galleysfield Ct TS24....**7** B3
Galloway Sands TS5 . **58** B3
Galsworthy Rd TS25....**8** B1
Ganstead Way TS23 . **17** C4
Ganton Cl TS22 ..... **16** A1
Ganton Ho TS10 ..... **70** C4
Garbutt St TS18...... **82** B4
Garden Cl TS17 ..... **47** A4
Garden Pl TS6 ...... **43** B1
Gardens The TS4..... **50** C4
Garforth Cl TS20..... **20** A1
Garmon Cl TS17 ..... **64** C4
Garnet Rd TS17 ..... **47** C3
Garnet St
  Middlesbrough TS1....**85** C2

Garnet St *continued*
  Saltburn-by-t-S TS12...**76** C4
Garrett Wlk TS1 .... **85** B2
Garrick Gr TS25...... **11** C4
Garrowby Rd TS3 ... **41** A1
Garsbeck Way TS7 .. **53** A3
Garsdale Cl TS15.... **66** B3
Garsdale Gn **5** TS3 .. **41** B2
Garside Dr TS24 ..... **5** C4
Garstang Ct TS17 ... **61** C3
Garston Gr TS25 .... **12** C2
Garth The
  Marske-by-t-S TS11 ...**74** C3
  Mount Pleasant TS8 ...**68** A4
  Stockton-on-T TS20....**26** A4
Garth Wlk TS3 ...... **41** A1
Garvin Cl TS3........ **41** A1
Gascoyne Cl TS7..... **61** B4
Gatenby Dr TS5..... **58** C4
Gatesgarth Cl TS24 .. **3** B1
Gatley Wlk TS16 .... **55** A4
Gatwick Gn **4** TS3... **41** B2
Gayle Moor Cl TS17 .. **65** B2
Gayton Sands TS5 .. **58** B3
Gedney Ave TS3 .... **51** C3
Geltsdale TS5 .... **58** C4
Geneva Dr TS10...... **70** C2
Gentian Way TS19 ... **24** C1
George St
  Hartlepool TS24 ..... **10** A4
  Redcar TS10 .... **71** A3
  Thornaby-on-T TS17 . . . **83** C1
Georgiana Cl TS17 . . . **83** C1
Georgian Theatre
  TS18 .... **82** B3
Gibb Sq TS24 ....**7** B3
Gibson Gr TS24 ...... **2** C2
Gifford St TS5 ...... **39** C2
Gilbert Pl TS25 ...... **3** B1
Gilkes St TS1 .... **84** C3
Gillbrook Coll TS6 ... **43** A3
Gillercomb TS10..... **72** C2
Gilling Rd TS19 ..... **34** C3
Gilling Way TS10..... **73** B4
Gilling Wlk **3** TS3... **41** A2
Gillpark Gr TS25 .... **13** B2
Gill St
  Guisborough TS14 .... **79** B4
  5 Hartlepool TS24.....**9** C3
  Saltburn-by-t-S TS12...**76** C2
Gilmonby Rd TS3 ... **51** C3
Gilmour St TS17 .... **47** B4
Gilpin Ho **1** TS20.... **26** A4
Gilpin Rd TS17....... **47** B3
Gilpin Sq TS19....... **25** C1
Gilside Rd TS23...... **17** C1
Gilsland Cl TS5 ..... **58** B4
Gilsland Gr TS6...... **43** B1
Gilwern Ct TS17 .... **64** C3
Girrick Cl TS8 ...... **58** C1
Girton Ave TS3....... **51** C3
Gisborne Gr **2** TS18 . **35** A1
Gisburn Ave TS3 .... **51** C4
Gisburn Rd TS3...... **17** C1
Gladesfield Rd TS20.. **26** B2
Gladstone Ind Est
  TS17 .... **83** C1
Gladstone St
  Eston TS6 .... **44** A2
  Hartlepool TS24 ...... **7** B2
  Stockton-on-T TS18.....**83** A1
Glaisdale Ave
  Middlesbrough TS5.....**50** A3
  Redcar TS10 .... **69** C1
  Stockton-on-T TS19....**25** B1
Glaisdale Cl TS6 .... **44** B3
Glaisdale Gr TS25.... **13** C2
Glaisdale Rd
  Eston TS6 .... **44** B3
  Yarm TS15.......... **93** B4
Glamis Gr TS4....... **50** C4
Glamis Rd TS23 ..... **16** C1
Glamis Wlk TS5 ..... **11** B2
Glamorgan Gr TS26 . . **4** C2
Glasgow St TS17 .... **83** C1
Glastonbury Ave TS6 . **43** C2

Glastonbury Ho **8**
  TS3 .... **52** A4
Glastonbury Wlk TS26 . **5** A2
Gleaston Cres TS4 ... **50** C3
Gleaston Wlk TS4.... **50** C3
Glebe Gdns TS8...... **58** C1
Glebe Prim Sch The
  TS20 .... **25** C4
Glebe Rd TS1 .... **85** B2
Glebe The TS20 ..... **19** C1
Glenbury Gr TS10 ... **73** C2
Glencairn Gr **5**
  TS25 .... **11** B2
Glen Ct TS5......... **50** A3
Glendale TS14....... **78** A1
Glendale Ave TS26 . . . **9** A3
Glendale Rd TS5..... **50** A3
Glendue Cl TS7...... **62** A2
Gleneagles Cl TS22 . . **16** A1
Gleneagles Ct TS4 ... **50** C3
Gleneagles Rd
  7 Hartlepool TS27 ... **2** B2
  Middlesbrough TS4.....**50** C3
Glenfall Cl TS22..... **16** A1
Glenfield Cl TS19 ... **34** B3
Glenfield Dr TS5..... **50** A3
Glenfield Rd TS19.... **34** B3
Glenhow **6** TS12 .... **76** C3
Glenluce Cl TS16..... **54** C1
Glenmoor Gr TS6 ... **43** A2
Glenn Cres TS7 ..... **61** A3
Glenside TS12 .... **77** A3
Glenston Cl TS26 .... **4** B1
Glen The TS16 ...... **63** C3
Glentower Gr TS25... **13** B2
Glentworth Ave TS3 . **42** B1
Glentworth Ho TS3 .. **42** B1
Gloucester Cl TS7.... **62** A3
Gloucester Rd TS14.. **79** A1
Gloucester St TS25....**9** B1
Gloucester Terr
  TS23 .... **22** A3
Glyder Ct TS17...... **64** B3
Goathland Dr TS25... **13** B1
Goathland Gr TS14... **79** A1
Goathland Rd TS6 ... **44** A3
Gofton Pl TS6........ **43** B4
Gold Crest TS14...... **78** B3
Goldcrest Cl
  1 Ingleby Barwick
    TS17 .... **56** B1
Golden Flatts Prim Sch
  TS25 .... **12** C1
Goldfinch Rd TS26 ... **4** C2
Goldsmith Ave TS24.. **3** A2
Goldsmith Cl TS23 ... **17** A3
Goodwin Cl TS10 ... **72** B2
Goodwin Wlk **15**
  TS24 .... **10** A3
Goodwood Rd TS10 . **73** A4
Goodwood Sq TS17 . . **38** B1
Goose Garth TS16.... **63** B4
Goosepastures TS15 . **61** A2
Gooseport Rd TS18 . . **82** C4
Gordon Cres TS6..... **33** B1
Gordon Rd TS10 ..... **70** A2
Gore Sands TS5...... **58** A3
Gorman Rd TS5...... **39** B2
Gorsefields Ct TS6... **53** C4
Gorton Cl TS23 ..... **16** C2
Gosford St TS2 ..... **86** A4
Gosforth Ave TS10 . . . **73** A4
Goshawk Rd TS26.... **4** C3
Gough Cl TS1....... **85** B2
Goulton Cl TS15 .... **64** C1
Gower Cl TS1........ **84** B3
Gower Wlk TS26 .... **4** B3
Grace Cl TS25 ...... **13** C1
Graffenberg St TS10 . **71** A4
Grafton Cl TS14...... **79** B2
Graham St TS24 ......**7** B2
Grainger Cl TS16.... **54** B2
Grainger St TS24..... **6** A1
Grammar School La
  TS15 .... **63** B1
Grampian Rd TS23 . . **21** B4

Grange Ave
  Billingham TS23 ...... **21** C1
  Hartlepool TS26 ...... **9** A4
  Stockton-on-T TS18.... **80** B4
Grange Bsns Ctr The
  TS23 .... **22** A2
Grange Cl
  Eston TS6 .... **33** B1
  Hartlepool TS26 ...... **8** C4
Grange Cres TS7..... **61** A2
Grange Farm TS8 .... **60** B3
Grange Farm Rd TS6 . **33** B1
GRANGEFIELD **80** B3
Grangefield Rd TS18 . **80** B3
Grangefield Sch & Tech
  Coll TS18 .... **80** A3
Grange Prim Sch
  TS25 .... **11** B1
Grange Rd
  Hartlepool TS26 ...... **9** A4
  Middlesbrough TS1.....**84** C3
  Middlesbrough TS1.....**86** A3
  Stockton-on-T TS20.... **26** B3
  Thornaby-on-T TS17 . . . **47** B4
GRANGETOWN **33** B2
Grangetown Prim Sch
  TS6 .... **33** A1
Grangetown Station Rd
  TS6 .... **33** B2
Grange View TS23.... **16** C3
Grangeville Ave
  TS19 .... **34** B3
Grange Wood TS8 ... **59** C3
Grantham Ave TS19.. **34** B3
Grantham Gn TS4.... **51** A1
Grantham Rd TS20 . . **20** A1
Grantley Ave TS3 ... **42** B3
Grant St TS10........ **70** C4
Granville Ave TS26 . . . **9** A4
Granville Gr TS20 ... **26** B2
Granville Rd
  Eston TS6 .... **33** A1
  Middlesbrough TS1.....**85** C1
  Stockton-on-T TS18.... **80** B3
Granville Terr TS10... **71** B4
Granwood Rd TS6 ... **44** A1
Grasby Cl TS3........ **42** B1
Grasmere Ave TS5 ... **49** B2
Grasmere Dr TS6 .... **43** A2
Grasmere Rd
  Redcar TS10 .... **70** C2
  Stockton-on-T TS18.... **80** B3
Grasmere St **4** TS25 . . **9** A4
Grassholme Rd TS26 . . **8** A4
Grassholme Way
  TS16 .... **54** A1
Grassholm Rd TS20 . . **26** B3
Grassington Gn TS17. **65** B2
Grassington Rd TS4 . . **50** C4
Graygarth Rd TS3 ... **41** A2
Gray's Rd TS18 ..... **80** B3
Gray St
  Hartlepool TS24 ...... **5** C1
  Middlesbrough TS2.....**86** A4
Great Ash TS14 ..... **78** B3
GREATHAM **14** C2
Greatham CE Prim Sch
  TS25 .... **14** B2
Greatham Cl TS25.... **59** A4
Greatham Hospl
  Almshouses TS25 .... **14** B2
  Greatham St TS25.... **10** A1
Greatham St TS25.... **58** B1
Greenacres Cl **3**
  TS11 .... **74** C2
Greenacres Rd TS5... **38** C2
Greenbank Ct TS26 . . **8** C4
Green Cl TS7 .... **62** A2
Greencroft TS10 .... **72** A3
Greencroft Wlk TS5 . **52** A4
Greenfield Dr TS16... **54** B1
Greenfields Way
  TS18 .... **34** B2
Greenfinch Cl TS26 . . **5** A3
Greenford Wlk TS3 . . **42** B1
Green Gables Primary
  Pupil Support Ctr
  TS19 .... **34** C4

Green Gates Prim Sch
  TS10 .... **72** B3
Greenham Cl TS23 .. **42** B1
Greenhead Cl TS8 ... **59** B3
Greenhow Gr TS25 . . **13** C2
Greenhow Rd TS3.... **41** A2
Greenhow Wlk TS10 . **72** C4
Green La
  Marske-by-t-S TS11 ...**74** A4
  Middlesbrough TS5.....**49** B4
  Redcar TS10 .... **73** C3
  Stockton-on-T TS19.... **25** B2
  Thornaby-on-T TS17 . . . **47** B2
  Yarm TS15.......... **66** C3
Greenland Ave TS5... **38** B1
Greenland Rd TS24 ...**6** B2
Greenlands Rd TS10 . **66** C3
Green Lane Prim Sch
  TS5 .... **49** C4
Greenlee **5** TS17.... **65** A3
Greenock Rd TS25 . . **11** C2
Green's Beck Rd
  TS18 .... **35** A1
Green Scar TS10 .... **73** B3
Greens Gr TS18...... **35** A1
Greenshank Cl TS26... **4** C3
Greenside
  Greatham TS25....... **14** B2
  Ingleby Barwick TS17... **56** B1
  Normanby TS6 .... **53** B3
Green's La TS18 ..... **35** A1
Green St TS25 ...... **10** A2
Greenstones Rd
  TS10 .... **73** B4
Greens Valley Dr
  TS18 .... **35** A1
Green Terr TS25..... **13** C2
Green The
  Billingham TS23 ...... **21** B1
  Egglescliffe TS16 .... **63** C3
  Greatham TS25....... **14** B2
  Middlesbrough TS4.....**50** C4
  Redcar TS10 .... **69** B1
  Saltburn-by-t-S TS12...**76** B1
  Seaton Carew TS25 . . . **13** C2
  Stockton-on-T TS20.... **20** C1
  Stockton-on-T TS20.... **26** A4
  Thornaby-on-T TS17 . . . **47** B1
  Wolviston TS22....... **16** C4
Green Vale Gr TS19... **34** B2
Greenway
  Eston TS6 .... **43** C2
  Ingleby Barwick TS17... **56** B1
  Green Way TS7 ..... **62** A2
Greenway Ct TS3 .... **42** A3
Greenway The TS3 . . **42** B2
Greenwood Ave TS5 . **49** C4
Greenwood Rd
  Billingham TS23 ...... **22** B3
  Hartlepool TS26 ...... **6** A1
  Stockton-on-T TS18.... **35** A1
Grenadier Cl TS18 . . **80** A3
Grendon Wlk TS3 ... **51** C3
Grenville Cl TS1..... **75** B1
Grenville Rd TS17.... **57** A4
Gresham Rd TS1..... **85** C2
Gresley Cl TS12 .... **76** C3
Greta Ave TS25 .... **12** B4
Greta Rd
  Redcar TS10 .... **70** A2
  Stockton-on-T TS20.... **26** A3
Greta St
  Middlesbrough TS1....**85** C2
  Saltburn-by-t-S TS12...**76** C2
Gretton Ave TS4 .... **51** A2
Grewgrass La TS10 . . **73** B2
Greylands Ave TS20 . **26** B3
Greymouth Cl TS18 . **35** A1
Greys Ct TS17....... **65** B4
Grey St **4** TS20 ..... **26** B2
Greystoke Dr TS10 . . **72** C3
Greystoke Rd TS10... **72** C3
Greystoke Wlk TS10 . **72** C3

Greystone Rd TS6..... 44 B4
Grey Towers Dr TS7 . 62 A1
Greywood Cl TS27 ..... 2 B3
Gribdale Rd TS3 ..... 41 B2
Griffin Rd TS4 .... 40 B2
Griffiths Cl TS15 ..... 66 B3
Griffiths Rd TS6...... 43 C4
Grimston Wlk TS3 ... 40 C2
Grimwood Ave TS3... 41 C4
Grinkle Ave TS3..... 51 C4
Grinkle Ct TS14 ..... 79 B4
Grinkle Rd TS10 ..... 69 C2
Grinton Rd TS18 ..... 45 A4
Grisedale Cl TS5..... 58 C4
Grisedale Cres
  Eaglescliffe TS16 ..... 63 C4
  Eston TS6 .... 44 A4
Gritten Sq TS24....... 6 B4
Groom Terr TS25..... 12 B1
Grosmont Cl TS10... 72 C3
Grosmont Dr TS23 ... 16 C1
Grosmont Pl TS6..... 44 A3
Grosmont Rd
  Eston TS6 .... 44 A3
  Hartlepool TS25 ..... 13 C2
Gross St TS23....... 23 B2
Grosvenor Ct TS17 .. 65 B3
Grosvenor Gdns
  Eston TS6 .... 43 B1
  12 Hartlepool TS26..... 9 B4
Grosvenor Ho TS17 . 83 B1
Grosvenor Pl TS14 .. 79 A3
Grosvenor Rd
  Billingham TS22 ..... 16 C1
  Middlesbrough TS5.... 39 A1
  Stockton-on-T TS19... 35 A2
Grosvenor Sq TS14... 79 A3
Grosvenor St **5** TS26 ..9 B4
Grove Cl TS26......... 9 A3
GROVE HILL 87 C1
Grove Rd
  Middlesbrough TS3.... 87 C2
  Redcar TS10 .... 71 A3
Groves St TS24 .... 7 B2
Grove St TS18 .... 81 C1
Groves The TS18 ..... 81 C1
Grove Terr TS27 ..... 26 B2
Grove The
  Greatham TS25....... 14 B2
  Guisborough TS14 ... 78 B1
  Hartlepool TS26 .... 9 A3
  Marton TS7 .... 52 A4
  Middlesbrough TS5.... 59 A3
  Yarm TS15.......... 66 C4
Grundales Dr TS11... 74 C2
Guernsey Wlk TS14 .. 79 A2
Guildford Ct TS14 ... 53 C3
Guildford Rd
  Billingham TS23 ..... 16 C1
  Normanby TS6 ...... 53 C3
Guillemot Cl TS26..... 4 C3
GUISBOROUGH 78 C4
Guisborough Cl **8** TS4 . 40 C1
Guisborough Ct **9**
  TS6 .... 44 A2
Guisborough General &
Maternity Hospl
  TS14 .... 79 B4
Guisborough Mus★
  TS14 .... 79 B4
Guisborough Priory★
  TS14 .... 79 C4
Guisborough Rd
  Nunthorpe TS7 ...... 62 B2
  Saltburn-by-t-S TS12... 76 B2
  Thornaby-on-T TS17 ... 47 C3
Guisborough Sports Ctr
  TS14 .... 79 C5
Guisborough St TS6.. 44 A2
Guiseley Way TS16... 84 C2
Gulliver Rd TS25..... 11 B4
Gunnergate Cl TS12.. 76 A3
Gunnergate La TS7,
  TS8 .... 60 C2

Gunnerside Rd TS19 . 34 B3
Gurney St TS1 .... 86 A3
Guthrie Wlk **6** TS25 . 11 B2
Guthrie Ave TS15 .... 48 C4
Gwynn Cl TS19....... 34 B4
Gypsy La
  Marton TS7 .... 61 B3
  Nunthorpe TS7 ...... 62 B4
Gypsy Lane Halt TS7 . 62 A4

H

Hackforth Rd TS18.... 45 A4
Hackness Wlk TS5 .... 50 A2
Hackworth Ct TS18 .. 82 A4
Hadasia Gdns TS19 ... 35 A3
Haddon Rd TS23 ..... 16 C1
Haddon St TS1....... 87 A2
Hadleigh Cres TS4 ... 40 B1
Hadleigh Wlk TS17... 56 A1
Hadlow Wlk **1** TS3 . 41 B2
Hadnall Cl TS15...... 48 C2
Hadrian Way TS17 ... 55 B2
Hadston Cl TS10 ..... 73 A3
Haffron Ave TS18 .... 82 B4
Hailsham Ave TS17... 57 A1
Haldane Gr TS25..... 11 C2
Hale Rd TS23 .... 17 B2
Halidon Way TS23 ... 17 C2
Halifax Cl TS11 ..... 74 B2
Halifax Rd TS17..... 57 A4
Hall Cl TS11 .... 74 C2
Hall Cl The TS7 ..... 52 C3
Hallcroft Cl TS23.... 21 B1
Hall Dr TS5 .... 49 C2
Hall Farm Cl TS22.... 16 B3
Hallgarth Cl TS15.... 58 C4
Hall Garth Com Arts
  Coll TS15........ 49 C2
Hallgate Cl TS18 ..... 45 A4
Hallifield St TS20 .... 26 B2
Halton Cl TS23....... 17 B4
Halton Ct
  6 Billingham TS23.... 17 B4
  Middlesbrough TS3.... 42 B3
Halyard The TS3 ..... 86 C4
Hambledon Rd TS5 .. 39 A1
Hambleton Ave TS10. 72 B4
Hambleton Cres
  TS11 .... 75 B1
Hambletonian Yd
  TS18 .... 83 A2
Hambleton Rd TS7.... 62 B3
Hambleton Sq TS23 .. 21 A4
Hamilton Gr
  Eston TS6 .... 42 C3
  Redcar TS10 .... 70 A3
Hamilton Rd
  Hartlepool TS25 ..... 11 C2
  Stockton-on-T TS19... 25 C1
Hammond Cl TS7 .... 60 C3
Hampden St TS6..... 32 A1
Hampden Way TS17... 57 A4
Hampshire Gn TS20.. 26 C3
Hampstead Gdns
  TS26 .... 8 C4
Hampstead Gr TS6... 53 B3
Hampstead Rd TS6 ... 53 B3
Hampstead The
  TS10 .... 73 B4
Hampton Cl TS7 ..... 62 A3
Hampton Gr TS10.... 71 C2
Hampton Rd TS18.... 81 B2
Hamsterley Rd TS19 . 24 C2
Hanbury Cl TS17 .... 56 B1
Handale Cl TS14 ..... 79 D3
Handley Cl TS18 ..... 46 B1
Hankin Rd TS3 ...... 87 C2
Hanover Ct TS20 ..... 25 C4
Hanover Gdns TS5 ... 39 C4
Hanover Ho **5** TS12. 76 A1
Hanover Par TS20.... 25 C4
Hanover Point TS20.. 25 C4
Hanson Gr TS3 ...... 42 A3
Harbottle Cl TS17.... 65 A3
Harbourne Gdns TS5. 59 A4
Harbour Wlk TS24 ... 6 B1

Harcourt Rd TS6..... 32 A1
Harcourt St TS26..... 9 A4
Hardale Gr TS10 ..... 70 A1
Harding Row TS20 ... 26 B3
Hardknott Gr TS10 .. 70 B2
HARDWICK.......... 24 B3
Hardwick Ave TS5 ... 49 B3
Hardwick Cl TS26..... 8 A2
Hardwick Prim Sch
  TS19 .... 24 B4
Hardwick Rd
  Billingham TS23 ..... 17 C1
  South Bank TS6...... 32 A2
  Stockton-on-T TS19... 24 C3
Hardy Gr TS23 ...... 17 A3
Harebell Cl TS17..... 56 B2
Harehills Rd TS5..... 38 C1
Haresfield Way TS17 . 65 B4
Hareshaw Cl TS17.... 65 A3
Harewood **9** TS4.... 40 C1
Harewood Cres TS19 . 24 B1
Harewood Prim Sch
  TS17 .... 47 C4
Harewood Rd TS17... 37 B1
Harewood St TS1.... 85 C1
Harewood Way TS10 . 73 B4
Harford St TS1....... 85 B1
Harker Cl TS15....... 66 B4
Harland Pl **1** TS20... 26 B3
Harlech Cl TS6....... 43 C3
Harlech Ct TS17 ..... 64 C4
Harlech Wlk TS26.... 5 A2
Harlow Cres TS17.... 48 A2
Harlsey Cres TS18.... 45 B4
Harlsey Gr TS18..... 45 B4
Harlsey Rd TS18 ..... 45 B4
Harpenden Wlk TS3.. 41 B2
Harper Par TS18 ..... 45 C4
Harper Terr TS18..... 45 C4
Harrier Cl
  Hartlepool TS26 ...... 4 C2
  Thornaby-on-T TS17 .. 47 B1
Harriet Ho TS17..... 83 B2
Harris Gr TS25....... 11 C2
Harrison Pl TS24..... 5 B4
Harrison St TS3...... 41 A4
Harris St TS1....... 84 C3
Harris Wlk TS14 ..... 79 A2
Harrogate Cres TS5 .. 39 C2
Harrow Ct TS5....... 49 C4
Harrowgate La TS19 . 24 B3
Harrow Gate Prim Sch
  TS19 .... 24 C3
Harrow Rd
  Middlesbrough TS5.... 49 C4
  Stockton-on-T TS18... 81 B2
Harrow St TS25....... 9 B1
Harsley Wlk TS3 ..... 41 B2
Hart Ave TS26 .... 5 A1
HARTBURN 81 A1
Hartburn Ave TS18... 81 B1
Hartburn Ct TS5..... 49 B1
Hartburn La TS18 ... 81 A1
Hartburn Prim Sch
  TS18 .... 81 A1
Hartburn Village
  TS18 .... 45 C4
Hart Cl TS19......... 25 A2
Harter Cl TS7....... 61 A2
Hartforth Ave TS5... 58 C4
Hartington Cl **7**
  TS17 .... 47 B4
Hartington Rd
  Middlesbrough TS1.... 84 C3
  Stockton-on-T TS18... 83 A2
Hart La TS26........ 5 A1
Hartland Gr TS3 ..... 52 A4
Hart Lane Cotts TS26.. 5 B1
HARTLEPOOL....... 10 C2
Hartlepool Cl TS19 ... 25 A2
Hartlepool Coll of F Ed
  TS24 .... 10 A3
Hartlepool Historic
  Quay & Heritage Ctr★
  TS24 .... 9 B1
Hartlepool Ind Est
  TS24 .... 6 A3

Hartlepool-Middleton
  Grange Sh Ctr TS24.. 9 C3
Hartlepool Sixth Form
  Coll TS25........ 9 A2
Hartlepool Sta TS24 . 10 A4
Hartlepool Utd FC
  (Victoria Pk) TS24 ... 9 C4
Hartlepool Workshops
  TS25 .... 12 C3
Hartley Cl **10** TS26 ....9 B4
Harton Ave TS22..... 16 B1
Hart Rd TS27....... 2 C1
Hartside Gdns TS26... 4 C1
Hartside Gr TS19..... 25 B2
HART STATION..... 2 C3
Hartville Rd TS24 ..... 2 B3
Hartwith Dr TS19 ... 24 B4
Harvard Ave TS17 ... 83 C2
Harvester Cl TS25.... 13 B4
Harvester St TS17.... 51 A1
Harvey Ct TS10 ..... 69 C1
Harvey Wlk TS25..... 11 B4
Harvington Cres TS8. 60 B2
Harwal Rd TS10..... 70 A3
Harwell Cl TS4...... 50 C4
Harwell Dr TS19 ..... 24 B1
Harwich Cl TS10 ..... 73 C4
Harwich Gr TS25..... 12 C2
Harwood Ct TS2..... 29 A3
Harwood St TS24 ..... 5 C1
Hasguard Way TS17.. 64 B3
Hastings Cl
  Nunthorpe TS7 ...... 62 A3
  Thornaby-on-T TS17 .. 56 C3
Hastings Ho TS3 ..... 51 C4
Hastings Pl TS24..... 5 B4
Hastings The **5** TS6.. 43 B1
Hastings Way TS3.... 18 A2
Haswell Ave TS25.... 12 C4
Haswell Ct **8** TS20... 26 B1
Hatchlands Pk TS17.. 56 A1
Hatfield Ave TS5..... 49 B3
Hatfield Cl
  Eaglescliffe TS16 .... 54 A1
  Hartlepool TS25 ..... 12 B1
Hatfield Rd TS23 ..... 22 A4
Hatherley Ct TS3.... 42 A3
Hatterall Ct TS17 ... 64 C3
Hauxley Cl TS10..... 73 C4
Hauxwell's Bldg
  TS15 .... 63 B2
Havelock St
  Hartlepool TS24 ..... 10 B3
  Thornaby-on-T TS17 .. 47 B4
Haven Wlk TS24 ..... 6 C4
Haverthwaite TS5.... 58 B4
HAVERTON HILL 23 A2
Haverton Hill Ind Est
  TS23 .... 23 B1
Haverton Hill Rd
  Middlesbrough
  TS23 .... 28 A3
  Stockton-on-T TS18... 27 C1
Havilland St TS17 ... 57 A4
Haweswater Rd
  TS10 .... 70 B2
Hawford Cl TS17..... 56 C1
Hawkesbury Cl **1**
  TS18 .... 35 A1
Hawkins Cl TS11..... 75 B1
Hawk Rd TS3 ...... 41 B4
Hawkridge Cl
  7 Hartlepool TS26 ... 5 C1
  Ingleby Barwick TS17.. 65 B2
Hawkridge St **2** TS26..9 B4
Hawkshead Rd TS10 . 70 C2
Hawkstone TS8...... 61 B1
Hawkstone Cl
  Billingham TS22 ..... 16 A1
  Guisborough TS14 ... 79 B1
Hawnby Cl TS19 ..... 34 B3
Hawnby Rd TS5...... 50 A4
Hawthorn Cres TS7 .. 61 B4

Hawthorne Ave **3**
  TS4 .... 40 A1
Hawthorne Dr TS14 . 78 B2
Hawthorne Gr TS15 . 25 C1
Hawthorn Gr TS15 ... 64 A1
Hawthorn Rd TS10 ... 71 B2
Hawthorn Terr TS6... 31 C2
Hawthorn Wlk TS24.. 5 C2
Haxby Cl TS15....... 50 A2
Haxby Ct TS14....... 79 C5
Haxby Wlk TS24 ..... 6 B3
Hayburn Cl
  Ingleby Barwick
  TS17 .... 65 C4
  Redcar TS10 .... 73 B4
Haydon Gn TS23 ..... 17 A4
Hayfield Cl TS26..... 8 C4
Hayling Way TS18.... 34 A2
Haymore St TS5 ..... 39 C2
Hayston Rd TS26..... 4 C1
Hazelbank TS8 ...... 60 B3
Hazel Ct TS1........ 86 A3
Hazeldene Ave TS18 . 46 A4
Hazel Gr
  Hartlepool TS24 ..... 5 C2
  Marton TS7 .... 61 C4
  Redcar TS10 .... 71 B3
  Thornaby-on-T TS17 .. 47 B3
Hazelhen Cl TS26..... 4 C3
Hazelmere Cl TS22... 16 A2
Hazel Rd TS19 ...... 25 C1
Hazel Slade TS16 .... 54 C1
Hazelwood Ct TS5 ... 59 B4
Hazelwood Rise TS3 . 7 A3
Headingley Ct TS25 .. 13 C1
Headlam Cl **5** TS20.. 26 B1
Headlam Rd
  Billingham TS23 ..... 17 C2
  Stockton-on-T TS20... 26 B1
Headlam Terr TS16... 63 B3
Headlands The TS11 . 75 A3
HEADLAND THE..... 7 C2
Head St TS1....... 84 C3
Healaugh Pk TS15 ... 67 A4
Heather Cl TS19 ..... 25 B3
Heather Dr TS5 ..... 49 B2
Heatherfields Rd
  TS6 .... 53 C4
Heather Gr TS24..... 5 B3
Heathfield Cl TS16... 54 B1
Heathfield Dr TS25... 9 B1
Heathrow TS17 ..... 48 A2
Heath The TS20 ..... 26 A2
Heaton Rd TS23..... 17 A3
Hebburn Rd TS19 ... 24 C2
Hebron Rd TS5...... 40 A1
Heddon Gr TS17 ..... 65 A2
Hedingham Cl **2**
  TS4 .... 40 B1
Hedley Cl TS15...... 66 B3
Hedley Ct TS15 ..... 63 B3
Hedleyhope Wlk
  TS19 .... 24 C2
Hedley St TS14 ..... 79 B4
Heighington Cl TS19. 24 C2
Helen Ho TS17....... 83 B2
Helmsley Cl TS5 ..... 50 A3
Helmsley Dr TS14 ... 79 B4
Helmsley Gr TS19.... 34 C4
Helmsley Ho TS14.... 79 B5
Helmsley Lawn TS10 . 71 B1
Helmsley St TS24 .... 5 C1
Helston Ct TS17..... 48 B2
Hemel Cl TS17...... 48 B3
Hemingford Gdns
  TS15 .... 67 A4
HEMLINGTON 59 C1
Hemlington Gn TS19 . 24 C2
Hemlington Hall Prim
  Sch TS8........ 59 A1
Hemlington Hall Rd
  TS8 .... 59 A2
Hemlington La TS8 .. 59 B3
Hemlington Rd TS8 . 59 B3
Hemlington Village Rd
  TS8 .... 60 A1

Hempstead Cl TS17 . . 48 A3
Henderson Gr TS24 . . . 6 A1
Henley Gr TS17 . . . . . . 47 B4
Henley Rd TS5 . . . . . . 39 A1
Henrhyd Cl TS17 . . . . 64 C3
Henrietta Cl TS17 . . . . 83 C1
Henrietta St TS24 . . . . 7 A3
Henry Smith's Terr
TS24 . . . . .7 B3
Henry St
Middlesbrough TS3. . . .41 A3
Redcar TS10 . . . . 70 B4
South Bank TS6. . . . . . 32 B2
Henry Taylor Ct TS7 . 52 C3
Henshaw Dr TS17 . . . . 65 A3
Hensley Cl TS20 . . . . . 19 C1
Heortnesse Rd TS24 . . .6 B4
Hepple Cl TS23 . . . . . . 17 A4
Herbert St TS3. . . . . . 41 A4
Herbert Wlk 7 TS24 . . 6 A1
Hereford Cl TS5. . . . . 39 C2
Hereford Rd TS14. . . . 79 A2
Hereford St 4 TS25. . . 9 C1
Hereford Terr TS23. . . 22 A3
Heriot Gr TS25. . . . . . 11 C2
Heriot Grange TS25 . . 11 C2
Hermitage Pl TS20 . . 20 B1
Herne Cl TS10 . . . . . . 73 B3
Heron Gate TS14. . . . 78 B3
Heronspool Cl TS24. . .6 B3
Herrington Rd TS23. . 17 B4
Hershall Dr TS3. . . . . 41 C2
Hertford Rd TS20 . . . 26 A3
Hesketh Ave TS4. . . . 51 A2
Hesleden Ave TS5. . . 58 B4
Hesledon Cl TS19 . . . . 25 A2
Heslington Gdns
TS14 . . . . 79 B5
Heslop St 5 TS17. . . . 47 C4
Heswall Rd TS23. . . . . 17 C1
Hetton Cl TS23. . . . . . 17 A2
Heugh Chare TS24 . . . 7 C2
Hewitt's Bldgs TS14. . 79 B4
Hewley St TS6. . . . . . . 43 B1
Heworth Dr TS20 . . . . 19 C1
Hexham Dr TS6 . . . . . 43 C3
Hexham Gn TS23. . . . 52 B4
Hexham Wlk TS23 . . . 17 A1
Heysham Gr TS10 . . . 73 C3
Heythrop Dr
Guisborough TS14 . . . . 79 C2
Middlesbrough TS5. . . . 48 C2
Heywood St TS1, TS5 . 85 A1
Hibernian Gr TS25 . . . 11 C2
Hickling Gr TS19. . . . . 24 B1
Hidcote Gdns TS17. . . 65 B4
Highbank Rd TS7 . . . . 53 A1
Highbury Ave TS5. . . . 50 A3
High Church Wynd
TS15 . . . . 63 B2
HIGH CLARENCE . . . 23 C1
High Clarence Prim Sch
TS2 . . . . 29 B4
Highcliff Prim Sch
TS14 . . . . 78 C2
High Farm View TS6. . 42 C4
High Fell TS10 . . . . . . 70 B1
Highfield Cl TS16 . . . . 54 B1
Highfield Cres TS18 . . 35 A1
Highfield Dr TS16. . . . 54 B1
Highfield Gdns TS16 . 54 C1
Highfield Rd
Eston TS6 . . . . 43 C2
1 Marske-by-t-S
TS11 . . . . 74 B2
Middlesbrough TS4. . . . 40 B2
Stockton-on-T TS18. . . . 35 A1
High Force Rd TS2. . . 28 C3
Highgate TS6. . . . . . . 44 B2
High Gill Rd TS7 . . . . 62 A3
High Grange Ave
TS23 . . . . 17 A3
High Grange Ho
TS23 . . . . 17 A2
Highland Rd TS25. . . . 11 C2
HIGH LEVEN 65 C1
Highlight The TS24. . . .6 B1

Highmead Wlk TS3 . . 51 C3
High Newham Ct
TS19 . . . . 24 C3
High Newham Rd
TS19 . . . . 24 B3
High Peak TS14. . . . . 79 C1
High Rifts TS8 . . . . . . 58 C1
High St E TS10. . . . . . 70 C4
High St W TS10 . . . . . 70 A4
High St
Billingham TS2 . . . . . . 29 C4
Eston TS6 . . . . 43 B2
Greatham TS25. . . . . . 14 B3
Hartlepool TS24 . . . . . . 7 B2
Marske-by-t-S TS11 . . 74 C2
Middlesbrough TS7. . . . 52 B3
Redcar TS10 . . . . 71 A4
Stockton-on-T, Norton
TS20 . . . . 26 B4
Stockton-on-T TS18. . . 82 B3
Wolviston TS22 . . . . . . 16 C4
Yarm TS15. . . . . 63 B2
High Stone Cl TS10 . . 73 B4
High Tunstall Coll of
Science TS26 . . . . 8 B4
Hilda Pl TS12 . . . . 76 C3
Hilda Wlk TS24 . . . . . 10 B3
Hilden Pk TS17 . . . . . 56 A2
Hilderthorpe TS7 . . . . 61 C3
Hillbrook Cres TS17. . 56 A1
Hillcott Cl TS17 . . . . . 56 A2
Hill Cres TS10 . . . . . . 69 B2
Hillcrest Ave TS18 . . . 81 A2
Hillcrest Dr TS7. . . . . 62 B4
Hillel Wlk TS5 . . . . . . 59 A4
Hillhouse Farm 13
TS20 . . . . 26 B2
Hillingdon Rd TS3 . . . 51 C3
Hill Rd TS23 . . . . 21 B1
Hill St Ctr TS1 . . . . . . 84 C4
Hill St E TS18 . . . . . . 82 C4
Hillside Ave TS4 . . . . 50 B4
Hillside Rd TS20 . . . . 26 B4
Hill St
Middlesbrough TS1. . . . 84 C3
Redcar TS10 . . . . 70 B4
Hillston Cl TS26. . . . . . 8 B1
Hills View Rd TS6 . . . 44 A2
Hill View
Greatham TS25. . . . . . 14 C1
Ingleby Barwick TS17. . 56 A1
Hillway TS17. . . . . . . 56 A2
Hilston Cl TS17 . . . . . 56 A2
Hinderwell Ave TS10. 70 A2
Hindhead TS16 . . . . . 54 C1
Hindpool Cl TS24 . . . . 6 A3
Hinton Ave TS5 . . . . . 38 C2
Hinton Cl TS14 . . . . . 79 C4
Hirdman Gr TS24 . . . . 3 A2
Hird Rd TS15 . . . . . . 66 A4
Hive Cl TS19 . . . . 25 C2
HM Bark Endeavour ★
TS18 . . . . 83 B2
HMS Trincomalee ★
TS24 . . . . 6 B1
Hob Hill Cl TS12 . . . . 76 B2
Hob Hill Cres TS12 . . 76 C2
Hob Hill La TS11,
TS12. . . . . 76 C2
Hobson Ave TS10 . . . 69 B1
Hodges Ho TS1. . . . . 86 A3
Hodgson Ct 3 TS6. . . 44 A1
Hogarth Cl TS23 . . . . 17 A3
Holbeck Ave TS5. . . . 59 A4
Holbeck Wlk TS17 . . . 57 B3
Holburn Pk TS19 . . . . 25 A2
Holdenby Dr TS3. . . . 51 C3
Holden Cl TS6 . . . . . . 33 A2
Holdforth Cl TS24. . . .5 B3
Holdforth Ct TS24. . . 5 C3
Holdforth Rd TS24 . . 5 B3
Holey Cl TS8. . . . . . . 59 A2
Holgate The TS5 . . . . 85 B1
Holland Rd TS20 . . . . 14 B4
Hollies The
Billingham TS23 . . . . . 21 B1
Redcar TS10 . . . . 71 B2

Hollinside Cl TS19 . . . 25 A2
Hollinside Rd TS23. . . 17 C2
Hollins La TS5 . . . . . . 39 A1
Hollis Ct TS8 . . . . 60 B2
Hollowfield TS8 . . . . . 60 A2
Hollowfield Sq TS8 . . 60 A2
Hollybush Ave TS17. . 56 C2
Holly Hill Cl TS7 . . . . 53 A2
Hollyhurst Ave 9
TS4 . . . . 50 B4
Holly La TS8 . . . . 58 C1
Hollymead Dr TS14 . . 79 B4
Hollymount
Billingham TS23 . . . . . 21 B1
Hartlepool TS26 . . . . . 8 C4
Holly St
Middlesbrough TS1. . . . 87 A2
3 Stockton-on-T
TS20 . . . . 26 B3
Hollystone Ct TS23. . . 17 B3
Holly Terr TS2 . . . . . . 23 C1
Hollytree Mews
TS14 . . . . 79 B3
Hollywalk Ave TS6 . . 53 C4
Hollywalk Cl TS6. . . . 53 B4
Hollywalk Dr TS6 . . . 43 B1
Holme Ct TS3. . . . . . . 52 B3
Holmefields Rd TS6 . . 53 C4
Holme House Rd
TS18 . . . . 27 B1
Holme Land TS17 . . . . 56 A3
Holmes Cl TS17 . . . . . 47 A2
Holmeside Gr TS23 . . 17 C3
Holmewood TS16 . . . 63 A1
Holmside Wlk TS19 . . 25 A2
Holmwood Ave TS4 . . 50 B4
Holmwood Sch
Middlesbrough,
Easterside TS4 . . . . . . 51 A1
Middlesbrough TS4. . . . 50 B3
Holnest Ave TS1 . . . . 41 B1
Holnicote Cl TS17. . . 65 B2
Holtby Wlk TS3 . . . . . 51 C3
Holt St TS24 . . . . 9 C2
Holwick Rd TS2 . . . . . 84 A4
Holyhead Ct TS6. . . . 43 B4
Holyhead Dr TS10. . . 73 C4
Holyport Cl TS17 . . . . 47 C4
Holy Rood Ct TS4. . . 40 B2
Holyrood La TS14. . . 40 B2
Holyrood Wlk 2
TS25 . . . . 11 C2
Holystone Dr TS17 . . 65 A3
Holy Trinity CE Prim
Sch TS25 . . . . 13 C2
Holy Trinity Rosehill CE
Prim Sch TS15 . . . . . 34 C1
Holywell Gr TS16 . . . 54 C1
Homerell Cl TS10 . . . 73 B4
Homer Gr TS25 . . . . . 11 C4
Homerton Rd TS3. . . 41 C2
Homestead Garth
TS17 . . . . 56 A3
Honddu Cl TS17 . . . . 64 C3
Honey Bee Cl TS19 . . 25 C2
Honeycomb Ave
TS19 . . . . 25 C2
Honeysuckle Ct
TS20 . . . . 26 A3
Honey Way TS19 . . . . 25 C2
Honister Cl TS19. . . . 80 C4
Honister Gr TS5 . . . . 49 A2
Honister Rd TS10 . . . 70 B2
Honister Wlk TS16 . . 63 C4
Honiton Way TS25 . . 12 B1
Hood Cl TS24 . . . . 3 A2
Hood Dr TS6. . . . . . . 32 B1
Hoope Cl TS15. . . . . . 66 B3
Hope St
Billingham TS23 . . . . . 23 B2
Hartlepool TS24 . . . . . 10 A4
Stockton-on-T TS18. . . 81 C1
Hopkins Ave TS3 . . . . 41 C1
Hopps St 3 TS26 . . . . 5 C1
Horden Rd TS23 . . . . 17 C1

Hornbeam Cl 8 TS7 . 53 A3
Hornbeam Wlk TS19 . 25 B3
Hornby Cl
Middlesbrough TS1. . . . 84 C3
Seaton Carew TS25 . . . 13 C4
Horndale Cl TS10 . . . 73 C2
Hornleigh Gr TS10 . . 70 A3
Hornsea Cl TS23 . . . . 17 C4
Hornsea Gr TS10. . . . 70 A3
Hornsea Rd TS8 . . . . 59 A1
Horsefield St TS1. . . . 86 B3
Horsley Pl TS24 . . . . . 5 B4
Horsley Way TS23 . . . 17 B4
Hoskins Way TS3 . . . 41 C2
Hough Cres TS17 . . . 47 B3
Houghton Banks
TS17 . . . . 56 A3
Houghton Gn TS19 . . 24 C2
Houghton St TS24 . . . 9 C2
Hoveton Cl TS19 . . . . 24 C1
Hovingham Dr TS14 . 79 B5
Hovingham St TS3 . . . 41 A4
Howard Ct TS4. . . . . 40 B1
Howard Dr TS11 . . . . 75 B1
Howard Pl TS20. . . . . 26 B1
Howard St
Hartlepool TS24 . . . . . 6 C4
Middlesbrough TS1. . . . 85 B2
Howard Wlk TS23 . . . 27 A4
Howbeck La TS24 . . . 5 C3
Howcroft Ave TS10. . 69 B1
Howden Dike TS15. . . 67 A4
Howden Rd TS24 . . . . 3 A2
Howden Wlk TS18 . . 82 A3
Howe St TS1 . . . . 85 C1
Howgill Wlk TS3 . . . . 41 A2
Howlbeck Rd TS14 . . 79 A4
Hoylake Rd TS20 . . . 50 B3
Hoylake Way TS16 . . 63 C4
Hubbard Wlk TS4 . . . 86 B3
Huby Ct TS14 . . . . . . 79 B5
Hucklehoven Ct 5
TS24 . . . . 10 A3
Hucklehoven Way
TS24 . . . . 10 A3
Hudson Ho 3 TS17 . . 47 C1
Hudson St TS2. . . . . . 29 C3
Hudswell Gr 4 TS18 . 35 A1
Hugill Cl TS15 . . . . . . 67 A4
Hulam Cl TS19 . . . . . 25 A2
Hulton Cl 2 TS7. . . . . 61 C3
Humber Gr TS22 . . . . 16 A2
Humber Rd TS17 . . . . 47 C2
Humbledon Rd TS19 . 25 A2
Hume Ho TS18. . . . . . 82 A4
Hume St TS18 . . . . . . 82 B4
Humewood Gr TS20. . 20 C1
Hummers Hill La
TS11. . . . . 75 B2
Hundale Cres TS10 . . 73 B4
Hunstanton Ave TS10 . 70 A2
Huntcliff Ave TS10. . . 70 A2
Huntcliff Sch TS12 . . 76 B2
Hunters Bldgs TS18 . . 83 A1
Huntersgate TS6. . . . 44 B2
Hunters Gn TS16. . . . 54 A1
Hunter St 11 TS26. . . .9 B4
Huntingdon Gn TS20 . 26 C2
Huntley Cl TS3. . . . . . 52 A3
Huntly Rd TS25 . . . . . 11 C2
Hunwick Cl TS5. . . . . 49 A1
Hunwick Wlk TS19 . . 25 A2
Hurn Wlk TS17 . . . . . 48 A1
Hurricane Ct TS18 . . 46 B2
Hurst Pk TS10 . . . . . . 73 A4
Hurworth Cl TS19. . . 34 B3
Hurworth Rd
Billingham TS23 . . . . . 18 A4
Middlesbrough TS4. . . . 50 C4
Hurworth St TS24 . . . 5 C1
Hury Rd TS20 . . . . . . 26 A4
Hustler Rd TS5 . . . . . 58 C2
Hutchinson St TS18 . . 82 A3
Hutone Pl TS24 . . . . . 3 A2
Hutton Ave TS26 . . . . .9 B3
Hutton Cl TS17 . . . . . 47 B3
Hutton 13 TS26. . . . . .9 B4
HUTTON GATE 78 B1

Hutton Gr
Redcar TS10 . . . . 69 B1
Stockton-on-T TS18. . . 81 A1
Hutton La TS14 . . . . . 78 C2
Hutton Rd
Eston TS6 . . . . 44 B3
Middlesbrough TS4. . . 87 C1
Hutton St TS24 . . . . . .6 B4
Hutton Village Rd
TS14 . . . . 78 B1
Huxley Wlk TS25 . . . . 11 C4
Hylton Gr TS20 . . . . . 26 A2
Hylton Rd
Billingham TS23 . . . . . 17 C1
Hartlepool TS26 . . . . . 8 B3
Hythe Cl TS10. . . . . . 73 C3

I

Ian Gr TS25 . . . . 11 C1
Ian Ramsey CE Comp
Sch TS18 . . . . 35 A2
Ian St TS17 . . . . 47 C4
Ibbetson St TS24. . . . .7 B3
Iber Gr TS25 . . . . 11 C1
Ibrox Gr TS25 . . . . . . 11 C1
Ibstock Ho TS3 . . . . . 41 A2
Ibstone Wlk TS19 . . . 24 C4
Ickworth Ct TS17 . . . 65 B4
Ida Rd TS3. . . . . 41 A3
Ida St TS20 . . . . 26 A2
Ilam Ct TS17 . . . . 65 B4
Ilford Cl TS19 . . . . . . 24 C4
Ilford Way TS3 . . . . . 51 C4
Ilfracombe Dr TS10 . . 72 A4
Ilkeston Wlk 3 TS19 . 24 C4
Ilkley Gr
Guisborough TS14 . . . . 79 A1
Hartlepool TS25 . . . . . 12 C2
Ilston Gn 2 TS3 . . . . 51 C4
Imeson St 2 TS6 . . . . 44 A1
Imperial Ave
Stockton-on-T TS20. . . 26 B2
Thornaby-on-T TS17 . . 47 C4
Imperial Cres TS20. . . 26 B2
Imperial Rd TS23 . . . . 27 A4
Inchcape Rd TS25. . . . 11 C1
Inch Gr TS25. . . . . 11 C1
Ingham Gr TS25 . . . . 14 A4
Ingleborough La
TS17 . . . . 65 B2
Ingleby 11 TS4. . . . . . 40 C1
Ingleby Cl TS6 . . . . . . 44 B3
Ingleby Gr TS10 . . . . 70 C4
Ingleby Gr TS18. . . . . 81 A1
Ingleby Mill Prim Sch
TS17 . . . . 65 B2
Ingleby Rd
Hartlepool TS25 . . . . . 13 C1
Middlesbrough TS4. . . 87 C1
Ingleby Way TS17 . . . 56 B2
Inglefield TS25 . . . . . . 12 B1
Ingleside Mews 5
TS12 . . . . 76 C3
Ingleton Rd TS19 . . . 24 C4
Inglewood Ave 2
TS11 . . . . 74 C1
Inglewood Cl TS3 . . . 42 B1
Ingoldsby Rd TS3 . . . 42 B1
Ingram Gr TS17. . . . . 47 B3
Ingram Rd TS3. . . . . . 41 A2
Ingrove Cl TS19 . . . . 24 C4
Ings Ave TS3. . . . . . . 41 C2
Ings Farm Prim Sch
TS10 . . . . 71 B2
Ings La TS15 . . . . 66 A4
Ings Rd TS10 . . . . 71 B2
Inkerman St TS18. . . 82 A3
Innes Rd TS25 . . . . . . 12 C1
Innes St TS2 . . . . 29 B3
Inskip Wlk 6 TS19. . . 24 C4
Institute Terr TS6 . . . 33 A2
Instow Cl TS19 . . . . . 24 C3

100 Int–Lan

Intrepid Cl TS25 ...... 13 B4
Inverness Rd TS25 ... 11 C1
Inwood Lo TS7...... 51 C2
Ipswich Ave TS3 ..... 51 C4
Ironstone Ct TS6..... 42 C4
Irstead Wlk [4] TS19 .. 24 C4
Irthing Cl TS17....... 65 A2
Irvin Ave TS12 ...... 76 B3
Irvine Rd
  Hartlepool TS25 ...... 11 C1
  Middlesbrough TS3.... 41 A3
Islay Ct TS17........ 47 C3
Islay Gr TS25 .... 11 C1
Islington Wlk TS4 .. 51 A1
Italy St TS2 .... 84 C4
Ivanhoe Cres TS25 ... 11 C1
Iveston Gr TS22...... 16 B1
Iveston Wlk [5] TS19 .. 24 C4
Ivy Cl TS20.......... 26 A2
Ivy Cotts TS16 ...... 63 C3
Ivy Gr TS24 .... 5 B2

J

Jack Hatfield Sq
  TS1 .... 86 A3
Jacklin Wlk TS16 .... 54 C1
Jackson Ho [5] TS5... 40 A1
Jacksons Landing
  TS24 ....6 B1
Jackson St
  Hartlepool TS25 ...... 9 B1
  [4] South Bank TS6... 32 A2
Jacques Ct TS24 ..... 7 C2
James Cook University
  Hosp l The TS4 ..... 51 A4
Jameson Rd
  Hartlepool TS25 ..... 11 B2
  Stockton-on-T TS20... 20 B1
James St
  Hartlepool TS24 ..... 10 B3
  Middlesbrough TS3.... 41 A4
Jane Wlk TS20....... 26 C1
Japonica Way TS20 .. 26 A2
Jarsling Ho TS24.... .6 B1
Jarvis Wlk [4] TS25 .. 11 B2
Jasmine Fields TS15 .. 67 B1
Jasmine Gr TS7...... 60 C4
Jasmine Rd TS19 .... 25 C1
Jaywood Cl TS27...... 2 B2
Jedburgh Rd TS25 ... 11 B2
Jedburgh St TS1..... 86 A3
Jefferson St TS3..... 41 A4
Jenner Dr TS19 ...... 24 C2
Jennings The TS6 .... 43 B1
Jersey St [6] TS24 ... 10 A4
Jersey Wlk TS14 ..... 79 A2
Jesmond Ave TS5.... 49 B4
Jesmond Est [1] TS24. 5 C2
Jesmond Gdns TS24 .. 5 B2
Jesmond Gr TS18 .... 45 B4
Jesmond Mews TS5... 5 C1
Jesmond Rd TS26.... 5 B1
Jesmond Road Prim
  Sch TS26 .... 5 B1
Jesmond Sq TS24..... 5 B2
Jobson St [6] TS26 ... 5 C1
John E Batty Prim Sch
  TS10 .... 71 B2
John Howe Gdns
  TS24 .... 5 A4
Johnson Gr TS20 .... 25 C4
Johnson St
  [2] Hartlepool TS26 ... 9 C3
  Middlesbrough TS1.... 84 C3
Johnson's Yd TS14 ... 79 B3
John St TS24 .... 10 A4
Johnston Ave TS12... 76 B3
John Walker Sq
  TS18 .... 83 B2
Joicey Ct TS26....... 9 C4
Jones Rd
  Hartlepool TS24 ...... 5 B4
  South Bank TS6...... 32 B2

Joppa Gr TS25....... 11 C2
Jowitt Rd TS24 ....5 B4
Joyce Rd TS24........ 3 A1
Jubilee Bank TS7 .... 52 C3
Jubilee Ct [7] TS6 .... 44 A1
Jubilee Gr TS22...... 16 C1
Jubilee Ho [3] TS26 .. 9 C3
Jubilee Rd TS6 ...... 44 A1
Jubilee St TS3 ...... 41 A4
Jubilee St TS3....... 41 A4
Junction Farm Prim
  Sch TS16 .... 54 B1
Junction Rd TS19,
  TS20 .... 19 C1
Juniper Cl [4] TS10... 73 B2
Juniper Gr TS7 ...... 61 C4
Juniper Wlk [3] TS25 . 11 B2
Jupiter Ct TS3 ...... 41 B4
Jura Gr TS25........ 11 C2
Jute Gr TS25........ 11 B2
Jutland Rd TS25 ..... 12 C2

K

Kader Ave TS5....... 49 B1
Kader Farm Rd TS5 .. 49 C1
Kader Prim Sch TS5 . 49 B1
Kathleen St TS25 .... 9 B1
Kearsley Cl TS16..... 45 C1
Keats Rd TS6 .... 43 C1
Keay St TS5......... 85 A1
Kebock Wlk [2] TS25 . 11 B2
Kedleston Cl TS19 ... 25 A1
Kedlestone Pk TS8... 61 B1
Kedward Ave TS3 .... 41 C3
Keel Ho TS24 .... 10 B4
Keepersgate TS6 .... 44 B2
Keepers La TS17 ..... 56 B1
Keighley Ave TS7 .... 51 A1
Keilder Cl TS10 ..... 72 B3
Keilder Rise TS8 .... 59 C2
Keir Hardie Cl TS6 ... 32 B2
Keir Hardie Cres
  TS6 .... 32 B1
Keithlands Ave TS20 . 26 B3
Keith Rd TS4........ 50 B4
Keithwood Cl [3] TS4. 50 B4
Kelbrook Wlk TS3.... 41 C2
Keld Cl TS17 .... 65 B2
Keld Gr TS19........ 34 B2
Kelfield Ave TS3 .... 41 C2
Kelgate Terr TS8 .... 58 C1
Kelling Cl TS23 ..... 17 B3
Kelloe Cl TS19 ...... 24 C3
Kells Gr TS25 .... 11 B2
Kelsall Cl TS3....... 52 A4
Kelso Ct TS3........ 41 A1
Kelso Gr TS25....... 11 B2
Kelsterne Ct TS15.... 67 B4
Kelvin Gr
  Hartlepool TS25 ..... 11 B2
  Middlesbrough TS3.... 41 A1
Kemplah Ho TS14 ... 79 B3
Kempston Way TS20 . 25 B4
Kendal Ct TS4 ...... 40 B1
Kendal Gr TS10 ..... 70 C1
Kendal Rd
  Hartlepool TS25 ...... 9 C1
  Stockton-on-T TS18... 80 B4
Kenilworth Ave TS3 .. 52 A4
Kenilworth Flats
  TS23 .... 17 B1
Kenilworth Rd TS23 .. 17 B1
Kenilworth Way
  TS10 .... 73 C4
Kenley Gdns TS20 ... 19 C1
Kenmore Rd TS3..... 42 B1
Kennedy Gdns TS23 .. 21 C4
Kennedy Gr TS20 .... 25 C3
Kennthorpe TS7 ..... 61 C3
Kensington Ave TS6.. 53 C3
Kensington Ct TS24... 5 B4
Kensington Rd
  Middlesbrough TS5.... 85 C1
  Stockton-on-T TS18... 81 C1
Kent Ave TS25 .... 9 C1

Kent Cl
  Nunthorpe TS7 ...... 62 B3
  Redcar TS10 .... 70 B1
Kent Gr TS20 .... 26 C3
Kentmere Rd TS3 .... 41 A1
Kenton Cl TS18 ..... 45 B4
Kentport Ct [10] TS18.. 82 C4
Kentra Cl TS10...... 73 B3
Kent Rd TS14 .... 79 A2
Kenville Gr TS19 .... 34 B4
Kepier Cl TS19 ...... 24 C3
Kepple Ave TS3 ..... 41 A1
Kepwick Cl TS5 ..... 50 A2
Kerr Gr TS25........ 11 B2
Kerridge Cl [1] TS11 . 74 C2
Kerry Cl TS6 .... 43 B4
Kesteven Rd
  Hartlepool TS25 ..... 11 C1
  Middlesbrough TS4.... 51 A1
Kestrel Ave TS3 ..... 41 C4
Kestrel Cl
  Hartlepool TS26 ..... 4 B3
  Stockton-on-T TS20.. 22 C2
Kestrel Hide TS14.... 78 B3
Keswick Gr TS5...... 49 B2
Keswick Rd
  Billingham TS23 ..... 21 B1
  Eston TS6 .... 43 A2
  Redcar TS10 .... 70 C1
Keswick St TS26 ...... 9 B2
Kettleness Ave TS10 .. 70 A2
Kettlewell Cl TS23 ... 17 B2
Ketton Rd TS19 ..... 25 A3
Ketton Row TS1 .... 84 B3
Keverstone Cl TS19 .. 25 A3
Keverstone Gr TS23.. 17 C4
Kew Gdns TS20 ..... 19 C1
Kew Rise TS6....... 53 B3
Keynsham Ave [9]
  TS3 .... 52 A4
Kielder Cl TS22 ..... 16 A1
Kielder Rd TS26 ..... 8 A4
Kilbride Cl TS17 ..... 48 A3
Kilburn Rd
  Middlesbrough TS4....50 C4
  Stockton-on-T TS18... 81 A1
Kildale [11] TS4 ...... 40 B1
Kildale Gr
  Hartlepool TS25 ..... 13 B1
  Redcar TS10 .... 70 A1
  Stockton-on-T TS19... 34 B2
Kildale Rd
  Billingham TS23 ..... 21 B3
  Middlesbrough TS4.... 40 B2
Kildare St TS1 ...... 85 B1
Kildwick Gr TS3 ..... 52 A4
Kilkenny Rd TS14 ... 79 B2
Killerby Cl [7] TS19 .. 25 A3
Killinghall Gr TS18... 34 B1
Kilmarnock Rd TS25 . 11 B2
Kilmory Wlk [1] TS25 . 11 B2
Kilmurich Cl TS23 ... 17 C4
Kilsyth Cl TS25 ..... 11 B2
Kilton Cl
  Redcar TS10 .... 71 C1
  Stockton-on-T TS19... 25 A3
Kilton Ct TS4 .... 40 A1
Kilwick St TS24 ...... 9 C2
Kimberley Dr TS3.... 41 B2
Kimberley St TS26 ... 9 B2
Kimble Dr TS17 ..... 56 C4
Kimblesworth Wlk [8]
  TS19 .... 25 A3
Kimmerton Ave TS5.. 49 B1
Kinbrace Rd TS25 ... 11 B2
Kindersley St TS3.... 41 A4
Kinderton Gr TS20 .. 25 B4
Kindlewood Gdns
  TS14 .... 79 B3
Kingcraft Rd TS7 .... 51 A1
King Edward's Rd
  TS1 .... 85 C2
King Edward's Sq
  TS1 .... 85 C2
King Edward Terr [1]
  TS11 .... 75 A2

King Edwin Sch
  TS20 .... 20 C1
Kingfisher TS26...... 4 C3
Kingfisher Dr TS14... 78 A3
Kingfisher Ho TS24 .. 10 B4
Kingfisher Way TS18 . 46 C2
King Georges Terr
  TS6 .... 31 C3
King Ho TS1 .... 86 A3
King Oswy Dr TS24... 2 C2
King's Acad The TS8 . 60 A2
Kings Ct TS20....... 26 B4
Kingsdale Cl TS15.... 66 B3
Kingsley Ave TS25 ... 12 A4
Kingsley Cl TS6...... 43 C4
Kingsley Prim Sch
  TS25 .... 12 A4
Kingsley Rd
  Eston TS6 .... 44 A4
  Stockton-on-T TS18... 35 A2
King's Manor Sch
  TS5 .... 49 C2
Kings Mews E TS3 ... 87 C2
Kings Mews W TS3... 87 C2
Kingsport Cl TS18.... 37 B4
Kings Rd
  Billingham TS22 ..... 16 C1
  Middlesbrough TS5.... 39 B2
King's Rd TS3 .... 41 A4
King St
  Hartlepool TS25 ..... 10 A1
  Redcar TS10 .... 71 A4
  South Bank TS6...... 32 A2
  Stockton-on-T TS18... 82 B3
  Thornaby-on-T TS17 .. 88 C3
Kingston Ave TS5 .... 49 C4
Kingston Rd TS20 ... 26 B1
Kingston St TS1 ..... 85 C2
Kingsway TS23 ...... 21 B4
Kingsway Ave TS6 ... 42 C3
Kininvie Cl TS10 .... 72 C2
Kininvie Wlk [6]
  TS19 .... 25 A3
Kinloch Rd TS6 ..... 43 A2
Kinloss Cl TS17 ..... 48 A1
Kinloss Wlk TS17 ... 48 A1
Kinmel Cl TS10 ..... 73 B3
Kinross Ave TS3 .... 52 A4
Kinross Gr TS25..... 11 B2
Kinterbury Cl TS25... 13 B4
Kintra Rd TS25...... 11 B2
Kintyre Dr TS17 .... 56 C4
Kintyre Wlk TS14 ... 78 C1
Kinver Cl TS3 .... 41 A1
Kipling Gr TS19 ..... 34 C2
Kipling Rd TS25..... 8 C1
Kirby Ave TS5....... 38 C1
Kirby Cl
  Billingham TS23 ..... 17 C1
  Eston TS6 .... 44 B3
Kirby Wlk TS10 ..... 72 C4
Kirkdale TS14 .... 78 A2
Kirkdale Cl TS19 .... 80 B4
Kirkdale Nursing Home
  TS17 .... 83 C2
Kirkdale Way TS5 ... 50 A2
Kirkfell Cl TS16 ..... 54 B2
Kirkgate Rd TS5 .... 49 B4
Kirkham Rd TS7 .... 62 B3
Kirkham Row TS14... 61 A2
Kirklands The TS11.. 75 A3
Kirkland Wlk [1] TS3 . 51 C4
KIRKLEATHAM 72 B1
Kirkleatham Ave
  TS11 .... 75 A2
Kirkleatham Hall Sch
  TS10 .... 72 B1
Kirkleatham La TS10 . 72 A4
Kirkleatham Owl
  Sanctuary★ TS10 ... 72 A1
Kirkleatham St TS10 . 70 B3
Kirkleavington Hall Dr
  TS15 .... 67 A2
Kirklevington Grange
  TS15 .... 67 A3
Kirklevington Wlk
  TS19 .... 24 C3

Kirkley Lo TS8 .... 60 B
Kirknewton Cl [5]
  TS19 .... 25 A
Kirknewton Gr [3]
  TS17 .... 65 A3
Kirknewton Rd TS6 .. 43 A
Kirk Rd TS15........ 67 B4
Kirkstall Ave [4] TS3 . 52 B4
Kirkstone Ct TS24.... 5 C3
Kirkstone Gr
  Hartlepool TS24 ..... 5 C
  Redcar TS10 .... 70 C
Kirkstone Rd TS3 .... 41 A
Kirkwall Cl TS19 .... 34 A4
Kirkwood Dr TS10 ... 73 B2
Kirriemuir Rd TS25 .. 11 B
Kittiwake Cl TS26 .... 4 C
Knaith Cl TS15...... 66 A3
Knapton Ave TS22 ... 16 A
Knaresborough Ave
  TS7 .... 61 B2
Knaresborough Cl
  TS27 .... 2 C
Knayton Gr TS19..... 34 B2
Knighton Ct TS17 ... 48 A2
Knightport Rd TS18 .. 82 C4
Knightsbridge Gdns
  TS26 .... 8 C4
Knitsley Wlk TS19.... 24 C3
Knole Rd TS23 ...... 17 C1
Knowles St TS18..... 82 B3
Kreuger Alley TS3 ... 87 C2
Kyle Ave TS25........ 9 B1

L

Laburnum Ave TS17.. 47 B2
Laburnum Ct TS18 .. 81 C2
Laburnum Gr TS2.... 29 C4
Laburnum Ho TS10 .. 70 B4
Laburnum Rd
  Eaglescliffe TS16 .... 54 C4
  Eston TS6 .... 43 A3
  Ormesby TS7........ 53 A2
  Redcar TS10 .... 71 B2
Laburnum St [6] TS26 . 9 B4
Lacey Gr TS25........ 5 B1
LACKENBY 44 C3
Lackenby La TS6 .... 44 B3
Ladgate Grange TS3 . 41 B1
Ladgate La TS8 ..... 51 B2
Ladle The TS4 ...... 51 C2
Ladyfern Way TS20... 25 C4
Lady Mantle Cl TS26 . 4 C4
Ladyport Gn [1] TS18 . 82 C4
Ladysmith St TS25 ... 10 A1
Lagonda Ct TS23..... 18 C1
Lagonda Rd TS23 ... 18 C1
Laindon Ave TS4.... 51 B1
Laing Cl TS6........ 33 A2
Laing St TS18....... 82 A3
Laird Rd TS25....... 11 B2
Lakes Ave TS10 ..... 70 C2
Lakes Prim Sch
  TS10 .... 70 C1
Lakeston Cl TS26 .... 4 C1
Lamberd Rd TS24 .... 3 B1
Lambeth Rd TS18 ... 39 B1
Lambfield Way TS17 . 56 A3
Lamb La TS17....... 65 A3
Lambourne Dr TS7... 61 B4
Lambton Rd
  Billingham TS23 ..... 17 C1
  Middlesbrough TS4.... 40 B2
  Stockton-on-T TS19... 25 C1
Lambton St
  Eston TS6 .... 43 B1
  [9] Hartlepool TS24... 10 A3
Lammermuir Rd
  TS23 .... 21 A4
Lamonby Cl TS7 .... 61 C2
Lamont Gr TS25 .... 11 A2
Lamport Cl TS18 .... 37 B4
Lamport St TS1 ..... 85 C2
Lanark Cl TS19...... 34 C4
Lanark Rd TS25 ..... 11 A2
Lanberry Gn TS4..... 40 C2

ancaster Ct TS24 . . . . 6 A2
ancaster Dr **4**
TS11 . . . . 74 B2
ancaster Ho TS6 . . . . 43 B4
ancaster Rd
Hartlepool TS24 . . . . 6 A2
Middlesbrough TS5 . . . 39 C1
ancaster Rd N TS24 . . 6 A3
ancaster Way TS17 . . 57 A3
ancefield Rd TS20 . . 20 C1
anchester Ave TS23 . 16 C2
anchester Rd TS6 . . . 33 B2
andseer Dr TS23 . . . . 17 A3
anehouse Rd TS17 . . 47 C4
aneside Rd TS18 . . . . 81 A1
angbaurgh Ct **3**
TS12 . . . . 76 C4
angdale TS14 . . . . 78 A2
angdale Cl TS16 . . . . 63 C4
angdale Cres TS6 . . . 44 A3
angdale Gr TS5 . . . . . 49 C3
angdale Rd TS3 . . . . . 21 C1
angdon Sq TS8 . . . . . 60 B3
angdon Way TS16 . . . 54 A1
angham Wlk TS19 . . 34 B3
angleeford Way
TS17 . . . . 65 A3
angley Ave TS17 . . . . 47 C4
angley Cl TS10 . . . . . . 72 C3
angley Ct **13** TS3 . . . . 51 C4
angley Ho TS10 . . . . . 72 C2
angridge Cres TS3 . . 41 B1
angsett Ave **1** TS3 . . 41 A1
angthorne Gr TS18 . . 34 B1
angthorpe TS7 . . . . . . 61 C3
angthwaite Wlk
TS10 . . . . 72 C3
angton Ave TS22 . . . . 16 B1
angton Cl TS4 . . . . . . 40 A2
anrood Gn TS4 . . . . . 40 C2
ansbury Cl TS6 . . . . . 32 A1
ansbury Rd TS24 . . . . 6 A1
ansdowne Ct **6**
TS26 . . . . 9 B3
ansdowne Rd
Hartlepool TS26 . . . . . . 9 B3
Middlesbrough TS4 . . . 40 C2
Thornaby-on-T TS17 . . 48 A3
Yarm TS15 . . . . 64 A1
ansdown Way TS3 . . 18 A2
anshaw Gn TS4 . . . . . 40 C2
anyard Ho TS14 . . . . . 10 A4
apwing La TS20 . . . . . 20 B2
apwing Rd TS26 . . . . . 4 C2
arch Cl TS17 . . . . 61 C4
arch Cres TS16 . . . . . 55 A4
arches The
Eston TS6 . . . . 42 C3
Ormesby TS7 . . . . 53 A2
Redcar TS10 . . . . 71 B2
arch Gr TS25 . . . . 5 C3
arch Rd
Guisborough TS14 . . . 79 A4
Stockton-on-T TS19 . . . 26 A1
ark Terr TS2 . . . . 29 C4
ark Dr TS14 . . . . 78 A3
arkhall Sq TS20 . . . . 26 B2
arkspur Cl TS26 . . . . 4 C4
arkspur Rd TS7 . . . . . 60 C4
arkswood Rd TS10 . . 72 C2
artington Way TS16 . . 54 A1
arun Beat The TS15 . . 64 A2
astingham Ave TS6 . . 43 C2
atham Rd TS5 . . . . . . 39 B2
atimer Cl TS15 . . . . . 66 A3
atimer La TS14 . . . . . 78 C2
auder Cl TS19 . . . . . . 34 C4
auderdale Dr TS14 . . 79 C2
auder Ho **1** TS19 . . . 34 C4
auder St TS24 . . . . . . 9 C4
aura St TS1 . . . . 87 A1
aurel Ave
Middlesbrough TS4 . . . 50 C4
Thornaby-on-T TS17 . . 47 B2
aurel Cl TS12 . . . . . . 76 C2

Laurel Rd
Eaglescliffe TS16 . . . . . 54 C4
Marton TS7 . . . . 61 A3
Redcar TS10 . . . . 71 C2
Saltburn-by-t-S TS12 . . 76 C2
Stockton-on-T TS19 . . . 25 C1
Laurel St TS1 . . . . 87 A2
Laurels The TS25 . . . . . 9 A2
Laurence Jackson Sch
TS14 . . . . 79 C5
Lavan Ct TS10 . . . . . . 73 B3
Lavan Sands TS5 . . . . 58 B3
Lavender Ct TS11 . . . . 75 A1
Lavender Flats TS10 . . . 4 C4
Lavender Rd TS3 . . . . . 41 A3
Lavender Way TS20 . . 26 A3
Lavernock Cl TS10 . . . 73 B4
Lawns The TS24 . . . . . . 7 B2
Lawnswood Rd TS3 . . 42 B2
Lawrence Rd TS17 . . . 47 A2
Lawrence St
Redcar TS10 . . . . 71 A3
Stockton-on-T TS18 . . . 83 A2
Lawrenny Gr TS17 . . . 64 C3
Lawson Cl
Middlesbrough TS3 . . . 30 C1
South Bank TS6 . . . . . 32 B1
Lawson Ind Est TS3 . . 30 C1
Lawson Rd TS25 . . . . . 13 C3
Lawson St TS18 . . . . . 83 A2
Lawson Way TS3 . . . . . 30 C1
Lawson Wlk TS18 . . . . 83 A2
Lax Terr TS22 . . . . 16 C4
Laxton Cl TS23 . . . . . . 17 A2
Laycock St TS1 . . . . . . 85 A2
Layfield Prim Sch
TS15 . . . . 66 B3
Lazenby Rd TS24 . . . . . 3 A2
Leahope Ct TS17 . . . . 57 B4
Lealholm Cres TS3 . . . 52 A3
Lealholme Gr TS19 . . 34 C2
Lealholm Rd TS25 . . . 12 C2
Lealholm Way TS14 . . 79 A1
Lealholm Wlk **2**
TS6 . . . . 44 A3
Leamington Dr **2**
TS25 . . . . 9 C1
Leamington Gr TS3 . . 52 B4
Leamington Par TS25 . 9 C1
Leam La TS19 . . . . 24 A1
Leas Gr TS24 . . . . 6 C4
Leas The TS10 . . . . . . 73 B4
Leas Wlk TS24 . . . . 6 C4
Leazon Hill TS17 . . . . 56 A2
Leckfell Cl TS7 . . . . . . 61 C2
Ledbury Dr
Middlesbrough TS5 . . . 59 A3
Thornaby-on-T TS17 . . 47 B2
Ledbury Way TS14 . . . 79 A1
Leeds St TS18 . . . . 82 A3
Leeholme Gdns
TS23 . . . . 22 A4
Leeholme Rd TS23 . . . 22 A4
Leeming Rd TS5 . . . . . 39 A1
Lee Rd TS6 . . . . 33 B2
Lees Rd TS1 . . . . 85 B2
Leeway The TS3 . . . . . 86 C3
Leicester Ho TS6 . . . . 43 C4
Leicester Rd TS20 . . . 26 C3
Leicester Way TS16 . . 63 A3
Leighton Rd
Eston TS6 . . . . 43 C4
Stockton-on-T TS18 . . . 34 B1
Leighton Terr TS27 . . . 2 C1
Leinster Rd TS1 . . . . . 85 A1
Leith Wlk TS17 . . . . . . 57 A3
Lenham Cl TS22 . . . . . 16 A1
Lennox Cres TS23 . . . 21 B3
Lennox Wlk TS25 . . . . . 9 C1
Leonard Ropner Dr
TS19 . . . . 34 B4
Lerwick Cl TS19 . . . . . 34 A3
Letch La TS21 . . . . 24 A4
Letch Rd TS20 . . . . . . 20 C1
Letchworth Dr TS19 . . 24 C3
Letitia Ind Est TS5 . . . 38 C4
LEVEN BRIDGE 65 B1

Leven Camping Site
TS17 . . . . 65 A2
Leven Cl TS16 . . . . . . 63 B3
Levendale Cl TS15 . . . 64 B1
Levendale Prim Sch
TS15 . . . . 64 B1
Leven Gr
Hartlepool TS25 . . . . . 11 B2
Thornaby-on-T TS17 . . 47 C2
Leven Rd
Guisborough TS14 . . . 79 A2
Middlesbrough TS3 . . . 41 A4
Stockton-on-T TS20 . . 26 A4
Yarm TS15 . . . . 64 A1
Leven St
Billingham TS23 . . . . . 23 B2
Middlesbrough TS1 . . . 85 A2
Saltburn-by-t-S TS12 . . 76 C3
South Bank TS6 . . . . . 32 A2
Levens Wlk TS10 . . . . 70 C1
Leveret Cl TS17 . . . . . 56 C2
Levick Cres TS5 . . . . . 49 A3
Levington Wynd TS7 . 62 A2
Levisham Cl
Middlesbrough TS5 . . . 50 A3
Stockton-on-T TS18 . . . 81 A1
Lewes Way TS23 . . . . 18 A3
Lewis Gr TS25 . . . . . . 11 B4
Lewis Rd TS5 . . . . 39 B2
Lewis Wlk TS14 . . . . . 79 A2
Lexden Ave TS5 . . . . . 49 A3
Lexington Ct **8** TS20 . 26 B2
Leybourne Terr TS18 . 81 C2
Leyburn Gr TS18 . . . . 45 A4
Leyburn St TS26 . . . . . . 9 B2
Libanus Ct TS17 . . . . 64 C4
Lichfield Ave
Eaglescliffe TS16 . . . . 54 A1
Eston TS6 . . . . 43 C3
Lichfield Rd TS5 . . . . . 40 A1
Liddel Ct TS24 . . . . 5 C4
Lightfoot Cres TS24 . . 5 B4
Lightfoot Gr TS18 . . . 83 A2
Light Pipe Hall Rd
TS18 . . . . 81 C2
Lilac Ave TS17 . . . . . . 47 B2
Lilac Cl TS12 . . . . 76 A2
Lilac Gr
Middlesbrough TS3 . . . 41 C3
Redcar TS10 . . . . 71 B2
Lilac Rd
Eaglescliffe TS16 . . . . 54 C4
Eston TS6 . . . . 43 A3
Ormesby TS7 . . . . 53 A2
Stockton-on-T TS19 . . . 25 C1
Limber Gn TS3 . . . . . . 52 C4
Limbrick Ave TS19 . . 34 B3
Limbrick Ct TS19 . . . 34 C3
Lime Cl TS7 . . . . 61 A4
Lime Cres
Eston TS6 . . . . 43 A2
Hartlepool TS24 . . . . . . 5 C2
Lime Gr TS19 . . . . 34 C3
Limeoak Way TS18 . . 82 C4
Lime Rd
Eaglescliffe TS16 . . . . 55 A4
Eston TS6 . . . . 43 A2
Guisborough TS14 . . . 79 A4
Redcar TS10 . . . . 71 B3
Limerick Rd TS10 . . . 69 A1
Limes Cres TS11 . . . . 75 A1
Limes Rd TS5 . . . . 38 C1
Limetree Ct **7** TS4 . . 50 B4
Limetrees Cl TS2 . . . . 23 C1
Limpton Gate TS15 . . 66 C4
Linby Ave TS3 . . . . . . 51 B4
Lincoln Cres TS23 . . . 22 A3
Lincoln Gr TS20 . . . . 26 C3
Lincoln Pl TS17 . . . . . 47 B3
Lincoln Rd
Guisborough TS14 . . . 79 A2
Hartlepool TS25 . . . . . 11 B1
Redcar TS10 . . . . 71 C1
Lincombe Dr TS5 . . . . 59 A3
Linden Ave TS18 . . . . 46 A4
Linden Cres TS7 . . . . 60 C3
Linden Ct TS17 . . . . . 47 B3

Linden Gr
Hartlepool TS26 . . . . . . 9 A3
Middlesbrough TS5 . . . 39 B1
Thornaby-on-T TS17 . . 47 B3
Lindisfarne Ave
TS17 . . . . 47 C3
Lindisfarne Cl TS27 . . 2 C1
Lindisfarne Rd TS3 . . 52 B4
Lindrick TS8 . . . . 61 B1
Lindrick Ct TS6 . . . . . 43 C1
Lindrick Dr TS27 . . . . 2 B2
Lindrick Rd **5** TS6 . . 43 C1
Lindsay Ho TS18 . . . . 82 B3
Lindsay Rd TS25 . . . . 11 A2
Lindsay St TS18 . . . . . 83 A1
Ling Cl TS7 . . . . 51 B1
Lingdale Cl TS19 . . . . 80 B4
Lingdale Gr TS10 . . . . 69 C1
Lingdale Rd TS17 . . . 47 C2
Lingfield Ash TS8 . . . 68 A4
Lingfield Dr TS16 . . . 44 A4
Lingfield Prim Sch
TS7 . . . . 61 A2
Lingfield Rd
Stockton-on-T TS19 . . . 34 C3
Yarm TS15 . . . . 64 B1
Lingfield Way TS8 . . . 60 C1
Lingholme TS10 . . . . . 70 B1
Lingmell Rd TS10 . . . 72 C4
Links Prim Sch The
TS16 . . . . 54 C1
Links The
Redcar TS10 . . . . 70 A4
Saltburn-by-t-S TS12 . . 76 B1
Seaton Carew TS25 . . 13 C1
Link The TS3 . . . . 52 B4
Linkway The TS23 . . . 21 C4
Linley Ct TS20 . . . . . . 20 B2
Linlithgow Cl TS14 . . 79 A1
Linmoor Ave TS3 . . . . 41 C2
Linnet Ct TS20 . . . . . 20 C2
Linnet Rd TS26 . . . . . . 5 A3
Linshiels Gr TS17 . . . 65 A3
Linsley Cl TS3 . . . . . . 86 C3
Linsley Rd TS18 . . . . 81 B1
LINTHORPE 39 B1
Linthorpe Com Prim
Sch TS5 . . . . 39 B1
Linthorpe Mews TS1 . 84 C4
Linthorpe Rd TS5 . . . 39 C2
Linton Ave TS7 . . . . . 60 C3
Linton Cl TS19 . . . . . 24 A1
Linton Rd TS6 . . . . . . 42 C1
Lismore Gdns TS17 . . 47 C3
Lister St TS26 . . . . 9 B3
Lithgo Cl TS25 . . . . . . 13 C4
Littleboy Dr TS17 . . . 48 A3
Little Crake TS14 . . . 78 B3
Little Grebe TS14 . . . 78 A3
Little Pasture TS17 . . 56 A2
Littondale TS8 . . . . . . 59 A1
Littondale Ct TS17 . . 65 A2
Liverton Ave TS5 . . . . 85 A1
Liverton Cres
Billingham TS22 . . . . . 16 B2
Thornaby-on-T TS17 . . 76 A3
Liverton Whin TS12 . . 76 A3
Livingstone Rd TS3 . . 41 A3
Lizard Gr TS24 . . . . . 10 A3
Lizard Wlk **12** TS24 . . 10 A3
Lloyd St TS2 . . . . 84 B4
Lobelia Cl **11** TS7 . . . 53 A3
Lobster Rd TS10 . . . . 70 B4
Loch Gr TS25 . . . . 11 B2
Lockerbie Wlk TS17 . . 56 C4
Locke Rd TS10 . . . . . . 70 B3
Lockheed Cl TS18 . . . 46 B1
Lockheed Ct TS18 . . . 46 B2
Lockton Cl TS8 . . . . . 58 C1
Lockton Cres TS17 . . 76 B3
Lockwood Ct TS6 . . . . 43 C1
Locomotion Cl TS6 . . 54 B2
Lodge Farm Rd TS6 . . 44 A2
Lodge Rd TS6 . . . . 43 C2
Lodge St TS18 . . . . . . 83 A2
Lodore Gr TS5 . . . . . . 49 A2
Loftus **10** TS4 . . . . . . 40 B1
Logan Dr TS19 . . . . . . 35 A3

Logan Gr TS25 . . . . . 11 B2
Lomond Ave TS23 . . . 21 C4
Londonderry Rd
TS19 . . . . 80 C4
Londonderry St TS24 . . 7 B2
Longbank Rd TS3 . . . 53 A2
Longbeck Rd TS11 . . 74 B1
Longbeck Sta TS11 . . 74 B1
Longbeck Trad Est
TS11 . . . . 74 B2
Longbeck Way TS17 . 57 B3
Longcroft Wlk TS3 . . 41 B3
Longfellow Rd TS23 . 17 A4
Longfellow Wlk
TS25 . . . . 5 A3
Longfield View TS6 . . 53 B3
Longford Cl TS23 . . . 17 B2
Longford St TS1 . . . . 85 A1
Longhill Ind Est
TS25 . . . . 10 A1
Longhirst TS8 . . . . . . 60 C1
Longlands Rd
Middlesbrough, Cargo
Fleet TS3 . . . . 41 B4
Middlesbrough, Grove Hill
TS4 . . . . 87 C1
Longleat Wlk TS17 . . 56 A1
Longscar Wlk **13**
TS24 . . . . 10 A3
Longshaw Cl **1**
TS17 . . . . 56 C1
Longworth Way
TS14 . . . . 79 C5
Lonsdale Ct **5** TS25 . . 9 C2
Lonsdale Cl TS10 . . . 69 B1
Lonsdale St TS1 . . . . 85 B2
Loraine Cl TS11 . . . . 75 B1
Lord Ave TS17 . . . . . . 57 A2
Lord Nelson Cl TS25 . 13 A4
Lorimer Cl TS17 . . . . 56 B1
Lorne Ct TS18 . . . . . . 46 A4
Lorne St TS5 . . . . 85 B2
Lorrain Gr TS20 . . . . 21 A1
Lorton Rd TS10 . . . . . 72 C4
Lothian Gr TS10 . . . . 70 A2
Lothian Rd TS4 . . . . . 87 B1
Lovaine St TS1 . . . . . 85 B2
Lovat Ave TS10 . . . . . 70 A2
Lovat Gr TS1 . . . . 11 B2
Low Church Wynd
TS15 . . . . 63 B3
Lowcross Ave TS14 . . 78 C1
Lowdale La TS24 . . . . . 2 B2
Lowell Cl **3** TS23 . . . 17 B4
Lower East St TS2 . . . 86 A4
Lower Feversham St
TS2 . . . . 86 A4
Lower Gosford St
TS2 . . . . 86 A4
Loweswater Cres
TS18 . . . . 80 A3
Loweswater Gr TS10 . 70 C2
Low Farm Dr TS10 . . 72 B4
Lowfield Ave TS3 . . . . 41 C3
Lowfields Ave TS17 . . 56 B2
Lowfields Gn TS17 . . 56 B1
Lowfields Wlk TS17 . . 56 B1
Low Fold TS10 . . . . . . 69 C2
Low Grange Ave
TS23 . . . . 18 A3
Lowick Cl TS19 . . . . . 34 C4
Low La
Middlesbrough TS5 . . . 59 A4
Stainton TS17 . . . . 57 C1
Thornaby-on-T TS17 . . 58 A1
Lowmead Wlk TS3 . . . 52 A3
Lowood Ave TS7 . . . . 60 C3
Lowther Cl TS22 . . . . 16 A2
Lowthian Rd TS24,
TS26 . . . . 9 C4
Loxley Rd TS3 . . . . . . 42 B2
Loyalty Cl TS25 . . . . . 12 C4
Loyalty Ct TS25 . . . . . 12 C4

Loyalty Rd TS25 . . . . **12** C4
Lucan St TS24 . . . . **9** C4
Luccombe Cl TS17 . . . **65** B2
Lucerne Ct TS7 . . . . **60** C4
Lucerne Dr TS14 . . . . . **78** B2
Lucerne Rd TS10 . . . . . **70** C2
Luce Sands TS5 . . . . . **58** B3
Lucia La TS14 . . . . **78** C2
Ludford Ave **11** TS3 . **51** C4
Ludham Gr TS19 . . . . . **24** C1
Ludlow Cres TS10 . . . **71** B1
Ludlow Rd TS23 . . . . . **17** A1
Luff Way TS10 . . . . . . **73** B4
Lufton Cl TS17 . . . . . . **55** B2
Lullingstone Cres
   TS17 . . . . **55** C3
Lulsgate TS17 . . . . . . **48** A1
Lulworth Cl TS10 . . . **73** B3
Lulworth Gr TS24 . . . . **2** C2
Lumley Rd
   Billingham TS23 . . . . **17** B1
   Redcar TS10 . . . . **71** A3
Lumley Sq TS24 . . . . . . **7** B2
Lundy Ct TS17 . . . . . **65** B4
Lundy Wlk TS14 . . . . . **79** A2
Lunebeck Wlk TS17 . **57** B3
Lunedale Ave TS5 . . . **50** A3
Lunedale Rd TS23 . . . **21** B3
Lunefield Ho **7** TS5 . **39** B1
Lune Rd
   Egglescliffe TS16 . . . **63** B3
   Stockton-on-T TS20 . . **26** A3
Lune St TS12 . . . . **76** C3
Lustrum Ave TS18 . . . **27** C1
Lustrum Ind Est
   TS18 . . . . **27** C1
Lutton Cres TS22 . . . . **16** A1
Luttrell Ho **5** TS3 . . **41** B1
Lycium Cl TS7 . . . . . . **51** B1
Lydbrook Rd TS5 . . . . **38** C2
Lydd Gdns TS17 . . . . . **48** A1
Lyndale TS14 . . . . . . **78** A1
Lyndon Way TS18 . . . **34** B3
Lynmouth Cl TS8 . . . **58** C2
Lynmouth Rd TS20 . . . **19** C1
Lynmouth Wlk TS26 . . **5** A2
Lynnfield Prim Sch
   TS26 . . . . **9** B4
Lynnfield Rd **8** TS26 . **6** A1
Lynn St S TS24 . . . . . . **10** B3
Lynn St TS24 . . . . **10** A4
Lynton Ct TS26 . . . . . . **5** A2
Lynwood Ave TS5 . . . **50** A3
Lysander Ct **5** TS11 . **74** B2
Lytham Wlk TS16 . . . **54** C1
Lythe Pl TS4 . . . . **50** C3
Lythe Wlk **8** TS6 . . . **44** A3
Lyttleton Dr TS18 . . . **35** A1
Lytton St TS4 . . . . . . **87** C2

M

MacAulay Rd TS25 . . . **11** C4
Mcauley Ct TS3 . . . . . **41** A2
MacBean St TS3 . . . . **41** A4
McClean Ave TS10 . . . **69** C2
McCreton St TS3 . . . . **41** B4
McDonald Pl TS24 . . . **7** C2
Mackie Dr TS14 . . . . . **79** C4
Macklin Ave TS23 . . . **18** B1
MacMillan Acad TS5 . **38** C3
Macnay St **3** TS12 . . **76** C3
Macrae Rd TS25 . . . . **11** A1
Maddern Way TS5 . . . **39** B2
Madison Sq **5** TS19 . . **34** C4
Magdalen St TS3 . . . . **87** C2
Magister Rd TS17 . . . **47** B1
Magnolia Ct
   18 Redcar TS10 . . . . . **73** B2
   Stockton-on-T TS18 . . **81** C2
Maidstone Dr TS7 . . . **61** B4
Mainsforth Dr
   Billingham TS23 . . . . **17** C4

Mainsforth Dr continued
   Middlesbrough TS5 . . . **59** A4
Mainsforth Flats
   TS24 . . . . **10** B3
Mainsforth Terr
   TS24 . . . . **10** B3
Major Cooper Ct
   TS25 . . . . **13** C2
Major St TS18 . . . . . . **82** B4
Majuba Rd TS10 . . . . . **70** A4
Malcolm Dr TS19 . . . . **24** A1
Malcolm Gr
   Redcar TS10 . . . . **71** B2
   Thornaby-on-T TS17 . . **47** C2
Malcom Rd TS25 . . . . . **11** B1
Malden Rd **3** TS20 . . **26** B4
Maldon Rd TS5 . . . . . **38** C2
Malham Gill TS10 . . . **70** B1
Malham Gr TS17 . . . . . **56** C1
Malin Gr TS10 . . . . . . **72** C2
Mallaig View **10**
   TS19 . . . . **34** C4
Mallard Cl TS14 . . . . . **78** A2
Mallard Ct TS10 . . . . . **69** C1
Mallard La TS20 . . . . . **20** B1
Mallards The TS8 . . . . **68** A4
Malleable Way TS18 . **37** B4
Malling Rd TS20 . . . . . **26** B4
Malling Wlk **3** TS3 . . **41** B2
Mallory Cl TS1 . . . . . **84** B3
Mallory Rd TS20 . . . . **26** A4
Mallowdale TS7 . . . . . **61** C2
Malltraeth Sands
   TS5 . . . . **58** A4
Maltby **9** TS4 . . . . . **40** B1
Maltby Ct TS14 . . . . . **79** A4
Maltby Pl TS17 . . . . . **47** B3
Maltby St TS3 . . . . . . **41** A4
Maltings The **7** TS25 . . **9** C2
Malton Dr TS19 . . . . . **24** A1
Malvern Ave TS10 . . . **70** A1
Malvern Dr TS5 . . . . . **59** A4
Malvern Rd
   Billingham TS23 . . . . **21** B4
   Stockton-on-T TS18 . . **81** B2
Mandale Ind Est
   TS17 . . . . **83** C1
Mandale Mill Prim Sch
   TS17 . . . . **47** C4
Mandale Rd
   Middlesbrough TS5 . . . **49** A3
   Thornaby-on-T TS17 . . **83** C1
Mandale Ret Pk
   TS18 . . . . **37** B4
Manfield Ave TS5 . . . **38** B1
Manfield St TS18 . . . . **81** C2
Manitoba Gdns TS4 . . **87** B1
Manners St TS24 . . . . **7** B2
Manning Cl TS17 . . . . **47** C1
Manning Way **6**
   TS17 . . . . **47** C1
Manor Cl TS22 . . . . . . **16** C3
Manor College of Tech
   TS25 . . . . **11** C1
Manor Ct TS22 . . . . . . **16** C3
Manor Farm Way
   TS8 . . . . **60** A2
Manor Gn TS6 . . . . . . **43** B2
Manor Pl TS19 . . . . . . **34** C4
Manor Rd TS6 . . . . **8** B4
Manor St TS1 . . . . **85** B2
Manor Way TS23 . . . . **22** C3
Manor Wood TS8 . . . . **59** C3
Mansepool Cl TS24 . . **6** A4
Mansfield Ave TS17 . . **47** C4
Mansfield Rd TS6 . . . . **43** C1
Manton Ave TS5 . . . . . **49** A4
Maple Ave
   Middlesbrough TS4 . . . **50** B4
   Thornaby-on-T TS17 . . **47** B2
Maple Cl TS19 . . . . . . **24** C1
Maple Rd TS19 . . . . . . **25** C1
Maple Sq TS10 . . . . . **71** B3
Maple St TS1 . . . . . . **87** A2
Mapleton Cl TS10 . . . **72** C2
Mapleton Cres TS10 . **72** C2

Mapleton Dr
   Hemlington TS8 . . . . . **59** A2
   Stockton-on-T TS20 . . **20** A1
Mapleton Rd
   1 Hartlepool TS24 . . . **6** A1
   Hartlepool TS24 . . . . . **6** A2
Maplin View **4** TS19 . **34** C4
Marchlyn Cres TS17 . **64** B4
Mardale TS8 . . . . **59** A1
Mardale Ave TS25 . . . **12** B1
Mardale Wlk TS10 . . . **72** C3
Margaret St TS3 . . . . **87** C2
Margill Cl TS7 . . . . . . **61** B4
Margrove Wlk **12**
   TS3 . . . . **51** C4
Marham Cl TS3 . . . . . **52** B4
Maria Dr TS19 . . . . . . **34** B4
Maria St TS3 . . . . **41** A4
Marigold Gr TS19 . . . **24** C1
Marina Ave TS10 . . . . **70** A4
Marina View TS24 . . . **10** A4
Marina Way TS24 . . . . **6** B1
Marine Cres TS24 . . . **7** B2
Marine Ct **1** TS12 . . **76** C4
Marine Dr TS24 . . . . . **7** A4
Marine Par TS12 . . . . **76** C4
Mariners Ct TS11 . . . . **74** C3
Mariners Point TS24 . . **6** C1
Marion Ave
   Egglescliffe TS16 . . . **63** B4
   Middlesbrough TS5 . . . **49** B4
Maritime Ave TS24 . . . **10** A4
Maritime Cl TS24 . . . . **10** B4
Maritime Rd TS18 . . . **82** B4
Mark Ave TS20 . . . . . . **20** B2
Markby Gn TS3 . . . . . **52** C4
Market Pl
   Guisborough TS14 . . . **79** B4
   Middlesbrough, North
     Ormesby TS3 . . . . . . **87** C2
   Middlesbrough TS2 . . . **29** C3
   Stockton-on-T TS18 . . **82** A3
Market St **6** TS6 . . . **32** A2
Markham Sq **2**
   TS19 . . . . **34** C4
Marland Bldgs TS4 . . **87** B1
Marlborough Ave
   TS11 . . . . **74** C3
Marlborough Cl
   TS23 . . . . **21** B1
Marlborough Rd
   Marton TS7 . . . . **60** C3
   Stockton-on-T TS18 . . **81** C1
Marlborough St TS25 . . **9** B1
Marley Cl TS19 . . . . . . **35** A4
Marley Wlk TS27 . . . . . **2** C1
Marlowe Rd TS25 . . . **11** C4
Marlsford Gr TS5 . . . . **49** A3
Marmaduke Pl TS20 . . **20** B1
Marmion Cl TS25 . . . . **13** A4
Marquand Rd TS6 . . . **32** B1
Marquis Gr TS20 . . . . **20** A1
Marquis St TS24 . . . . . **7** B2
Marrick Rd
   Middlesbrough TS3 . . . **51** C4
   Stockton-on-T TS18 . . **45** A4
Marsden Cl
   Ingleby Barwick
     TS17 . . . . **65** C4
   Middlesbrough TS4 . . . **50** C4
Marshall Ave TS3 . . . . **41** C3
Marshall Cl
   Hartlepool TS24 . . . . . **3** A1
   Saltburn-by-t-S TS12 . . **76** B3
Marshall Ct TS3 . . . . . **42** A4
Marshall Gr TS18 . . . . **80** B4
Marsh House Ave
   TS23 . . . . **17** B2
Marsh Rd
   Middlesbrough, Cargo
     Fleet TS3 . . . . **30** C1
   Middlesbrough TS1 . . . **84** B3
   Middlesbrough TS1 . . . **84** C4
Marsh St TS1 . . . . **84** B3
MARSKE-BY-T-SEA . **75** B3
Marske La TS19 . . . . . **24** A2
Marske Mill La TS12 . **76** C2

Marske Mill Terr
   TS12 . . . . **76** C2
Marske Par TS19 . . . . **24** A1
Marske Rd
   Saltburn-by-t-S
     TS12 . . . . **76** A3
   Thornaby-on-T TS17 . . **47** C3
Marske St TS25 . . . . . **9** C2
Marske Sta TS11 . . . . **74** C1
Marston Gdns TS24 . . **5** C2
Marston Rd TS18 . . . . **37** C4
Martham Cl TS19 . . . . **24** C1
Martindale TS5 . . . . . **58** B4
Martindale Gr TS16 . . **63** C3
Martindale Pl TS6 . . . **43** C4
Martindale Rd TS6 . . . **43** C4
Martindale Way
   TS10 . . . . **72** C3
Martinet Ct TS17 . . . . **47** B1
Martinet Rd TS17 . . . . **47** B1
Martin Gr TS25 . . . . . **9** A1
Martinhoe Cl TS17 . . . **65** B2
MARTON **61** A4
Marton Ave TS4 . . . . . **51** C2
Marton Burn Rd TS4 . **40** B1
Marton Cres TS6 . . . . **44** A1
Marton Dale Ct TS7 . . **61** B3
Marton Dr TS22 . . . . . **16** B1
Marton Gill TS12 . . . . **76** A3
MARTON GROVE . . . **40** B1
Marton Grove Prim Sch
   TS4 . . . . **40** B2
Marton Grove Rd
   TS4 . . . . **40** B2
Marton Manor Prim Sch
   TS7 . . . . **60** C4
Marton Moor Rd TS7 . **62** B2
Marton Rd TS4 . . . . . . **40** B2
Martonside Way TS4 . **51** A4
Marton St TS24 . . . . . **5** C1
Marton Sta TS4 . . . . . **52** A2
Marwood Sq **7**
   TS19 . . . . **34** C4
Mary Jaques Ct TS4 . . **40** B2
Marykirk Rd TS17 . . . **57** A3
Maryport Cl TS18 . . . **82** C4
Mary Rose Cl TS25 . . **13** B3
Mary St
   Hartlepool TS26 . . . . . **9** B4
   Stockton-on-T TS18 . . **81** C2
Masefield Rd TS25 . . . **8** B1
Masham Gr TS19 . . . . **34** B2
Mason St **2** TS6 . . . . **43** B1
Mason Wlk **5** TS24 . . **6** A1
Massey Rd TS17 . . . . **83** C2
Master Rd TS17 . . . . . **47** C1
Masterton Dr **3**
   TS18 . . . . **35** A1
Mastiles Cl TS17 . . . . **65** A2
Matfen Ave TS7 . . . . . **62** A3
Matford Ave TS3 . . . . **41** C3
Matlock Ave TS7 . . . . **61** A2
Matlock Gdns TS22 . . **16** C2
Mattison Ave TS5 . . . **38** C2
Maxton Rd TS6 . . . . . **32** A1
Maxwell Court Flatlets
   TS25 . . . . **11** B1
Maxwell Ct **3** TS18 . . **46** B4
Maxwell Pl TS10 . . . . **69** B1
Maxwell Rd
   Hartlepool TS25 . . . . . **11** B1
   Middlesbrough TS3 . . . **41** C4
Mayberry Gr TS5 . . . . **50** A4
Maybray King Wlk **5**
   TS20 . . . . **26** B4
Mayes Wlk TS15 . . . . **66** B3
Mayfair Ave
   Middlesbrough TS4 . . . **40** B2
   Normanby TS6 . . . . . . **53** B3
Mayfield Cl TS16 . . . . **54** A1
Mayfield Cres TS16 . . **54** A1
Mayfield Rd TS7 . . . . **62** A4
Mayflower Cl TS24 . . **10** B4
Mayflower Ho TS24 . . **10** B4
Maygate TS6 . . . . **44** B2
May St TS24 . . . . **6** A2
Maze La TS17 . . . . . . **37** C2

Mead Cres TS17 . . . . . **48** A
Meadfoot Dr TS5 . . . . **58** C
Meadowbank Rd
   TS7 . . . . **53** A
Meadow Cl
   Guisborough TS14 . . . **79** B
   Ormesby TS7 . . . . **52** C
Meadowcroft Rd
   TS6 . . . . **42** C
Meadowdale Cl TS2 . . **23** C
Meadow Dr
   Hartlepool TS26 . . . . . **8** B
   Ormesby TS7 . . . . **53** A
Meadow End TS16 . . . **54** B
Meadowfield Ave
   TS4 . . . . **50** B
Meadowfield Ct
   TS25 . . . . **13** C
Meadowfield Dr
   TS16 . . . . **54** B
Meadowgate TS6 . . . **44** B
Meadowgate Dr TS26 . **5** A
Meadowings The
   TS15 . . . . **66** B
Meadow Rd
   Marske-by-t-S TS11 . . **75** A
   Stockton-on-T TS19 . . **35** A
Meadows The
   Coulby Newham
     TS8 . . . . **60** C
   Redcar TS10 . . . . **70** B
Meadowsweet La
   TS19 . . . . **24** B
Meadowsweet Rd
   TS26 . . . . **4** C
Meadow The TS25 . . . **12** B
Meadow View Rd
   TS5 . . . . **38** C
Meadway TS10 . . . . . **72** B
Measham Cl TS20 . . . **25** C
Meath St TS1 . . . . . . **85** A
Meath Way TS14 . . . . **79** A
Medbourne Cl **4**
   TS25 . . . . **44** A
Medbourne Gdns
   TS5 . . . . **59** A
Medina Cl TS19 . . . . . **34** C
Medina Gdns TS5 . . . **59** B
Medway Ho TS23 . . . . **21** B
Megarth Rd TS5 . . . . **39** B
Meggitts Ave TS10 . . **69** B
Melbourne Cl TS7 . . . **61** B
Melbourne St TS18 . . **82** A
Melbreak Gr TS5 . . . . **49** A
Meldrum Sq **9** TS19 . **34** C
Meldyke La TS8 . . . . . **58** C
Meldyke Pl TS8 . . . . . **58** C
Melford Gr TS17 . . . . **65** B
Melksham Sq **6**
   TS19 . . . . **34** C
Mellanby La TS25 . . . **14** B
Mellor St TS19 . . . . . **80** C
Melrose Ave
   Billingham TS23 . . . . **17** B
   Middlesbrough TS5 . . . **49** B
Melrose Cres TS14 . . **79** D
Melrose Dr TS18 . . . . **46** A
Melrose St
   Hartlepool TS26 . . . . . **9** B
   Middlesbrough TS1 . . . **86** A
Melsonby Ave TS3 . . . **52** A
Melsonby Ct TS23 . . . **18** A
Melsonby Gr TS18 . . . **34** B
Melton Rd TS19 . . . . . **34** C
Melton Wlk TS8 . . . . . **59** A
Melville Wlk TS20 . . . **26** C
Memorial Dr TS7 . . . . **61** A
Mendip Dr TS10 . . . . **72** A
Mendip Rd TS23 . . . . **21** B
Merchant Ho TS24 . . **10** B
Meredith Ave TS6 . . . **53** B
Mereston Cl TS26 . . . . **4** B
Merganser Rd TS26 . . **4** C
Meridian Way TS18 . . **80** A
Merioneth Cl TS17 . . . **64** B
Merlay Cl TS15 . . . . . **66** A
Merlin Cl TS14 . . . . . **78** A

Merlin Rd
Middlesbrough TS3.... **41** C4
Stockton-on-T TS19.... **34** C4
Merlin Way TS26..... **4** C3
Merriman Gn TS24.... **2** C1
Merring Cl TS18 .... **34** B2
Merrington Ave TS5.. **58** B4
Merryweather Ct
TS15 .... **63** C2
Mersehead Sands
TS5 .... **58** B4
Mersey Rd TS10.... **70** B2
Merville Ave TS19.... **35** A2
Meryl Gdns TS25.... **12** B1
Metcalfe Cl TS15.... **66** B3
Metcalfe Rd TS6.... **31** C1
Metz Bridge Rd TS2.. **84** B4
Mews The TS11 .... **74** C2
Mexborough Cl TS19. **25** A1
Meynell Ave TS14.... **78** B2
Meynell Ho TS16.... **63** B3
Meynell's Wlk TS15.. **66** B4
Mickleby Cl TS7 .... **61** C2
Mickledales Dr TS11. **74** C2
Mickleton Dr TS16... **54** A1
Mickleton Rd TS2.... **28** C4
Micklow Cl TS10 .... **72** C3
Midbourne Rd TS19.. **26** A1
Middle Ave TS23 .... **21** B1
Middle Bank Rd TS7. **53** A2
Middlefield Rd
Marske-by-t-S TS11 ... **74** B2
Stockton-on-T TS19.... **24** C2
Middlegate TS24..... **7** B2
Middleham Rd TS19.. **35** A2
Middleham Way
TS10 .... **71** C1
Middle Rd TS17..... **56** B1
MIDDLESBROUGH .. **87** A1
Middlesbrough Art
Gallery★ TS1 ..... **85** C1
Middlesbrough Coll
Middlesbrough,
Linthorpe TS5 ...... **39** B1
Middlesbrough TS4... **87** B1
Middlesbrough Coll
(Acklam Campus)
TS5 .... **49** C2
Middlesbrough Coll
(Marton Campus)
TS4 .... **51** B3
Middlesbrough Inst of
Modern Art★ TS1... **86** A3
Middlesbrough Rd
South Bank TS6....... **31** C2
South Bank TS6....... **32** A2
Thornaby-on-T TS17 ... **37** C1
Middlesbrough Rd E
TS6 .... **32** B3
Middlesbrough Road E
5 TS6........... **32** A2
Middlesbrough Sta
TS1 .... **86** A4
Middlesbrough Wharf
Trad Est TS2.... **29** B4
Middle St TS18 .... **82** A3
MIDDLETON **7** A2
Middleton Ave
Billingham TS22 ...... **16** B1
Middlesbrough TS5.... **49** A4
Thornaby-on-T TS17 ... **56** C3
Middleton Ct TS15... **66** C4
Middleton Dr TS14... **79** C2
Middleton Grange La **2**
TS24 .... **9** C4
Middleton Rd TS24... **6** A1
Middleton Wlk TS18.. **81** C2
Middleway TS17..... **83** C1
Middlewood Cl **3**
TS27 ....**2** B2
Middridge Gr TS23... **17** C3
Midfield The TS5.... **85** B1
Midfield View **3**
TS19 .... **34** C4
Midhurst Rd TS3.... **42** B2
Midlothian Rd TS5... **11** A2
Midville Wlk TS3..... **52** C4

Midvill Wlk TS3...... **42** B1
Miers Ave TS24 ..... **5** C4
Milbank Ct TS18 .... **82** A3
Milbank Rd TS24..... **6** A2
Milbank St
3 South Bank TS6.... **32** A2
Stockton-on-T TS18.... **82** A3
Milburn Cres TS20 ... **26** A2
Mildenhall Cl TS25... **14** B4
Miles St TS6 .... **32** A2
Milfoil Cl TS7....... **60** B4
Milford Ho TS3 ..... **41** B4
Milford Wlk TS10 ... **72** B4
Millais Gr TS23 .... **17** A4
Millbank La TS17 .... **47** B1
Millbeck Ho TS20 ... **26** B4
Millbeck Way TS7... **53** A3
Millbrook Ave TS3 ... **42** A4
Mill Cl TS23 .... **27** A4
Miller Cl TS15 ..... **67** A4
Miller Cres TS24 .... **2** C1
Millfield Cl
Egglescliffe TS16 ..... **63** B4
Thornaby-on-T TS17 ... **48** A4
Millfield Rd TS3 .... **41** A3
Millford Rd TS20 ... **25** C3
Millgin Ct TS17 .... **56** A2
Millington Cl TS23 .. **17** C5
Mill La
Billingham TS23 ...... **21** C1
Stockton-on-T TS20.... **20** C1
Wolviston TS22....... **16** B3
Mill Lane Prim Sch
TS18 .... **82** A3
Mill Meadow Ct **10**
TS20 .... **26** B4
Millpool Cl TS24 .....**6** B4
Mill St E TS18...... **82** B3
Mill St W TS18...... **82** A3
Mills St TS1 .... **85** A2
Mill St
Guisborough TS14 .... **79** B3
Stockton-on-T TS20.... **26** A4
Millston Cl TS26 .....**4** B2
Millstone Cl **3** TS10 . **73** B2
Mill Wynd **3** TS15.... **63** B2
Milner Gr TS24 ..... **6** A1
Milner Rd TS20 .... **20** B1
Milne Wlk TS25 .... **11** A2
Milton Ct TS1...... **84** B3
Milton Rd TS26 ......**9** B4
Milton St TS12 .... **76** C3
Minch Rd TS25 .... **11** B1
Miniott Wlk TS8 .... **59** A2
Minskip Cl TS14 ... **79** B5
Minsterley Dr TS5... **48** C2
Missenden Gr TS3 .. **52** B4
Mitchell Ave TS17... **48** A2
Mitchell St **1** TS26 ...**9** B3
Mitford Cl TS7 .... **53** A3
Mitford Cres TS19.... **24** A2
Moat The TS23...... **22** C3
Moffat Rd TS25.... **11** B1
Monach Rd TS25.... **11** B1
Monarch Gr TS7 ... **61** B4
Mond Cres TS23 .... **27** A4
Mond Ho **3** TS3 .... **41** B1
Monkland Cl TS1 ... **84** C3
Monkseaton Dr TS22. **16** C1
Monkton Rd TS25... **11** A1
Monkton Rise TS14 .. **79** C5
Monmouth Dr TS16 .. **54** C1
Monmouth Gr TS26 .. **5** A2
Monmouth Rd TS6... **43** C4
Monreith Ave TS16... **54** C1
Montague St TS24 ....**7** B3
Montagu's Harrier
TS14 .... **78** B3
Montgomery Gr TS26 . **5** A2
Montreal Pl TS4 .... **40** B2
Montrose Cl TS7.... **60** C3
Montrose St
Middlesbrough TS1....**86** A4
Saltburn-by-t-S TS12... **76** C4
Moorbeck Way TS7 .. **53** A3

Moorcock Cl
Eston TS6 .... **44** A1
Normanby TS6 ..... **44** A1
Moore St
Hartlepool TS24 ..... **5** C2
Redcar TS10 .... **71** A4
Moorgate TS6 ..... **44** B2
Moor Gn TS7 ...... **62** A1
Moorhen Rd TS26... **4** C3
Moorhouse Est TS18 . **45** C2
Moor Par TS24.......**7** B3
Moor Pk
Egglescliffe TS16 ..... **63** C4
Nunthorpe TS7 ...... **62** A2
Moorsholm Way
TS10 .... **72** C4
Moorside Cl TS10.... **73** C2
Moorston Cl TS26....**4** B1
Moor Terr TS24 ..... **7** C2
Moortown Rd TS4 ... **50** C3
Moor View TS6...... **53** C4
Moray Cl TS4 ...... **40** B1
Moray Rd TS20 .... **25** C3
Mordales Dr TS11.... **75** B2
Moreland Ave TS23 .. **21** C4
Moreland Cl TS22.... **16** C4
Moreland St TS24.... **10** A3
Moresby Cl TS4 .... **51** A4
Morgan Dr TS14 .... **79** B2
Morison Gdns TS24 ...**7** B3
Morlais Ct TS17..... **64** C3
Morland Fell TS10 ... **70** C1
Morpeth Ave TS4 ... **51** A1
Morrison Rd TS14.... **79** C4
Morris Rd **6** TS6 .... **43** C1
Mortain Cl TS15 .... **67** B4
Mortimer Dr TS20 ... **25** C4
Morton Carr La TS7 .. **62** C3
Morton Cl TS14 .... **78** C2
Morton St **8** TS26 ....**9** B4
Morven View **8**
TS19 .... **34** C4
Morville Ct TS17 .... **65** B4
Mosedale Rd TS6.... **43** C3
Moses St TS3...... **87** C2
Mosman Terr TS3 ... **87** C2
Mossbrough Cl TS19 . **25** A1
Mossdale Gr TS14.... **78** B2
Moss Gdns TS8 .... **59** A2
Mosston Rd TS19.... **35** A4
Moss Way TS18 .... **46** A2
Mosswood Cres TS5 . **49** A1
Motherwell Rd TS25 . **11** B1
Moulton Ct TS19..... **34** B2
Mountbatten Ct TS24.. **6** B3
Mount Gr TS20...... **20** C1
Mount Leven Rd
TS15 .... **64** B2
MOUNT PLEASANT
Middlesbrough **68** C4
Stockton-on-Tees **26** C2
Mount Pleasant Ave
TS11 .... **75** A2
Mount Pleasant Grange
TS18 .... **46** C4
Mount Pleasant Rd
TS20 .... **26** B2
Mountston Cl TS26.... **4** C1
Mount The TS6 .... **53** B4
Mowbray Dr TS8.... **59** A2
Mowbray Gr TS19 ... **34** C1
Mowbray Ho **12** TS4.. **50** B4
Mowbray Rd
Hartlepool TS25 ..... **14** B4
Stockton-on-T TS20.... **26** B2
Mowden Cl TS19.... **35** A4
Moyne Gdns **4** TS25.. **9** C2
Muirfield TS7....... **62** A2
Muirfield Cl TS27 .....**2** B2
Muirfield Rd TS16.... **54** C1
Muirfield Way TS4 ... **50** C4
Muirfield Wlk TS27 ...**2** B2
Muir Gr TS25 ...... **11** B1
Muker Rd TS19...... **34** B2
Mulberry Ct **2** TS4 .. **50** B4
Mulgrave Cl TS14.... **79** B5

Mulgrave Rd
Hartlepool TS26 ..... **9** A4
Middlesbrough TS5.... **39** C1
Mulgrave Wlk
9 Eston TS6 ...... **44** A3
Redcar TS10 .... **72** C4
Mullroy Rd TS25 ... **11** A1
Munro Gr TS25 .... **11** B1
Murdock Rd TS3..... **42** A4
Muriel St
Middlesbrough TS1.... **87** A1
Redcar TS10 .... **71** A3
Murray St TS26 ..... **9** B4
Murton Cl TS17 .... **56** B4
Murton Gr TS22.... **16** B1
Museum Rd TS24 ... **9** C4
Musgrave St TS24... **10** B3
Musgrave Terr TS22.. **16** C4
Musgrave Wlk **10**
TS24 .... **10** A3
Mus of Hartlepool &
Gray Art Gal★ TS24.. **6** B1
Muston Cl TS15 .... **66** C4
Myrddin-Baker Rd
TS6 .... **43** C3
Myrtle Ct TS17...... **47** B3
Myrtle Gr TS17 .... **47** B3
Myrtle Rd
Egglescliffe TS16 ..... **54** C4
Stockton-on-T TS19.... **25** C1
Myrtle St TS1....... **87** A2
Myton Park Prim Sch
TS17 .... **64** C4
Myton Rd TS17 .... **65** A4
Myton Wlk TS8 .... **59** A2

N

Nab Cl TS6 .... **43** C1
Nairnhead Cl TS8.... **59** A2
Nantwich Cl TS8 .... **59** A2
Napier St
Middlesbrough TS5.... **85** C1
2 South Bank TS6.... **32** A2
Stockton-on-T TS20.... **26** B2
Naseby Ct TS23 .... **18** A3
Nash Gr TS25 ...... **11** C4
Nature's World★
TS5 .... **59** B4
Navenby Gr TS25 ... **14** A4
Navigation Point
TS24 .... **6** C1
Navigation Way
TS17 .... **37** C2
Navigator Ct TS18.... **46** C3
Neasham Ave
Billingham TS23 ..... **17** C3
Marton TS7 .... **61** A2
Neasham Cl TS18 ... **82** B3
Neath Ct TS17 .... **64** C4
Nederdale Cl TS15... **66** B3
Needles Cl TS10 .... **72** B2
Nelson Ave TS23 ... **23** A2
Nelson Cl TS6 ..... **32** A2
Nelson St Ind Est
TS6 .... **31** C2
Nelson Sq TS20 .... **20** B1
Nelson St TS6 ..... **31** C2
Nelson Street Ind Est
TS6 .... **32** A2
Nelson Terr
Redcar TS10 .... **70** B4
Stockton-on-T TS18.... **82** A3
Neptune Cl TS25 ... **13** B4
Neptune Ho TS24 ... **6** C1
Nesbyt Rd TS20 .... **33** B1
Nesham Ave TS5.... **38** C1
Nesham Rd
Hartlepool TS24 ..... **7** B3
Middlesbrough TS1.... **85** A2
Netherby Cl TS15 ... **64** B1
Netherby Gate TS26.. **5** A1
Netherfields Cres
TS3 .... **52** A4
Netley Gr TS3....... **52** B4
Nevern Cres TS17 ... **64** B3

Neville Gr TS14 ..... **78** C2
Neville Rd TS18..... **28** A1
Neville's Ct TS5..... **49** C4
Newark Rd TS25 ... **14** A4
Newark Wlk TS26 ... **26** C3
Newbank Cl TS7 .... **53** A2
Newbiggin Rd **8**
TS23 .... **17** B4
Newbridge Ct TS5 .. **50** A3
Newburn Bridge Ind Est
TS25 .... **10** B2
Newbury Ave TS5 ... **38** C1
Newbury Way TS23 .. **17** C2
NEWBY............. **68** A1
Newby **8** TS4 ..... **40** B1
Newby Cl
Middlesbrough TS5.... **50** A3
5 Stockton-on-T
TS20 .... **26** A4
Newby Gr TS17 .... **47** C3
Newcomen Ct TS10 .. **70** C4
Newcomen Gn TS4 .. **40** B2
Newcomen Cl TS10.. **70** C4
Newcomen Prim Sch
TS10 .... **70** B1
Newcomen Rd TS6... **31** C1
Newcomen Terr
TS10 .... **70** B4
Newfield Cres TS5 .. **49** A1
Newgale Cl TS17.... **64** B3
Newgate TS6 ...... **44** A2
Newham Ave TS5 ... **50** A3
Newham Bridge Prim
Sch TS5 .... **50** A3
NEWHAM GRANGE.. **80** B4
Newham Grange Ave
TS19 .... **80** B3
Newham Grange
Leisure Farm★
TS8 .... **60** A3
Newham Way TS8.... **60** B3
Newhaven Cl TS8 ... **59** A2
Newhaven Ct **3**
TS24 .... **10** A3
Newholm Ct TS25.... **12** B2
Newholme Ct TS14... **79** A4
Newholm Way TS10.. **72** C4
Newick Ave TS3 .... **41** B2
Newington Rd TS4... **50** C2
Newlands Ave
Hartlepool TS26 ..... **9** A3
Stockton-on-T TS20.... **26** B3
Newlands Cl TS16 ... **70** B2
Newlands RC Sch The
TS4 .... **50** B2
Newlands Rd
Egglescliffe TS16 ..... **63** B4
Middlesbrough TS1.... **87** B2
Newley Ct TS3 ..... **42** B1
Newlyn Gn TS3 .... **52** A4
Newlyn Way TS10 ... **73** C3
Newmarket Ave
TS17 .... **38** A3
Newmarket Rd TS10 . **71** A4
NEWPORT.......... **85** A1
Newport Cres TS1 .. **84** C3
Newport Prim Sch
TS1 .... **85** B2
Newport Rd TS1, TS5 . **84** B3
Newport South Bsns Pk
TS1 .... **85** A2
Newport Way TS1.... **84** B3
Newquay Cl
Hartlepool TS26 ..... **5** A1
Hemlington TS8....... **59** A2
New Rd
Billingham TS23 ..... **27** B4
Guisborough TS14 ... **79** B3
Newsam Cres **4**
TS16 .... **29** C1
Newsam Rd TS16 ... **63** B4
New St TS17....... **83** C1

Newstead Ave TS19 . . 25 A1
Newstead Rd TS4 . . . . 87 B1
Newton Cl TS6 . . . . 44 A1
Newtondale TS14 . . . . 78 A2
Newton Dr TS17 . . . . . 56 C4
Newton Gr TS22 . . . . . 16 B1
Newton Mall TS1 . . . . 84 C3
Newton Rd TS10 . . . . . 72 B4
Newton Wlk **7** TS20 . 26 B1
NEWTOWN 80 B4
Newtown Ave TS19 . . 80 C4
Nicholson Way TS24 . . 3 A1
Nicklaus Dr TS16 . . . . 55 A1
Nightingale Cl TS26 . . . 4 B3
Nightingale Dr TS19 . 24 C2
Nightingale Rd TS6 . . 43 C3
Nightingale Wlk
　TS20 . . . . 20 B1
Nile St TS2 . . . . 84 C4
Nimbus Cl TS7 . . . . . . 60 C4
Nolan Ho TS18 . . . . . . 82 A4
Nolan Pl TS18 . . . . . . 82 A4
Nolton Ct TS17 . . . . . 64 C3
Nookston Cl TS26 . . . . 4 C2
Norcliffe St TS3 . . . . . 41 A4
Norfolk Cl
　Hartlepool TS25 . . . . . 9 C1
　Redcar TS10 . . . . 70 B1
Norfolk Cres TS3 . . . . 52 B3
Norfolk Pl TS3 . . . . . . 41 B2
Norfolk St TS18 . . . . . 81 C2
Norham Wlk TS7 . . . . 52 C3
Norlyn **5** TS16 . . . . . . 63 B4
NORMANBY 43 B1
Normanby Ct TS7 . . . . 60 C3
Normanby Hall Pk
　TS6 . . . . 53 B4
Normanby Prim Sch
　TS6 . . . . 53 C4
Normanby Rd
　Eston TS6 . . . . 42 C4
　Ormesby TS7 . . . . 53 A4
Norman Terr TS6 . . . . 31 C2
North Albert Rd
　TS20 . . . . 20 B1
Northallerton Rd
　TS17 . . . . 47 C3
Northampton Ho
　TS6 . . . . 43 C4
Northampton Wlk **9**
　TS25 . . . . 9 C2
North Ave TS12 . . . . . 76 B3
North Bank Cres
　TS7 . . . . 53 A2
Northbourne Rd
　TS19 . . . . 25 C1
Northbrook Ct TS26 . . . 8 C3
Northcote St TS18 . . . 83 A1
Northdale Ct TS3 . . . . 41 C2
North Dr
　Hartlepool TS26 . . . . . 8 C4
　Ormesby TS7 . . . . 52 C3
Northern Rd TS5 . . . . 38 C2
North Fen TS10 . . . . . 70 B1
Northfield Rd
　Billingham TS22 . . . . 16 C1
　2 Marske-by-t-S
　TS11 . . . . 74 B2
Northfield Sch & Sports
　Coll TS22 . . . . 16 C2
Northfleet Ave TS3 . . 41 C4
Northgate
　Guisborough TS14 . . . 79 B4
　Hartlepool TS26 . . . . . 7 A3
Northgate Rd TS5 . . . 49 C4
Northiam Cl TS8 . . . . 59 A2
Northland Ave TS26 . . 9 A3
Northleach Dr TS8 . . . 59 A2
North Mount Pleasant
　St **9** TS20 . . . . 26 B2
NORTH ORMESBY . . 87 C2

North Ormesby Prim
　Sch TS3 . . . . 41 A4
North Ormesby Rd TS1,
　TS4 . . . . 86 B3
Northpark TS23 . . . . . 17 B4
Northport Rd TS18 . . . 82 C4
North Rd
　Middlesbrough TS2 . . . 86 B4
　Seaton Carew TS25 . . . 13 C3
North St
　Middlesbrough TS2 . . . 29 C3
　South Bank TS6 . . . . . 32 A3
　Stockton-on-T TS18 . . . 82 A3
North Tees Ind Est
　Middlesbrough
　TS18 . . . . 28 A1
　Stockton-on-T TS18 . . . 27 C1
North Terr TS10 . . . . . 70 C4
Northumberland Gr
　12 Hartlepool TS25 . . . 9 C2
　Stockton-on-T TS20 . . . 20 C2
Northumberland Rd
　TS17 . . . . 47 B3
Northumberland Wlk **13**
　TS25 . . . . 9 C2
Northwold Cl TS25 . . 14 B4
North Wood TS5 . . . . 49 C2
NORTON 20 C2
Norton Ave TS20 . . . . 26 A3
Norton Ct **12** TS20 . . 26 B2
Norton Dr TS19 . . . . . 24 A1
Norton Hall TS20 . . . . 20 C1
Norton Junction Cotts
　TS20 . . . . 19 B1
Norton Prim Sch
　TS20 . . . . 26 C2
Norton Rd
　Billingham TS20,
　TS23 . . . . 21 A1
　Stockton-on-T TS20 . . . 26 B2
Norton Sch Humanities
　Coll The TS20 . . . . . . 26 C2
Norwich Ave TS19 . . . 24 C1
Norwich Rd
　Middlesbrough TS5 . . . 39 C2
　Redcar TS10 . . . . 71 C1
Norwood Cl TS19 . . . 24 B1
Norwood Rd TS3 . . . . 52 B2
Nottingham Dr TS10 . 71 B1
Nottingham Wlk **10**
　TS25 . . . . 9 C2
Nuffield Rd TS23 . . . . 22 B4
Nugent Ave TS1 . . . . 85 A2
Nuneaton Dr TS8 . . . . 59 A2
Nunnington Cl TS17 . 56 B1
Nuns St TS24 . . . . 7 B2
NUNTHORPE 62 B2
Nunthorpe Gdns TS7 . 62 B2
Nunthorpe Oaks TS7 . 62 B2
Nunthorpe Prim Sch
　TS7 . . . . 62 C3
Nunthorpe Sch TS7 . 62 C3
Nunthorpe Sta TS7 . 62 B3
Nursery Gdns TS15 . . 67 A4
Nursery La
　Middlesbrough TS5 . . . 39 A2
　Stockton-on-T TS18 . . . 81 B2
Nutfield Cl TS8 . . . . . 59 A2
Nuthatch Cl TS26 . . . . 4 C2
Nut La TS4 . . . . 40 B2
Nutley Rd TS23 . . . . . 17 C1

O

Oak Ave TS7 . . . . 61 B3
Oakdale TS7 . . . . 53 A3
Oakdene Ave TS18 . . 46 A4
Oakdene Cl TS6 . . . . . 43 B1
Oakdene Prim Sch
　TS23 . . . . 17 C2
Oakenshaw Dr TS5 . . 49 B1
Oakesway TS24 . . . . . . 6 A3
Oakfield Ave TS16 . . . 54 B2
Oakfield Cl TS16 . . . . 54 B2
Oakfield Gdns TS7 . . 42 C1
Oakfield Rd TS3 . . . . 87 C2
Oak Gr TS24 . . . . 5 B2

Oakham Gn TS20 . . . . 26 C3
Oak Hill TS8 . . . . 60 C2
Oakhurst Cl **5** TS17 . . 56 C1
Oakland Ave TS25 . . . 12 B4
Oaklands Ave **6**
　TS20 . . . . 26 B3
Oaklands Rd TS6 . . . . 53 C4
Oaklea Cl TS20 . . . . . 26 A4
Oakley Cl
　Guisborough TS14 . . . 79 C1
　Hemlington TS8 . . . . . 59 A2
Oakley Gdns TS24 . . . . 5 C1
Oakley Wlk
　Eston TS6 . . . . 43 C1
　Normanby TS6 . . . . . . 53 C4
Oak Rd
　Eaglescliffe TS16 . . . . 55 A4
　Guisborough TS14 . . . 79 B4
　Redcar TS10 . . . . 71 C2
Oakridge **1** TS7 . . . . 53 A3
Oakrise TS7 . . . . 53 A3
Oaksham Dr TS23 . . . 17 C4
Oak St
　Middlesbrough TS1 . . . 86 A3
　South Bank TS6 . . . . . 32 A2
Oakstead TS25 . . . . . . 13 A3
Oaks The TS8 . . . . 59 A2
Oaktree Gr TS18 . . . . 45 A4
Oak Tree Prim Sch The
　TS19 . . . . 80 B4
Oakwell Gdns TS20 . . 26 A4
Oakwell Rd TS20 . . . . 26 A4
Oakwood Cl TS27 . . . . 2 B2
Oakwood Ct TS7 . . . . 61 C3
Oakworth Gn TS4 . . . 50 C4
Oatfields Ct TS6 . . . . 53 C4
Oban Ave TS25 . . . . . . 9 B1
Oban Rd TS3 . . . . 41 B2
Oberhausen Mall
　TS1 . . . . 84 C3
Occupation Rd
　Eston TS6 . . . . 44 A1
　Normanby TS6 . . . . . . 44 A1
Ocean Rd TS24 . . . . . . 2 B3
Ochil Terr TS23 . . . . . 21 C3
Offerton Dr TS8 . . . . . 59 B2
Okehampton Dr TS7 . 60 C3
Old Brew Ho TS14 . . . 79 C3
Oldbury Gr TS8 . . . . . 59 B2
Old Cemetery Rd
　TS24 . . . . 6 B4
Old Custom Ho The
　TS24 . . . . 10 A4
Old Docks Office The
　TS24 . . . . 10 A4
Oldford Cres TS5 . . . 49 B2
Oldgate TS6 . . . . 44 B2
Old Market The TS15 . 63 B2
Old Middlesbrough Rd
　TS6 . . . . 31 C2
Old Municipal Blgs **6**
　TS24 . . . . 9 C4
Old Rd TS23 . . . . 21 B1
Old Rectory Gdns
　TS15 . . . . 63 B1
Old Row **6** TS6 . . . . . 44 A2
Old School Complex
　TS1 . . . . 85 A2
Old Station Mews
　TS16 . . . . 63 B3
Old Station Rd TS6 . . 31 C3
Oldstead Ct TS8 . . . . 59 A2
OLD TOWN 10 B3
Oliver St
　Middlesbrough TS5 . . . 39 C2
　South Bank TS6 . . . . . 32 A2
Olive St
　Hartlepool TS24 . . . . . 7 B2
　Middlesbrough TS2 . . . 84 C4
Olliver St TS10 . . . . . 71 A3
Olney Wlk TS3 . . . . . 51 C4
Ontario Cres TS10 . . . 70 C2
Onyx Cl TS25 . . . . . . 13 B4
Orange Gr TS20 . . . . . 26 A2
Orchard Dr TS14 . . . . 79 C3
Orchard Gr TS6 . . . . . 43 B2

Orchard Mews TS16 . . 63 A4
Orchard Rd
　Middlesbrough TS5 . . . 39 C1
　Redcar TS10 . . . . 70 C2
　Stockton-on-T TS19 . . . 35 A3
　Thornaby-on-T TS17 . . . 47 A1
Orchard The
　Ingleby Barwick
　TS17 . . . . 56 A2
　Yarm TS15 . . . . 63 B2
Orchard Way TS7 . . . 52 C2
Orde Wingate Way
　TS19 . . . . 22 A4
Ordsall Gn **5** TS3 . . . 52 A4
Oriel Cl TS5 . . . . 49 C4
Orkney Way TS17 . . . 47 C3
Orkney Wlk TS14 . . . 78 C1
Orleans Gr TS7 . . . . . 61 B4
ORMESBY 53 B4
Ormesby Bank TS7 . . 53 A1
Ormesby Hall ★ TS7 . 52 B2
Ormesby Prim Sch
　TS7 . . . . 52 C3
Ormesby Rd
　Eston TS6 . . . . 43 A1
　Hartlepool TS25 . . . . 12 B2
　Middlesbrough TS3 . . . 41 B2
Ormesby Sch
　Eston TS3 . . . . 42 C1
　Ormesby TS3 . . . . 53 A4
Ormston Ave **4** TS3 . 52 A4
Orpington Rd TS3 . . . 52 A4
Orton Gr TS22 . . . . . . 16 B1
Orwell Gdns TS19 . . . 34 C2
Orwell St TS1 . . . . . . 85 A2
Orwell Wlk TS25 . . . . 11 C4
Osborne Rd
　Hartlepool TS26 . . . . . 9 B3
　Middlesbrough TS5 . . . 39 B2
　Stockton-on-T TS18 . . . 81 C2
Osbourne Cl TS8 . . . . 59 A2
Osprey Cl
　Guisborough TS14 . . . 78 A3
　Stockton-on-T TS20 . . . 20 C2
Osprey Ho TS24 . . . . 10 B4
Ostler Cl TS17 . . . . . . 56 B1
Oswestry Gn TS4 . . . 51 A1
Otley Ave TS3 . . . . . . 52 A4
Ottawa Rd TS4 . . . . . 40 B2
Otterburn Gdns TS5 . 59 A4
Otterburn Way TS23 . 17 C3
Otterhill Ct TS8 . . . . 59 A3
Otterpool Cl TS24 . . . 6 A3
Otter Way TS17 . . . . 56 C2
Oughton Cl TS15 . . . 67 B4
Oulston Rd TS18 . . . . 81 A2
Our Lady of the Most
　Holy Rosary RC Prim
　Sch TS23 . . . . 16 C1
Our Lady & St Bede RC
　Sch TS19 . . . . 35 A4
Ouseport Rd TS18 . . . 82 C4
Ouston St TS24 . . . . . . 9 C3
Outhwaite St TS5 . . . 85 A1
Outram St
　Middlesbrough TS1 . . . 85 B2
　Stockton-on-T TS18 . . . 83 A2
Ouzel Cl TS26 . . . . 4 C2
Oval Grange TS26 . . . . 8 C4
Oval The
　Hartlepool TS26 . . . . . 9 A3
　Middlesbrough TS5 . . . 58 C3
Overdale TS14 . . . . . . 78 A1
Overdale Cl TS10 . . . 72 C2
Overdale Rd TS3 . . . . 51 C4
Overfields Prim Sch
　TS7 . . . . 53 A4
Overton Way TS18 . . 83 A1
Owens Rd TS6 . . . . . . 31 C1
Owington Gr TS23 . . 18 A4
Owletts Ct TS17 . . . . 65 B3
Owls Gr TS17 . . . . . . 64 C3
Owton Cl TS25 . . . . . 12 A2
OWTON MANOR . . . 11 C2
Owton Manor La
　TS25 . . . . 11 B1

Owton Manor Prim Sch
　TS25 . . . . 11 B1
OXBRIDGE 81 B1
Oxbridge Ave
　Stockton-on-T,
　Grangefield TS18 . . . 80 A4
　Stockton-on-T, Hartburn
　TS18 . . . . 81 A1
Oxbridge Ct TS18 . . . 81 A1
Oxbridge Ind Est
　TS18 . . . . 81 C1
Oxbridge La TS18 . . . 81 B1
Oxbridge Lane Prim Sch
　TS18 . . . . 81 C1
Ox Close Cotts TS12 . 76 A1
Oxfield TS18 . . . . 60 B1
Oxford Rd
　Hartlepool TS25 . . . . . 9 B1
　Middlesbrough TS5 . . . 39 A1
　Thornaby-on-T TS17 . . . 47 B2
Oxford St
　Hartlepool TS24 . . . . . 9 C1
　Hartlepool TS25 . . . . 10 A2
　Middlesbrough TS1 . . . 85 B1
　Saltburn-by-t-S TS12 . . 76 C1
　1 South Bank TS6 . . . 32 A2
　Stockton-on-T TS18 . . . 82 B4
Oxgang Cl TS10 . . . . 72 C2
Oxley St TS10 . . . . . . 71 A4
Oysterman Ho TS24 . . 6 B3

P

Paddock The
　Eaglescliffe TS16 . . . . 54 C2
　Seaton Carew TS25 . . . 13 C2
Paddock Wood TS8 . . 60 A3
Padstow Cl TS26 . . . . . 4 C2
Paignton Cl TS8 . . . . 60 B4
Paignton Dr TS25 . . . 12 A1
Palace Cl TS20 . . . . . 20 B3
Palin Cl TS4 . . . . 86 B3
Palladium Bldgs **1**
　TS4 . . . . 40 A3
PALLISTER 41 A3
Pallister Ave TS3 . . . 41 C4
Pallister Ct TS3 . . . . . 42 A4
Pallister Park Prim Sch
　TS3 . . . . 85 C2
Palmer St TS1 . . . . . . 85 C2
Palmerston Ct **2**
　TS17 . . . . 47 B4
Palmerston St TS18 . 82 A1
Palmer Wlk TS16 . . . 54 C3
Palm Gr TS19 . . . . . . 34 C2
Palm St TS1 . . . . 87 A2
Pamoor Terr TS22 . . . 23 C1
Panmore Wlk TS16 . . 54 C2
Pannal Wlk TS16 . . . 54 C2
Pannell Ave TS5 . . . . 49 A4
Pannell Cl **5** TS27 . . . 2 B2
Pannell Pl **4** TS27 . . . 2 B2
Parade The TS26 . . . . 8 C4
Paris Pl TS7 . . . . 60 C2
Park Ave
　Eston TS6 . . . . 42 C3
　Hartlepool TS26 . . . . . 8 C3
　Redcar TS10 . . . . 71 B3
　Thornaby-on-T TS17 . . . 47 C4
Park Ave N **6** TS3 . . 52 B4
Park Ave S TS3 . . . . . 52 C4
Park Ct TS10 . . . . 69 B1
Parkdale Way TS5 . . 50 A3
Park Dr
　Hartlepool TS26 . . . . . 8 B4
　Stockton-on-T TS19 . . . 25 A2
PARK END 53 A4
Park End Prim Sch
　TS3 . . . . 52 C4
Parkfield Ave TS5 . . . 50 A3
Parkfield Ct TS16 . . . 63 B3
Parkfield Rd TS18 . . . 83 A1
Parkfield Way **7**
　TS18 . . . . 83 A1
Parkgate TS6 . . . . . . 44 B2
Parkinson Ho TS1 . . . 86 A4
Parkin St TS18 . . . . . 82 B3

ark La
Guisborough TS14 .... 79 A3
Middlesbrough TS1.... 87 A1
Parklands TS10....... 73 A3
Parklands Ave TS23 . 21 B2
Parklands CI TS23 .... 41 B2
Parklands Way TS26 . . 8 A3
Park Mews TS26 ...... 8 C4
Park Rd
Hartlepool TS26 .... 9 B3
Middlesbrough TS5.... 85 C1
Stockton-on-T TS18...81 C1
Thornaby-on-T TS17 . . 47 B2
Park Rd N TS1........ 87 A1
Park Rd S TS5 .... 40 A2
Parkside
Guisborough TS14 .... 79 B4
Middlesbrough TS3.... 52 A3
Parkside Ct TS17 .... 48 A2
ark Sq TS26 ....5 B1
Park St TS1.......... 84 C3
Parkstone Gr TS24.... 2 C2
Parkstone Pl TS16 .... 63 C4
Parkston Ho TS23.... 21 B2
Park Terr
Stockton-on-T TS18... 83 B2
Thornaby-on-T TS17 . . 47 B4
Park The TS22 .... 16 C4
Park Vale Rd TS4..... 87 B1
Park View
Stockton-on-T TS18...81 C1
Yarm TS15........... 66 B4
Park View Apartments
TS1 .... 85 C1
Parkview Ind Est
TS25 .... 12 C2
Parkview Rd E TS25. 13 A2
Parkview Rd W TS25. 12 C2
Park View Terr TS14 . . 79 A3
Parkway Ctr TS8...... 60 B2
Parkway Dr TS6 ..... 53 C4
Parkway Gr TS3 ..... 41 B2
Parkway The TS12 ... 76 A3
Parkwood Dr TS18.... 45 C4
Parliament CI TS18 .. 83 A1
Parliament Rd TS1.... 85 B2
Parliament St TS18 ... 83 A1
Parliament Wlk **4**
TS18 .... 83 A1
Parracombe CI TS17 . 65 B2
Parsons Ct TS6 ...... 42 B4
Parton St TS24........ 5 C2
Partridge Ave TS5 .... 58 C4
Partridge CI **3** TS17 . 56 B1
Passfield Cres TS6.... 32 B2
Pasture CI TS11...... 74 A2
Pastures The TS18 .... 60 C1
Pasture The TS17 .... 56 A2
Patey Ct **2** TS5 ...... 39 B1
Pathway Specl Sch
TS6 .... 43 C4
Patten La TS14 ...... 79 B4
Patten St **3** TS6 .... 43 B1
Patterdale Ave
Middlesbrough TS5.... 49 B3
Stockton-on-T TS19.... 80 B4
Patterdale St TS25 .... 9 C1
Pauntley Dr TS5 ..... 58 C3
Pavilion CI TS25 ..... 13 C1
Paxton CI TS18 ...... 82 B4
Peacock St TS1...... 86 A3
Peakston CI TS26 .... 4 C1
Pearl Rd TS17 ...... 47 C3
Pearl St
Middlesbrough TS1.... 85 C2
Saltburn-by-t-S TS12... 76 C4
Pearson Ct TS18 ..... 83 A1
Pearson Rd TS17 .... 83 C2
Pearson St TS1 ...... 84 A3
Pearson Way TS17 ... 83 C2
Pearson Wlk **2**
TS18 .... 83 A1
Pease Ct
Eaglescliffe TS16 .... 54 B2
Guisborough TS14 .... 78 B1
Peaton St TS3 ...... 41 A4
Peebles Ave TS25 .....9 B1

Peelers Ct TS14...... 79 B5
Peel St
Middlesbrough TS1.... 85 C2
Thornaby-on-T TS17 . . . 47 B4
Pegman CI TS14 ..... 79 C5
Peirse CI TS4 .... 86 B3
Peirson Ct TS10...... 70 B4
Peirson St TS10...... 70 B4
Pelham St
Hartlepool TS24 .... 5 C2
Middlesbrough TS1.... 85 C2
Pelton CI TS23....... 17 A4
Pemberton Cres TS4 . 58 C4
Pembroke Dr TS17... 65 A2
Pembroke Rd TS26.... 3 A3
Pembroke Rd TS20.... 26 A3
Pembroke Way TS10 . 71 B2
Penarth CI TS26..... 4 C2
Penberry Gdns TS17 . 64 C3
Penderyn Cres TS17 . 64 C3
Pendle Cres TS23 .... 21 C4
Pendock CI TS5...... 59 A4
Penhill CI TS3 ...... 41 A2
Penhill Rd TS18...... 34 C1
Penistone Rd TS3.... 52 A3
Penllyn Way TS8..... 59 B3
Pennal Gr TS17 ..... 64 B4
Pennard Gn TS3 ..... 41 C2
Pennine Ave TS18.... 27 C1
Pennine Cres TS10... 70 B1
Pennine Way TS17 ... 65 B3
Pennington CI TS23.. 17 B2
Penny La **3** TS24.... 83 A1
Pennyman CI TS6.... 43 A1
Pennyman St TS3.... 52 B3
Pennyman Prim Sch
TS3 .... 52 C4
Pennyman Way TS8.. 58 C1
Pennyman Wlk TS1.. 75 A2
Pennypot La TS16.... 45 C1
Pennyroyal Rd TS18.. 46 C1
Penrhyn St TS26..... 9 C2
Penrith CI TS10 ..... 70 C1
Penrith Rd TS3 ..... 41 B1
Penrith St TS24...... 6 C4
Pensby Ave TS4..... 51 A1
Penshaw CI **3** TS17. 56 C1
Penshaw Ct TS23 ... 17 C1
Penshurst Pl TS23 ... 17 C1
Pentilly St TS24.......7 B3
Pentland Ave
Billingham TS23 ..... 21 B4
Redcar TS10 .... 72 A4
Pentland Prim Sch
TS23 .... 21 B3
Penton Ct TS23 ..... 17 B3
Penwick CI TS15..... 66 B4
Penyghent Way TS17. 65 B2
Percy St
Hartlepool TS26 .... 5 B1
Middlesbrough TS1.... 85 C2
Peregrine CI TS14 ... 78 B3
Perry Ave TS17 ..... 57 A2
Perth Cres TS7 ..... 61 A2
Perth Gr TS18 ...... 81 A1
Perth St TS24........ 5 C1
Pert Rd TS24 .... 3 A2
Petch CI TS1........ 85 B2
Petch St TS18....... 82 A3
Petrel Cres TS20..... 20 B2
Petworth Cres TS17... 65 B4
Pevensey CI TS4..... 50 C3
Peveril Rd TS23...... 17 A1
Pexton CI TS8 ...... 59 B3
Pheasant CI **2** TS17 . 56 B1
Phillida Terr TS5 ..... 40 A2
Phillips Ave TS5 .... 50 A4
Phillips Ho TS1..... 86 A3
Phoenix CI TS25 .... 11 C1
Phoenix Gdns TS18 .. 81 A2
Phoenix Pk TS8..... 59 B2
Phoenix Sidings
TS19 .... 82 A3
Phoenix Wlk TS18 ... 81 A2
Phoenix Workshops
TS19 .... 82 A3

Phyllis Mohan Ct **10**
TS3 .... 51 C4
Pickering Gr TS25.... 12 B2
Pickering Ho **13** TS4 . 50 B4
Pickering Rd TS17 ... 48 A3
Picktree Gdns TS25 . . 12 A3
Picton Ave
Billingham TS22 ..... 16 B2
Middlesbrough TS5.... 49 A4
Picton Cres TS17 .... 56 B4
Picton Pl **2** TS20 .... 26 B4
Picture House Bldgs
TS23 .... 21 B1
Piercebridge CI
TS19 .... 24 C1
Pikeston CI TS26..... 4 C1
Pilgrim St TS24...... 10 A3
Pilkingtons Bldgs **5**
TS5 .... 39 B1
Pilkington St TS3 .... 41 A4
Pilot Ho TS24........ 10 B4
Pinder CI TS20....... 26 A4
Pine Ct TS19........ 24 C1
Pineda CI TS5 ...... 59 A3
Pine Gr TS24 ....5 B2
Pine Hill TS8 .... 60 C2
Pine Rd
Guisborough TS14 .... 79 B4
Ormesby TS7......... 53 A3
Pinero Gr TS25 ...... 11 B4
Pine St
Middlesbrough, Cargo
Fleet TS3 .... 31 A1
Middlesbrough TS1.... 86 A3
Stockton-on-T TS20... 26 B4
Pine Tree CI TS5..... 55 C1
Pinewood Ave TS4 ... 50 B4
Pinewood CI TS27 ....2 B2
Pinewood Rd
Eaglescliffe TS16 .... 54 C4
Marton TS7......... 61 C4
Pinfold St TS18 ..... 82 B4
Pintail CI TS15....... 4 C2
Piper Knowle Rd
TS19 .... 24 B4
Pipit CI TS17........ 56 A1
Pippins The TS22 .... 16 C4
Pirbright Gr TS8..... 59 B2
Planetree Ct TS7..... 61 B4
Plantation Rd TS10 .. 72 C2
Player CI TS15....... 54 C1
Playlin CI TS15...... 67 B4
Plumer Dr TS20..... 26 A4
Plymouth Gr TS26 ... 5 A2
Plymouth Wlk TS26 . . 5 A2
Pochin Rd
Eston TS6 .... 33 A2
Eston TS6 .... 33 B2
Poldon Terr TS23..... 21 C3
Pope Ct TS25 ....8 B1
Poplar Gr
Redcar TS10 .... 71 B3
South Bank TS6...... 42 C4
Stockton-on-T TS18...81 C1
Poplar Pl TS14 ..... 78 C4
Poplar Rd
Eaglescliffe TS16 .... 63 B4
Thornaby-on-T TS17 . . 47 B3
Poplars Rd TS5 ..... 39 C1
Poplars The TS22 .... 16 C4
Poplar Terr TS2 ..... 23 C1
Poppy La TS19...... 24 C1
Porchester CI TS17 .. 55 B2
Porlock Rd TS3...... 16 C1
Porrett CI TS24 ..... 3 A2
PORT CLARENCE .. 30 A4
Port Clarence Rd
Billingham TS2 ..... 29 C4
Middlesbrough TS2... 23 C1
Porthleven Way
TS10 .... 73 C3
Portland CI
Eaglescliffe TS16 .... 63 C4
Marton TS7......... 60 C3
Redcar TS10 .... 72 C2
Portland Gr TS24 .... 2 C2
Portland Ho TS3..... 41 C4

Portland Wlk TS10 ... 72 C2
Portmadoc Wlk TS26.. 4 C2
Portman Rd TS20 .... 26 A3
Portman Rise TS14... 79 B1
Portman St TS1...... 85 C2
PORTRACK 27 B1
Portrack Back La
TS18 .... 27 B2
Portrack Ct TS18..... 82 C4
Portrack Grange CI
TS18 .... 38 A4
Portrack Grange Rd
TS18 .... 38 A4
Portrack Ind Est
TS18 .... 38 A4
Portrack Interchange
Bsns Pk TS18....... 27 B1
Portrack La TS18 .... 37 B4
Portrack Ret Pk
TS18 .... 27 B1
Portrush CI TS4...... 50 B3
Potter Wlk **6** TS24.... 6 A1
Pottery Mews TS5 ... 39 B2
Pottery St TS18...... 47 A4
Potto CI TS15....... 64 B1
Pounder Pl TS24..... 5 B4
Powburn CI TS19 .... 24 A1
Powell St TS26....... 9 B2
Powlett Rd TS24 .... 5 C3
Pragnell Ct TS10..... 73 C3
Preen Dr TS5 .... 49 A3
Premier Par TS19 .... 34 B2
Premier Rd
Middlesbrough TS3... 41 C2
Ormesby TS7......... 52 C1
Prescot Rd TS3 ..... 52 B4
Preseli Gr TS17 ..... 64 C3
Preston Farm Ind Est
TS18 .... 46 A2
Preston Hall Mus *
TS16 .... 55 A4
Preston La TS18 .... 46 A1
PRESTON-ON-T 55 B4
Preston Prim Sch
TS16 .... 54 C4
Preston Rd TS18 .... 35 A2
Prestwick CI TS4.... 50 C3
Prestwick CI TS16 ... 63 C4
Price Ave TS5....... 49 A4
Price Rd TS10 ...... 69 B1
Priestcrofts TS11..... 75 B2
Priestfield Ave TS13... 52 A3
Primrose CI TS14 .... 78 B2
PRIMROSE HILL 26 A1
Primrose Hill Ind Est
TS19 .... 82 A4
Primrose Rd TS26.... 4 C4
Primrose St TS19 .... 80 C4
Princeport Rd TS18 .. 82 C4
Prince Regent St
TS18 .... 83 A2
Princes Rd
Middlesbrough TS1.... 85 B2
Saltburn-by-t-S TS12... 76 C3
Princess Ave TS18 ... 82 B4
Princes Sq TS17 .... 57 A3
Princess St
Hartlepool TS24 ..... 7 C2
Middlesbrough TS2... 84 C4
Thornaby-on-T TS17 .. 83 C1
Princes St TS1....... 85 C2
Princeton Dr TS17 ... 37 B2
Prior Ct TS23....... 17 B2
Prior CI TS15....... 64 B1
Prior Pursglove Coll
TS14 .... 79 B4
Priors Mill CE Prim Sch
TS22 .... 16 B2
Priorwood Gdns
TS17 .... 65 B3
Priory CI TS14 ..... 79 B4
Priory Ct
Guisborough TS14 .... 79 B4
Hartlepool TS24 ..... 7 B2
Stockton-on-T TS20... 26 B4
Priory Dr TS5....... 58 C1
Priory Gdns TS20 ... 26 A4

Par–Rad | 105

Priory Gr TS10....... 70 A3
Priory Rd TS5........ 48 C4
Prissick St TS24 ..... 7 C2
Pritchett Rd TS3..... 52 B4
Prospect Pl **7** TS20.. 26 B2
Prospect Terr **2**
TS6 .... 44 A2
Prospect The TS5 .... 50 A4
Prospect Way TS25 . . 12 C2
Protear Gr TS20 .... 21 A1
PS Wingfield Castle *
TS24 .... 6 B1
Puddlers Rd TS6..... 32 B3
Pulford Rd TS20 .... 25 C4
Punch St TS1....... 84 A3
Purslglove Terr
TS14 .... 79 C4
Purves Pl TS24...... 5 C4
Pym St TS6 .... 32 A1
Pytchley Rd TS14 ... 79 B2

Q

Quarry Dr TS8 ...... 58 C1
Quarry Rd TS16...... 55 A3
Quayside Rd TS18.... 83 B2
Quebec Gr
Billingham TS23 ..... 17 B3
Middlesbrough TS4.... 40 B2
Quebec Rd TS18 .... 45 C4
Queen Anne Terr
TS18 .... 81 A1
queen Elizabeth Way
TS17, TS19......... 56 A4
Queens Ave TS17 ... 83 C1
Queensberry Ave
TS26 .... 9 A3
Queensbury CI TS10 . 72 A3
Queen's Campus
(Durham Univ)
TS17 .... 83 C2
Queens Ct TS24.......5 B4
Queens Dr TS22 .... 16 C1
Queensland Ave
TS10 .... 71 A2
Queensland Gr TS18 . 81 A1
Queensport CI TS18.. 27 A1
Queens Rd TS5 ..... 39 B1
Queen's Sq TS2..... 86 A4
Queen St
Hartlepool, Middleton
TS24 .... 6 C1
Hartlepool, The Headland
TS24 .... 7 C2
Redcar TS10 .... 70 B4
Seaton Carew TS25 . . 13 C3
South Bank TS6...... 32 A4
Stockton-on-T TS18... 82 B4
Queen's Terr
Billingham TS2 ..... 29 C4
Middlesbrough TS2... 86 A4
Queensway
Billingham TS23 ..... 21 B4
Greatham TS25....... 14 B2
Middlesbrough TS5... 41 C4
Saltburn-by-t-S TS12... 76 A2
Queens Wlk TS18 ... 82 B3
Queen Terr TS25 .... 13 C3
Quenby Rd TS23 .... 17 B1
Quorn CI TS14 ..... 79 B1

R

Raby Gdns TS24 ..... 5 C2
Raby Rd
Hartlepool TS24,
TS26 .... 6 A1
Redcar TS10 .... 71 B1
Raby St TS18....... 81 A2
Raby Sq **6** TS24 .... 5 C2
Raby St TS24 ....7 B2
Radcliffe Ave TS19 .. 25 B3
Radcliffe Cres TS17 . . 83 C2

Radcliffe Terr TS24.... **7** C2
Radford Cl TS19 ..... **19** B1
Radlett Ave TS19..... **25** A3
Radnor Cl TS19 ...... **25** B3
Radnor Gn TS3 ...... **52** A4
Radnor Gr TS26....... **4** C2
Radstock Ave TS19.... **25** B3
Radyr Cl TS19........ **19** A1
Raeburn St **3** TS26 .. **9** A4
Rafton Dr TS27 ...... **2** C1
Raglan Cl TS19 ...... **19** A1
Raglan Terr TS23..... **17** B1
Ragpath La TS19...... **25** A3
RAGWORTH **25** B2
Ragworth Pl **3** TS20 . **26** A4
Ragworth Rd TS20 ... **26** A4
Railway Cotts TS16 .. **63** B3
Railway Hos TS2..... **30** A3
Railway Pl TS6....... **33** A1
Railway St TS18...... **82** B4
Railway Terr
  Eaglescliffe TS16 .... **54** C3
  Thornaby-on-T TS17 .. **83** C1
Raincliffe Ct TS8.... **60** B2
Rainford Ave TS19 ... **25** B3
Rainham Cl
  Ingleby Barwick
    TS17 .... **65** B3
  Middlesbrough TS3... **42** B3
Rainsford Cres TS3 .. **42** B3
Rainton Ave TS5 ..... **49** B1
Rainton Dr TS17 ..... **56** B4
Rainton Gr TS18 ..... **34** B1
Raisbeck Cl TS11 .... **74** C2
Raisby Cl TS5........ **58** B4
Raisdale Cl TS17..... **47** C1
Raisegill Cl TS3..... **40** C2
Raithwaite Cl TS14... **79** A4
Raithwaite Ho TS14 . **79** B4
Rake Ave TS19 .... **25** A4
Raleigh Cl TS11...... **75** C1
Raleigh Ct TS2....... **84** A4
Raleigh Rd TS20 ..... **26** A3
Ralfland Way TS7 .... **62** A2
Ralph Sq TS19 .... **25** A1
Rampside Ave TS19 .. **19** B1
Ramsbury Ave TS19 .. **25** A4
Ramsey Cres TS15 ... **66** B4
Ramsey Gdns TS17... **64** B3
Ramsey Rd TS10 ..... **69** C1
Ramsey View TS20 ... **26** C3
Ramsey Wlk TS14.... **79** A2
Ramsgate TS18 ...... **83** A2
Randolph St TS12.... **76** C2
Raskelf Ave **2** TS19 . **25** A3
Rathnew Ave TS19 ... **24** C4
Raunds Ave TS19 ..... **25** A3
Raven Cl TS14 .... **78** A2
Ravendale Rd TS3 ... **42** A1
Raven La TS20........ **20** B1
Ravenscar Cres TS19 . **25** C3
Ravenscroft Ave TS5 . **50** A4
Ravensdale TS5...... **58** B4
Ravensworth Ave
  TS6 .... **43** A2
Ravensworth Cres
  TS24 .... **2** C3
Ravensworth Gr
  TS18 .... **34** B1
Ravensworth Jun Sch
  TS6 .... **43** A2
Ravensworth Rd
  TS23 .... **17** B1
Ravenwood Cl TS27... **2** A2
Rawcliffe Ave TS5.... **58** C3
Rawley Dr TS10 ...... **72** A3
Rawlings Ct TS24 .... **5** C4
Rawlinson Ave TS23.. **21** C1
Ray Ct TS19.......... **24** C3
Raydale TS8 .... **59** A1
Raydale Beck TS17... **65** B2
Raylton Ave TS7 ..... **61** A2
Reading Rd TS20..... **26** A2
Rectory Ave TS14 .... **79** A3

Rectory Cl TS14...... **79** A3
Rectory La TS14 ..... **79** B3
Rectory Way TS25.... **13** C1
Red Admiral Cl TS19 . **24** B1
Redbrook Ave TS19 .. **25** B4
Redbrook Prim Sch
  TS19 .... **25** A4
REDCAR............. **71** A4
Redcar Ave
  Marske-by-t-S TS11 .. **74** B2
  Stockton-on-T TS19.. **25** B3
Redcar Beach Cvn Pk
  TS10 .... **70** A4
Redcar Cl TS25 ......**9** B2
Redcar & Cleveland Coll
  Redcar TS10 .... **70** B3
  Redcar TS10 .... **73** A4
Redcar Com Coll
  TS10 .... **70** A1
Redcar East Sta
  TS10 .... **71** B2
Redcar La TS10 ...... **71** A1
Redcar Rd
  Guisborough TS14 .... **79** C4
  Marske-by-t-S TS11 ... **74** B2
  South Bank TS6...... **32** A2
  Thornaby-on-T TS17 .. **47** B2
  Thornaby-on-T TS17 .. **47** C3
Redcar Rd E TS6...... **32** B2
Redcar St TS18 ...... **82** A4
Redditch Ave TS19 ... **25** B4
Redesdale Ct TS2 .... **29** A4
Redesdale Gr **2**
  TS17 .... **65** A3
Redhill Rd TS19...... **25** A4
Red House Sch TS20 . **20** B1
Redland Ct TS18 ..... **34** B2
Redlion St TS10...... **70** C4
Redmayne Ct TS23 ... **17** B2
Redmire Rd TS18 .... **80** B3
Redruth Ave TS19 .... **25** B3
Redshank Cl TS26.... **4** C3
Redstart Cl TS26 .... **5** A4
Redwing La TS20 .... **20** C2
Redwing Rising TS14. **78** B3
Redwood Cl TS27 .... **2** B2
Redwood Ct TS7 ..... **61** B4
Redwood Dr TS12.... **76** A2
Redworth Rd TS23 ... **17** C1
Redworth St TS24.... **10** A3
Reed Cl TS20 .... **26** C3
Reedsdale Cl TS10 ... **73** C2
Reed St
  Hartlepool TS24 ...... **10** A3
  Thornaby-on-T TS17 ... **47** B1
Reedston Rd TS26 .... **4** B1
Reef Ho TS24 .... **2** A3
Reepham Cl **7** TS19 . **24** C4
Reeth Rd
  Middlesbrough TS5.... **49** B4
  Stockton-on-T TS18... **45** B4
Regal Cl TS25........ **13** D1
Regency Ave TS6 .... **53** C4
Regency Dr TS25 .... **12** C3
Regency Mans The
  TS10 .... **70** B4
Regency Mews TS10 . **70** C4
Regency Pk TS17 .... **65** C3
Regency West Mall
  TS18 .... **83** A2
Regent Ct TS6 .... **43** C4
Regent Mews TS18... **83** A2
Regent Rd TS4....... **40** B1
Regent Sq TS24.......**7** B2
Regent St
  Hartlepool TS24 ...... **7** B4
  Stockton-on-T TS18... **82** A3
Regents Wlk TS10 ... **70** C4
Reid Terr TS14 .... **79** B4
Reigate Ave TS5 ..... **50** A4
Reigate Ct TS19 ..... **25** A4
Relton Way TS26..... **8** C3
Renfrew Rd TS20 .... **26** B4
Rennie Rd TS6....... **42** A4
Renown Wlk TS6..... **32** B1
Renvyle Ave TS19 ... **24** C4
Repton Ave TS19..... **25** A3

Repton Rd TS3....... **42** B3
Resolution The TS7 .. **62** A3
Resource Cl TS6 ..... **32** B1
Retford Cl **4** TS19 ... **25** A4
Retford Gr TS25...... **11** C1
Rettendon Cl TS19 ... **25** B4
Revesby Rd TS3...... **52** B4
Reynolds Ct TS23 .... **17** A3
Reynoldston Ave
  TS19 .... **19** B1
Rhinog Gr TS17...... **55** C1
Rhobell View TS17 ... **64** B4
Rhodes Ct TS17...... **57** A4
Rhondda Ave TS19 ... **25** B3
Rhoose Gate TS17 ... **48** A2
Rhyl Cl TS19 .... **25** B4
Ribble Cl TS22....... **16** A2
Ribbleton Cl **3** TS7 . **61** C3
Ribchester Cl **1**
  TS19 .... **25** A4
Riccarton Cl TS19.... **24** C4
Richard Ct TS26...... **9** B3
Richard Hind Wlk **4**
  TS18 .... **46** B4
Richardson Rd
  Stockton-on-T TS18... **81** C1
  Thornaby-on-T TS17 .. **47** A2
Richardson St **5**
  TS26 ....**5** C1
Richmond Cl TS6 .... **43** B2
Richmond Cres TS23 . **21** C4
Richmond Ct TS6 .... **43** C4
Richmond Ho TS19 .. **80** C4
Richmond Pl TS17 ... **48** A2
Richmond Rd
  Redcar TS10 .... **71** B1
  Stockton-on-T TS18... **81** B2
Richmond St
  Hartlepool TS25 ...... **9** C1
  Middlesbrough TS2... **29** B3
Rickman Ho TS1 ..... **86** A3
Ricknall Cl TS5 ...... **58** B4
Ridge The
  Mount Pleasant
    TS8 .... **68** A3
  Saltburn-by-t-S TS12... **76** C1
Ridgeway TS8 .... **60** A1
Ridley Ave TS5....... **49** B3
Ridley Ct
  8 Hartlepool TS26 ... **5** C1
  Stockton-on-T TS25... **26** A4
Ridley Dr TS20....... **25** C4
Ridley Mews **6** TS20. **26** B4
Ridley St TS10 .... **70** C4
Ridlington Way TS24.. **3** A2
Ridsdale Ave **3**
  TS19 .... **25** A3
Rievaulx Ave TS23 ... **17** A2
Rievaulx Cl TS19..... **25** A4
Rievaulx Dr TS5...... **50** A3
Rievaulx Way TS14... **79** C3
Rievaulx Wlk TS6 .... **43** B2
RIFT HOUSE **11** C4
Rift House Prim Sch
  TS25 ....**8** C1
Rifts Ave TS12 .... **76** B3
Riftswood Dr TS11 ... **74** B2
Rigby Ho TS15 .... **63** B1
Riggston Pl TS26 .... **4** C1
Rigg The TS15 .... **66** C4
Riley St TS18 .... **81** C2
Rillington Cl **9** TS19 . **24** C4
Rillston Cl TS26..... **4** C1
Rillstone Way **10**
  TS10 .... **73** B2
Rimdale Dr TS19 .... **34** B4
Rimswell Dr TS11 ... **74** B2
Rimswell Rd TS19.... **34** B4
Rings The TS17 ...... **55** C2
Ringway TS17 .... **48** A1
Ringwood Cres TS19 . **25** B3
Ringwood Rd TS3.... **42** B2
Ripley Ct TS13 ...... **42** B3
Ripley Rd TS20....... **20** A1
Ripon Cl TS19 .... **25** A3
Ripon Rd
  Nunthorpe TS7 ...... **62** B3

Ripon Rd continued
  Redcar TS10 .... **71** C1
Ripon Way TS6 ...... **44** A2
Rise The TS7........ **62** A3
Rishton Cl TS19...... **25** A3
Rissington Wlk TS17 . **48** A1
Rium Terr TS24 ......**9** C4
River Ct TS2 .... **28** C4
Riverdale Ct **1** TS5 .. **38** C1
Riverdale Prim Sch
  TS10 .... **72** B4
Riverhead Ave TS19 .. **25** A3
Riverside TS10....... **83** B2
Riverside Park Ind Est
  TS2 .... **29** A4
Riverside Park Rd
  TS2 .... **28** C3
Riverside Stadium
  (Middlesbrough FC)
  TS3 .... **86** C4
Riverside View TS18.. **47** A3
Riverston Cl TS26.....**4** B1
Riversway TS7 .... **61** B4
Robert Ave TS6 ...... **33** A1
Roberts Ct TS7 ...... **53** A4
Roberts Row TS7 .... **53** A4
Roberts St TS6....... **33** A1
Robert St TS17....... **83** C1
Robin Cl TS17 .... **56** B1
Robson Ave TS17 .... **57** A1
Robson Ct TS24...... **5** C3
Robson St TS23...... **23** B2
Rochdale Ave TS19... **26** A4
Rochdale Cl TS3 ..... **41** B1
Rochester Ct
  Ingleby Barwick
    TS17 .... **65** A3
  Thornaby-on-T TS17 .. **83** C2
Rochester Dr TS10 .. **71** B1
Rochester Rd
  Billingham TS23 ..... **17** B2
  Middlesbrough TS5.... **39** C1
  Stockton-on-T TS19... **25** B3
Rockall Ave **10** TS19 . **24** C4
Rockbourne Way
  TS17 .... **55** C3
Rocket Terr TS10..... **70** A4
Rockferry Cl TS19.... **24** C4
Rockingham Ct TS5 .. **49** A3
Rockliffe Rd TS5..... **39** B1
Rockpool Cl TS24 ....**6** A4
Rockport Ct TS18 .... **82** C4
Rockwood Ct TS14... **79** C2
Rodmell Cl TS3 ...... **42** B1
Rodney Cl TS23...... **27** A4
Rodney St TS26.......**9** B4
Roebuck Cl TS17..... **56** C2
Roecliffe Gr TS19 .... **24** B4
Roedean Dr TS16 .... **63** C4
Rogeri Pl TS24.......**3** B1
Rokeby Ave TS4...... **50** C4
Rokeby St
  Hartlepool TS24 ......**6** B4
  Stockton-on-T TS18... **81** C1
Roker St TS24........**6** B4
Roker Terr TS18...... **81** C1
Rolleston Ave TS19 .. **24** C4
Romaine Pk TS24 ....**6** B4
Romaldkirk Rd TS2 .. **84** B4
Romanby Ave TS19... **25** B3
Romanby Cl TS24 ....**6** B4
Romanby Gdns TS5 .. **59** B3
Roman Rd TS5........ **39** B1
Romford Rd TS19 .... **25** B4
Romney Cl TS10 ..... **73** B4
Romney Gn TS20.... **20** A1
Romney St TS1 ...... **85** C2
Romsey Rd TS19 .... **25** B3
Rona Gdns TS17 .... **47** C3
Ronaldshay Terr
  TS11 .... **75** B2
Rook La TS20........ **20** C2
Rookwood Rd TS7 ... **62** B2
Ropery Rd TS24...... **6** B4
Ropery St TS18...... **82** A3
Ropner Ave TS18..... **81** B1
Roscoe Rd TS23 ..... **21** C1

Roscoe St TS1 .... **87** B4
Rose Ave TS11 ...... **74** A4
Rosebank TS26 ......**9** A4
Rosebay Ct TS14.... **78** B3
Roseberry Cres
  Eston TS6 .... **44** B3
  Stockton-on-T TS20... **20** C4
Roseberry Dr TS8.... **58** C4
Roseberry Flats
  TS23 .... **21** B4
Roseberry Mews **1**
  TS26 ....**9** A4
Roseberry Mount
  TS14 .... **78** C4
Roseberry Prim Sch
  TS23 .... **21** C4
Roseberry Rd
  Billingham TS23 ..... **21** C1
  Middlesbrough TS4... **40** C1
  Middlesbrough TS4... **87** B4
  Redcar TS10 .... **72** B4
  Stockton-on-T TS20... **20** C4
Roseberry View
  TS17 .... **47** B4
Roseberry Rd TS26 .. **9** A4
Rosecroft Ave **4**
  TS4 .... **40** A2
Rosedale Ave
  Hartlepool TS26 ..... **9** A4
  Middlesbrough TS5.... **40** A1
Rosedale Cres TS14.. **78** B2
Rosedale Ct TS14 ... **87** C2
Rosedale Gdns
  Billingham TS23 ..... **17** A2
  3 Stockton-on-T
    TS19 .... **25** A4
Rosedale Gr TS10 ... **69** C3
Rosedale Rd TS7..... **62** B2
Rose Hill TS15 ...... **63** C3
Roseland Cres TS7 .. **52** A1
Roseland Dr TS7 .... **52** A1
Rosemary Cotts
  TS11 .... **75** A1
Rosemoor Cl TS7 ... **60** C3
Roseneath Ave TS19 . **19** B1
Rose St TS1 .... **84** C3
Rose Terr TS16...... **63** C3
Roseway The TS12 ... **76** C2
Rosewood Cl TS17 .. **53** A3
Rosewood Ct TS7.... **61** B4
Rose Wood Prim Sch
  TS8 .... **68** A4
ROSEWORTH **25** A4
Roseworth Prim Sch
  TS19 .... **24** C4
Rosgill TS10 .... **70** B1
Rosiere Gr TS10 .... **70** C2
Roslyn Ave TS3 ..... **41** B1
Rossall St TS25...... **9** B1
Rossendale Cl **1**
  TS11 .... **74** C1
Rossetti Way TS23 ... **17** A2
Rossett Wlk
  2 Middlesbrough
    TS3 .... **41** A1
  Middlesbrough TS3... **51** B4
Ross Gr TS25 .... **12** C2
Rosslare Rd TS19 ... **24** C4
Rosslyn Ct TS18..... **46** A4
Rossmere Prim Sch
  TS25 .... **12** A2
Rossmere Way TS25 . **12** A2
Ross Rd TS18 .... **37** B4
Ross St TS1 .... **85** B2
Rosthwaite TS5...... **58** B4
Rosthwaite Ave TS19 . **25** B4
Rosthwaite Cl TS24 ..**6** A3
Rostrevor Ave TS19 .. **19** B1
Rothbury Ave TS19... **25** A4
Rothbury Cl TS17.... **65** B3
Rothbury Rd TS3..... **41** A1
Rothbury St TS23 ... **21** B4
Rotherham Ave TS19 . **25** A3
Rothesay Dr TS10.... **73** B4
Rothesay Gr TS7 .... **62** B4
Rothwell Cres TS19 .. **25** A3
Rothwell Mews TS6... **43** A4

ottingdean Cl TS19 . . 25 A4
oundhay Dr TS16 . . . 54 C1
oundhill Ave TS17 . . 64 C3
oundhill Cl TS26 . . . . 8 A4
OUNDHILL
VILLAGE 64 B3
ounton Gn TS3 . . . . . 41 A1
ounton Gr TS19 . . . . 34 C2
ousham Gdns 4
TS5 . . . . 38 C1
outledge Ct TS24 . . . . 5 C3
outledge Rd TS20 . . 26 C1
owallane Gdns
TS17 . . . . 65 B3
owan Ave TS14 . . . . . 78 B2
owan Gr TS8 . . . . 58 B1
owan Rd
Egglescliffe TS16 . . . . 63 B4
Stockton-on-T TS19. . . . 26 A4
owanwood Ct TS5 . . 59 B4
owell St TS14 . . . . 7 C2
owen Cl TS17. . . . . . 64 C4
owland Keld TS14 . . 78 B1
owlands Gn TS23 . . . 18 A4
oworth Rd TS3 . . . . . 42 B1
oxburgh Cl TS16 . . . . 42 C3
oxby Ave
Guisborough TS14 . . . 79 A1
Middlesbrough TS3. . . 52 A3
oxby Cl
Hartlepool TS25 . . . . . 13 B1
Redcar TS10 . . . . 72 C4
Stockton-on-T TS19. . . . 25 C3
oyal George Dr
TS16 . . . . 54 B2
oyal York Apartments
TS10 . . . . 70 B4
oyce Ave TS23 . . . . . 18 B1
oyce Ct TS23 . . . . . . 18 B1
oyd The TS15 . . . . . . 66 B4
oyston Ave TS3 . . . . 52 A3
oyston Cl TS19 . . . . 25 C3
oyston Gr TS25 . . . . 14 A4
uberry Ave 8 TS19 . 24 C4
uby Rd TS17 . . . . 47 C3
uby St
Middlesbrough TS1. . . 85 C2
Saltburn-by-t-S TS12. . 76 C4
udby Cl TS15 . . . . . . 64 B1
udd's Pl TS3 . . . . 39 C2
udland Wlk 1 TS6. . 44 A3
udson Ave TS26 . . . . 16 B2
udston Cl TS17 . . . . 56 B4
udyard Ave TS19. . . . 24 C4
ufford Cl
Guisborough TS14 . . . 79 B1
Ingleby Barwick TS17. . 56 C1
1 Marton TS7 . . . . . . 61 C3
uff Tail TS14 . . . . 78 B3
ugby Rd TS18 . . . . . 81 C2
ugby St TS25 . . . . 9 B1
ugby Terr TS2 . . . . . 23 C1
ugeley Cl 4 TS19. . 25 A3
uislip Cl TS19 . . . . . 25 A3
unciman Rd TS24. . . . 5 B4
uncorn Ave TS19 . . 25 A3
unfold Cl TS19. . . . . 19 B1
unnymead Gn TS3. . 52 A3
unnymede TS7 . . . . . 62 A2
unnymede Ct TS19. . 25 A4
unswick Ave
Middlesbrough TS5. . . 58 C4
Redcar TS10 . . . . 70 A2
Stockton-on-T TS19. . . . 25 A3
unswick Ho TS1. . . . 84 C3
unswick Rd TS6 . . . 44 A2
upert St TS18 . . . . . 82 B4
ushleigh Ave TS5. . . 49 A2
ushmere TS8 . . . . . . 61 B1
ushmere Heath
TS16 . . . . 63 C4
ushpool Cl TS10 . . . 72 B4
ushyford Ave TS19 . 25 A3
uskin Ave
Middlesbrough TS5. . . 49 A3
Saltburn-by-t-S TS12. . 76 B3

Ruskin Gr TS25 . . . . 9 A1
Russell St
Hartlepool TS24 . . . . . . 7 A3
Middlesbrough TS1. . . . 86 A3
Stockton-on-T TS18. . . . 82 A3
Russell Wlk
8 Hartlepool TS25 . . . . 9 C2
4 Thornaby-on-T
TS17 . . . . 47 B4
Rustington Cl TS19 . . 25 A4
Ruswarp Ave 1
TS19 . . . . 25 A3
Ruswarp Cl 1 TS6. . . 44 A2
Ruswarp Gr TS25 . . . 13 C1
Ruswarp Rd TS6 . . . . 44 A2
Ruth Ave TS3 . . . . . . 41 C2
Rutherglen Wlk
TS16 . . . . 63 C4
Ruthin Cl TS19. . . . . . 25 A4
Rutland Ave TS7 . . . . 60 C3
Rutland Cl TS19. . . . . 25 A4
Rutland Ct TS11 . . . . 86 A3
Ryan Ave TS18 . . . . . 82 B4
Ryan Ct TS26 . . . . 9 B4
Ryan's Row TS11. . . . 74 B2
Ryan Wlk TS18. . . . . 82 B4
Rydal Ave
Billingham TS23 . . . . 21 C1
Eston TS6 . . . . 44 A4
Middlesbrough TS5. . . 49 B3
Redcar TS10 . . . . 70 C2
Rydal Rd TS18 . . . . . . 80 B3
Rydal St TS26. . . . . . . 9 B2
Ryde Rd TS19 . . . . . . 25 B3
Rye Cl TS16. . . . . 63 B3
Ryedale TS14 . . . . . . 78 B1
Ryedale Cl TS15 . . . . 66 B3
Ryedale St TS3 . . . . . 41 A4
Ryefields Ho TS6. . . . 53 C4
Ryehill Cl TS7. . . . . . 62 A1
Ryehill Gdns TS26. . . . 5 A1
Ryehills Dr TS11 . . . . 75 B2
Rye Hills Sch TS10. . 71 A1
Rye Hill Way TS8. . . 68 B3
Ryhill Wlk TS7 . . . . . . 62 A1
Ryhope Ave 2 TS19. . 25 A4
Rylstone Ct TS4. . . . . 50 C4
Ryton Cl TS17. . . . . . 56 B4

S
Sabatier Cl TS17 . . . . 83 C2
Sacred Heart RC Prim
Sch
Hartlepool TS26 . . . . . 7 C1
Middlesbrough TS1. . . 85 B1
Sacred Heart RC Sch
TS10 . . . . 70 B2
Sacriston Cl TS23. . . . 16 C2
Sadberge Gr TS19. . . 34 B2
Sadberge Rd TS18 . . 46 C4
Sadberge St TS3. . . . . 41 A4
Saddler Cl 4 TS17. . 56 B1
Saddleston Cl TS26 . . 4 C1
Sadler Dr TS7 . . . . . . 60 C3
Sadler Forster Way
TS17 . . . . 57 A1
Saffron Wlk TS25 . . . 13 C3
Sailport Ind Est TS17 47 A3
St Abbs Wlk 7 TS24 . 10 A3
St Aidan's CE Meml
Prim Sch TS25. . . . . 12 C4
St Aidan's Cres TS22 . 21 A3
St Aidans Dr TS1. . . . 84 C3
St Aidan's St
1 Hartlepool TS25 . . . 9 C1
Middlesbrough TS1. . . 85 C2
St Alphonsus' RC Prim
Sch TS3 . . . . 41 A4
St Andrews Cl TS16 . . 63 C4
St Andrews Dr TS27. . . 2 C2
St Andrew's RC Prim
Sch TS5 . . . . 49 C3
St Andrews Rd TS7. . 61 A3
St Andrew's Rd E
TS6 . . . . 33 B1

St Andrew's Rd W
TS6 . . . . 33 B1
St Ann's Ct TS24 . . . 10 B3
ST ANN'S HILL. 82 C4
St Anns Ind Est TS18. 82 C4
St Ann's Terr TS18 . . 82 B4
St Augustine's RC Prim
Sch TS7 . . . . 60 C2
St Austell Cl TS8 . . . 58 C2
St Barnabas' Rd TS5 . 39 B2
St Bede's RC Prim Sch
Marske-by-t-S TS11 . . 74 C2
Stockton-on-T TS19. . . 80 C4
St Bees Wlk 8 TS4 . . 10 A3
St Bega's Glade TS26 . 8 C2
St Bega's RC Prim Sch
TS24 . . . . 7 A4
St Benedicts RC Prim
Sch TS10 . . . . 70 B2
St Bernadette's RC Prim
Sch TS7 . . . . 61 C3
St Bernard Rd TS18 . . 83 A2
St Brides Ct TS17 . . . 64 C3
St Catherines Ct TS3 . 41 A2
St Catherine's Ct
TS24 . . . . 10 B3
St Clare's RC Prim Sch
TS5 . . . . 58 B4
St Columba's Ave
TS22 . . . . 21 A3
St Crispins' Ct TS19 . 25 B3
St Cuthbert Ave TS7. . 61 C2
St Cuthbert Ct 6
TS17 . . . . 47 B4
St Cuthbert's Ave
TS23 . . . . 21 A3
St Cuthbert's RC Prim
Sch
Hartlepool TS25 . . . . . 9 C1
Stockton-on-T TS18. . . 83 A1
St Cuthbert's Rd
TS18 . . . . 83 A1
St Cuthbert St TS24. . . 7 A3
St David's Gr TS17. . . 64 C3
St David's RC Tech Coll
TS5 . . . . 49 C1
St David's Rd TS6 . . . 33 B2
St Davids Way TS5 . . 49 C2
St David's Wlk TS26. . . 4 C2
St Edwards RC Prim
Sch TS5 . . . . 39 C1
St Francis Gate TS25. 12 C4
St Francis of Assisi CE
Sch TS17 . . . . 56 A2
St Gabriel's RC Prim
Sch TS3 . . . . 52 C4
St Georges Bglws
TS6 . . . . 33 B2
St George's Ho TS1 . . 85 C2
St George's Rd E
TS6 . . . . 33 B1
St George's Rd W
TS6 . . . . 33 B1
St Gerards RC Prim Sch
TS8 . . . . 59 C2
St Germain's Gr
TS11 . . . . 75 A2
St Germain's La
TS11 . . . . 75 A3
St Gregorys RC Prim
Sch TS19 . . . . 25 A2
St Helen's Cl TS6 . . . 43 B2
St Helen's Prim Sch
TS24 . . . . 7 A3
St Helen's St TS24 . . . 7 A3
St Hilda Chare TS24. . 7 C2
St Hild's CE Sch TS24. 3 B1
St Ives Cl
Middlesbrough TS8. . . 60 B4
Redcar TS10 . . . . 73 C3
St James Ct
Eston TS6 . . . . 33 A2
Stockton-on-T TS19. . . 25 A3
St James Gdns TS2 . . 86 A4
St James' Ho TS18 . . 82 C4
St James Mews TS1. . 85 B1

St Joan's Gr TS25 . . . 12 C4
St Johns Cl
Middlesbrough TS4. . . 86 B3
Stockton-on-T TS18. . . 82 A4
St John's Gr TS10. . . 71 A2
St John's Way TS1. . . 85 A3
St John the Baptist CE
Prim Sch TS19 . . . . 25 B2
St John the Evangelist
RC Prim Sch TS23 . . 21 C2
St John Vianney RC
Prim Sch TS24. . . . . 3 B1
St Josephs Ct TS10 . . 70 B2
St Joseph's Ct 14
TS26 . . . . 9 B4
St Joseph's RC Prim
Sch
Billingham TS23 . . . . 17 C2
Hartlepool TS24 . . . . 10 A3
Middlesbrough TS4. . . 87 B1
Stockton-on-T TS20. . . 26 A4
St Leonards Rd TS14 . 78 C2
St Luke's Ave TS17 . . 47 C4
St Luke's Cotts 7
TS4 . . . . 40 B1
St Lukes Ct TS26 . . . . 5 B1
St Luke's Hosp TS4 . 51 A4
St Margarets Gr 1
TS17 . . . . 47 C1
St Margaret's Gr
Hartlepool TS25 . . . . 12 C4
Middlesbrough TS5. . . 49 C3
Redcar TS10 . . . . 71 A1
South Bank TS6. . . . . 42 C4
St Mark's Cl
2 Marske-by-t-S
TS11 . . . . 74 C2
Stockton-on-T TS19. . . 34 C4
St Mark's Ct TS17 . . . 83 B2
St Mark's Elm Tree CE
Prim Sch TS19 . . . . 34 C4
St Mary's Cath TS8 . . 60 B1
St Mary's Cl TS18 . . 82 B4
St Mary's Coll TS4 . . 50 B2
St Marys Ct
Eston TS6 . . . . 33 B1
Middlesbrough TS5. . . 49 C4
St Mary's Ct TS24. . . . 7 B2
St Mary's Gate Bsns Pk
TS20 . . . . 82 B4
St Mary's RC Prim Sch
TS6 . . . . 33 B1
St Mary St TS24. . . . . 7 B2
St Mary's Wlk TS5 . . 49 C3
St Matthews Ct TS6 . 33 A2
St Mawes Ct TS26 . . . 4 C1
St Michael's Ct 3
TS20 . . . . 26 B2
St Michael's Gr 5
TS20 . . . . 26 B2
St Michael's RC Comp
Sch TS23 . . . . 18 A2
St Nicholas Ct TS6 . . 33 A2
St Nicholas Gdns
TS15 . . . . 67 B4
St Oswald's Cres
TS22 . . . . 21 A3
St Oswald's St TS24. . . 5 C1
St Patrick's RC Comp
Sch TS17 . . . . 47 C4
St Patrick's RC Prim
Sch
Stockton-on-T TS19. . . 34 C3
Thornaby-on-T TS17 . . 47 B4
St Patrick's Rd TS6 . . 33 A2
St Paulinus RC Prim
Sch TS14 . . . . 78 B2
St Pauls Ct TS19 . . . . 80 C4
St Paul's RC Prim Sch
TS22 . . . . 16 C2
St Paul's Rd
Hartlepool TS26 . . . . . 9 B3
Middlesbrough TS1. . . 84 B3
Stockton-on-T TS19. . . 80 C4
Thornaby-on-T TS17 . . 47 B4
St Paul's St TS19. . . . 80 C3

St Paul's Terr TS19 . . 80 C4
St Peter's Gr TS10 . . 71 A2
St Peter's RC Comp Sch
TS6 . . . . 32 B1
St Peter's RC Prim Sch
TS6 . . . . 42 C4
St Peter's Rd TS18 . . 81 C1
St Peters Sq TS17 . . . 47 C1
St Pius X RC Prim Sch
TS5 . . . . 51 C4
St Stephens Cl TS20. . 20 B2
St Teresa's RC Prim Sch
TS25 . . . . 12 A2
St Therese of Lisieux
RC Prim Sch TS14 . . 65 A3
St Thomas Gr TS10. . 71 A2
St Thomas More RC
Prim Sch TS4. . . . . . 51 A1
St Vincent Terr TS10. . 70 B3
Salcombe Cl TS8 . . . 60 B4
Salcombe Dr TS25 . . 12 B3
Salcombe Way TS10 . 73 B3
Salisbury Gr TS10. . . 71 C2
Salisbury Pl TS26 . . . 13 B4
Salisbury St 6 TS17 . 47 C4
Salisbury Terr
Middlesbrough TS6. . . 31 C2
South Bank TS6. . . . . 32 A2
Stockton-on-T TS20. . . 26 B2
Saltaire Terr TS25. . . 14 C1
Saltburn Bank TS12. . 77 A3
Saltburn-by-t-
SEA 76 B4
Saltburn La TS12. . . . 77 A1
Saltburn Miniature
Rly★ TS12 . . . . 77 B3
Saltburn Prim Sch
TS12 . . . . 76 B3
Saltburn Rd
Saltburn-by-t-S
TS12 . . . . 77 B3
Thornaby-on-T TS17 . . 47 C3
Saltburn Smugglers
The★ TS12 . . . . 77 B4
Saltburn Sta TS12 . . 76 C3
Saltburn Valley
Woodland Ctr★
TS12 . . . . 77 A3
Saltcote TS7 . . . . 61 B4
Saltersgill Ave
Middlesbrough,
Beechwood TS4. . . . . 50 B3
Middlesbrough, Easterside
TS4 . . . . 51 A1
Saltersgill Cl TS4 . . . 50 B4
Salter Wlk TS24. . . . . . 7 A3
Saltholme Cl TS2 . . . 23 C1
Saltney Rd TS20 . . . . 25 C4
Salton Cl TS5 . . . . . . 38 C1
Saltram Cl TS17. . . . 65 B4
Saltram Gr TS7 . . . . . 60 C4
Saltscar TS10 . . . . . . 73 B4
Saltview Terr TS2 . . . 30 A4
Saltwells Cres TS4 . . 87 C1
Saltwells Rd TS4 . . . 87 C2
Samaria Gdns TS5 . . 59 B4
Sambrook Gdns TS5 . 59 B4
Samphire St TS22 . . . 20 C1
Samuelson Ho 3
TS3 . . . . 41 A1
Samuel St TS19. . . . . 80 C4
Sandalwood Ct TS5. . 59 B4
Sandbanks Dr TS24 . . 2 C2
Sandford Cl TS4 . . . . 50 C3
Sandgate Ind Est
TS25 . . . . 10 B2
Sandhall Cl 4 TS23. . 17 A4
Sandling Ct TS7 . . . . 61 B4
Sandmartin La TS20 . 20 C2
Sandmoor Cl TS6 . . . 43 C1
Sandown Pk TS10. . . 71 A1
Sandown Rd TS23. . . 17 A4
Sandown Way TS17 . . 38 C4
Sandpiper Cl TS10 . . 73 B3

Sandpiper Ho TS24 . . **10** B4
Sandport Wlk 🫥
　TS18 . . . . **82** C4
Sandringham Rd
　Eston TS6 . . . . **43** C4
　Hartlepool TS26 . . . . . . **9** B4
　Middlesbrough TS3 . . . . **52** A4
　Stockton-on-T TS18. . . **81** C2
　🔟 Thornaby-on-T
　TS17 . . . . **47** C4
Sandsend Rd
　Eston TS6 . . . . **44** A3
　Redcar TS10 . . . . **70** A2
Sandwell Ave TS3 . . . . **52** B4
Sandwell Chare TS24 . . **7** B2
Sandwich Gr TS27 . . . . **2** C2
Sandwood Pk TS14 . . **78** B1
Sandy Flatts Ct TS5 . . **59** B4
Sandy Flatts La TS5 . . **59** B4
Sandy La TS22 . . . . . . **20** C4
Sandy La W TS22 . . . . **16** A2
Sapley Cl TS17 . . . . . . **56** C4
Sarah St TS25 . . . . . . **10** A1
Sark Wlk TS14 . . . . . . **79** A2
Satley Rd TS23 . . . . . . **17** C4
Saunton Ave TS10. . . **73** B3
Saunton Rd TS23 . . . . **22** A4
Sawley Gr TS18 . . . . . . **34** B1
Sawtry Rd 🫥 TS3 . . **52** B4
Saxby Rd TS20 . . . . . . **26** B2
Saxonfield TS8 . . . . . . **60** B2
Scalby Gr
　Redcar TS10 . . . . **73** B4
　Stockton-on-T TS19. . . **34** B3
Scalby Rd TS3 . . . . . . **40** C2
Scalby Sq TS17 . . . . . . **47** C3
Scaling Ct TS14 . . . . . **79** A4
Scampton Cl TS17 . . **56** B4
Scanbeck Dr TS11 . . **75** A2
Scarborough St
　🫥 Hartlepool TS24 . . **10** A4
　South Bank TS6. . . . . **32** A1
　🔟 Thornaby-on-T
　TS17 . . . . **47** B4
Scarteen Cl TS14 . . . . **79** A2
Scarth Wlk TS18 . . . . **82** A3
Scarthwood Cl 🫥
　TS17 . . . . **56** C1
Scawfell Gr TS25. . . . . **9** C1
Scholars Ct TS15. . . . . **63** B2
Scholars Gate TS14 . . **79** A1
School Ave 🫥 TS5 . . **38** C1
School Cl
　Marske-by-t-S TS11 . . **75** A2
　Stockton-on-T TS18. . . **83** A1
School Croft TS1. . . . **86** A4
School Wlk TS18. . . . . **83** A1
Schooner Ct TS24. . . **10** B4
Scotforth Cl 🫥 TS7 . . **61** C3
Scotney Ct 🫥 TS5. . . **38** C1
Scotney Rd TS23 . . . . **17** A1
Scott Dr TS20. . . . . . . **25** C4
Scott Gr TS25. . . . . . . **11** B4
Scotton Cl TS18. . . . . **34** B1
Scotton Ct TS3 . . . . . . **42** B1
Scott Rd TS6 . . . . **42** C1
Scott's Rd TS2 . . . . . . **86** B4
Scott St TS10 . . . . **71** A3
Scrafton Pl TS11 . . . . **75** A2
Scruton Cl TS18 . . . . **34** C1
Scugdale Cl TS15 . . . . **66** B3
Scurfield Rd TS19. . . . **24** B3
Seaford Cl TS10. . . . . **73** B3
Seaham Cl
　Redcar TS10 . . . . **73** C3
　Stockton-on-T TS19. . . **19** C1
Seaham St TS20 . . . . **82** B4
Sealand Cl TS17 . . . . **57** A3
Seamer Cl TS5. . . . . . . **50** A3
Seamer Gr TS18 . . . . **81** A1
Seathwaite TS5. . . . . . **58** B3
SEATON CAREW **13** D2

Seaton Carew Sta
　TS25 . . . . **13** B2
Seaton Cl
　Redcar TS10 . . . . **73** C4
　Stockton-on-T TS19. . . **34** B3
Seaton La TS25 . . . . . . **13** A2
Seatonport Ct 🫥
　TS18 . . . . **82** C4
Seaton St TS1 . . . . . . **87** A2
Seaview Rd TS26 . . . . . **9** B4
Sea View Terr TS24 . . . . **7** B3
Sedgebrook Gdns
　TS3 . . . . **52** C4
Sedgefield Rd TS5 . . . **58** C4
Sedgefield Way
　TS18 . . . . **27** B1
Sedgemoor Rd TS6 . . **53** C4
Sedgemoor Way
　TS23 . . . . **18** A3
Sedgewick Cl TS24. . . . **3** C1
Sefton Rd TS3 . . . . . . **42** B2
Sefton Way TS15. . . . . **66** A4
Selbourne St TS1 . . . . **85** B2
Selby Gr TS25. . . . . . . **12** C3
Selby Rd TS7 . . . . **62** B3
Selkirk Cl TS4 . . . . **50** B3
Selset Ave TS3. . . . . . . **52** A3
Selset Ct TS26 . . . . **8** A4
Selwood Cl TS17. . . . . **57** A4
Selworthy Gn TS17. . . **65** B2
Selwyn Dr TS19 . . . . . **24** A2
Semmerwater Gr
　TS10 . . . . **70** C2
Sennybridge Gr
　TS17 . . . . **64** C3
Serpentine Gdns TS26 **5** A1
Serpentine Rd
　Hartlepool TS26 . . . . . . **5** A1
　Hartlepool TS26 . . . . . . **8** C4
Severn Dr TS14 . . . . . **78** C2
Severn Gr TS22 . . . . . . **16** A2
Severn Rd TS10 . . . . . **70** A3
Severn St TS1 . . . . . . **87** B2
Severs Dr TS8 . . . . . . **58** C1
Seymour Ave TS16 . . . **63** A3
Seymour Cl TS11. . . . . **75** C1
Seymour Cres TS16 . . **63** A4
Seymour Dr TS16 . . . **63** A4
Seymour Gr TS16 . . . . **63** B4
Shackleton Cl TS17 . . **57** A4
Shadforth Dr TS23 . . **17** C3
Shadwell Cl TS6 . . . . . **61** B1
Shaftesbury Rd TS6. . **43** B3
Shaftesbury St TS18 . **83** A2
Shakespeare Ave
　Eston TS6 . . . . **44** A4
　Hartlepool TS25 . . . . . . **9** B1
Shaldon Cl TS10 . . . . **73** C3
Shandon Pk TS8 . . . . **61** B1
Shannon Cres TS19 . . **34** B4
Shannon Ct TS25 . . . . **14** B2
Sharp Cres TS24 . . . . . **5** C4
Sharrock Ct TS3 . . . . **87** C2
Shaw Cres TS6. . . . . . . **44** A4
Shawcross Ave TS6 . . **33** A1
Shaw St TS25 . . . . **11** B4
Shearwater La TS20. . **20** B2
Sheepfoote Hill
　TS15 . . . . **66** B4
Sheerness Gr TS24. . . **10** A3
Sheerness Way TS10 . **73** B3
Shelley Cl TS23 . . . . . . **17** A4
Shelley Cres TS6. . . . . **43** A3
Shelley Gr TS25. . . . . . . **9** A1
Shelley Rd TS4 . . . . . . **50** B4
Shelton Ct TS3. . . . . . . **42** B1
Shepherd Cl TS17. . . . **47** A2
Shepherdson Ct 🫥
　TS6 . . . . **32** A2
Shepherdson Way
　TS3 . . . . **86** C3
Shepton Cl TS17. . . . . **48** A2
Sheraton Ho TS20 . . . **20** C1
Sheraton Pk TS19. . . . **25** B2
Sheraton St TS18 . . . . **81** C2
Sherborne Wlk 🫥
　TS5 . . . . **38** C1

Sherburn Ave TS23. . . **17** C3
Sherburn Cl TS5 . . . . . **58** C4
Sheridan Gr TS25. . . . . **9** A1
Sheriff St TS26. . . . .**9** B4
Sheringham Ct TS10 . **73** C3
Sherwood Cl TS7 . . . . **53** A1
Sherwood Dr TS11. . . **74** C1
Sherwood Rd TS17. . . **56** C4
Shetland Ave TS17 . . . **47** C3
Shetland Cl TS5 . . . . . **59** A3
Shevington Gr TS7. . . **61** B3
Shibden Rd TS3. . . . . . **41** A3
Shields Terr TS24 . . . . .**6** B4
Shildon Cl TS23. . . . . . **17** A2
Shincliffe Rd TS23 . . . **17** C3
Shinwell Cres TS6 . . . **32** A1
Shipham Cl TS10. . . . . **73** B3
Ship Inn Yd TS18. . . . **83** A2
Shirley Ave TS5 . . . . . . **38** C1
Shoreham Cl TS3 . . . . **73** C3
Shoreswood Wlk
　TS5 . . . . **59** A4
Short Cl TS18. . . . . **46** B3
Shotley Cl TS23 . . . . . . **17** A2
Shotton Cl TS23 . . . . . **17** C1
Shrewsbury Rd TS3 . . **42** B1
Shrewsbury St TS25. . .**9** B1
Shropshire Wlk 🫥
　TS25 . . . .**9** C2
Sidcup Ave TS3. . . . . . **52** A3
Siddington Wlk TS3. . **41** B1
Sideling Tails TS15 . . . **66** C4
Sidlaw Rd TS23 . . . . . . **16** C1
Sidmouth Cl TS8. . . . . **51** A1
Silton Cl TS10 . . . . **69** C1
Silton Gr TS18 . . . . . . **81** A1
Silverdale TS7 . . . . **61** C2
Silver St
　Hartlepool TS24 . . . .**9** C3
　Middlesbrough TS2. . . . **29** B3
　Stockton-on-T TS18. . . **82** B3
　Yarm TS15. . . . . **63** B2
Silverton Rd TS14 . . . **79** C1
Silverwood Ct TS27 . . .**2** B2
Silverwood Ct 🫥
　TS17 . . . . **87** B4
Simcox Ct TS2 . . . . . . **84** A4
Simonside Gr TS17. . . **65** B3
Simonside Wlk TS3 . . **52** C4
Simpson Cl TS6. . . . . . **32** B1
Simpson Gn TS6. . . . . **32** A1
Simpson St TS5 . . . . . **39** C2
Sinclair Rd TS25 . . . . . **11** B4
Sinderby Cl TS23 . . . . **17** B2
Sinnington Cl TS14 . . **79** B2
Sinnington Rd TS17. . **56** C4
Sir Douglas Pk TS17 . **47** B1
Sir Hugh Bell Ct
　TS10 . . . . **69** B4
Sir William Turner's
　Homes TS10 . . . . **72** A1
Siskin Cl
　Hartlepool TS26 . . . . . . **4** C2
　Stockton-on-T TS20. . . **20** B2
Sitwell Wlk TS25. . . . . **11** C4
Skeeby Cl TS18 . . . . . . **45** A4
Skelton Ct TS14. . . . . . **79** B5
Skelton Dr
　Marske-by-t-S TS11 . . **75** B2
　Redcar TS10 . . . . **71** B1
Skelton Rd TS17 . . . . **47** C3
Skelton St TS24 . . . .**3** B1
Skelwith Rd TS3 . . . . **41** A1
Skerne Rd
　Hartlepool TS24 . . . .**5** C4
　Stockton-on-T TS20. . . **26** B3
Skerries Cres TS10. . . **72** B3
Skiddaw Cl TS16 . . . . **54** B2
Skiddaw Ct TS7. . . . . . **61** C2
Skinner St TS18. . . . . . **83** A2
Skiplam Cl TS18 . . . . **58** C2
Skipper's La
　Eston TS6. . . . . **42** C2
　South Bank TS6. . . . . . **42** B4
Skippers La Ind Est
　TS6 . . . . **42** B4

Skipper's Lane Ind Est
　TS6 . . . . **31** C1
Skipton Rd TS23 . . . . **17** B1
Skirbeck Ave TS3 . . . . **52** C4
Skirlaw Rd TS15 . . . . . **66** B4
Skomer Ct TS10. . . . . . **73** B3
Skripka Dr TS22 . . . . . **16** A1
Skye Wlk TS14 . . . . . . **78** C1
Skylark Cl TS26. . . . .**5** A3
Slake Terr
　Hartlepool, Middleton
　TS24 . . . .**6** C1
　Hartlepool TS24 . . . . . **10** B4
Slater Rd TS6. . . . . **44** A4
Slater Wlk TS6. . . . . . . **44** A4
Slayde The TS15 . . . . . **66** C4
Sledmere Cl TS23 . . . . **17** C4
Sledmere Dr TS5 . . . . **50** A3
Sledwick Rd TS23 . . . . **17** C1
Sleights Cres TS6 . . . . **44** A3
Sleights Ct TS14 . . . . . **79** B4
Slingsby Cl TS5 . . . . . . **50** A3
Smirks Yd 🫥 TS20 . . . **26** B4
Smith's Dock Park Rd
　TS6 . . . . **43** A1
Smith's Dock Rd TS6. . **32** A3
Smith St
　Middlesbrough TS1. . . . **84** C3
　Stockton-on-T TS18. . . **82** A3
Smyth Pl TS24 . . . .**3** C1
Snipe St TS10. . . . . **69** B4
Snowberry Cl TS20. . . **26** A3
Snowden St TS6 . . . . . **43** B2
Snowdon Cres TS10. . **70** B1
Snowdon Gr
　Hartlepool TS24 . . . .**2** C2
　Ingleby Barwick TS17. . **64** C4
Snowdon Rd TS2 . . . . **29** B3
Snowdrop Cl TS19 . . . **24** C1
Snowdrop Rd TS26. . . . **4** C4
SOBER HALL. **65** A3
Sober Hall Ave TS17 . . **65** A3
Somerby Terr TS3. . . . **41** B2
Somersby Cl TS24 . . . . **6** B4
Somerset Rd
　Eston TS6 . . . . **43** C4
　Guisborough TS14 . . . . **79** A2
　Stockton-on-T TS20. . . **26** A3
Somerset St TS1. . . . . . **86** B3
Somerset Terr TS23 . . **22** A3
Somerville Ave 🫥
　TS3 . . . . **52** B4
Sopwith Cl TS18 . . . . **46** B3
Sorbonne Cl TS17. . . . **83** B2
Sorrel Cl TS19 . . . . . . **24** B1
Sorrel Ct TS7 . . . . **51** B1
Sorrell Gr TS14 . . . . . . **78** B2
Sotherby Rd
　Middlesbrough TS3. . . . **41** C4
　South Bank TS6. . . . . . **32** A1
Southampton St
　TS10 . . . . **71** A3
South Ave
　Billingham TS23 . . . . . **27** A4
　Redcar TS10 . . . . **69** B1
SOUTH BANK. **32** A2
South Bank Bsns Ctr
　TS6 . . . . **32** A2
South Bank Rd TS3 . . **31** B1
South Bank Sta TS6 . . **32** A2
Southbrooke Ave
　TS25 . . . . **12** A4
Southburn Terr TS25 . . **9** C2
South Cres TS24 . . . . . **7** C2
South Ct 🫥 TS6. . . . . . **32** A2
Southdean Cl TS8. . . . **59** C3
Southdean Dr TS8 . . . **59** C3
South Dr
　Hartlepool TS26 . . . .**9** A4
　Marton TS7 . . . . **61** A4
　Ormesby TS7. . . . . **52** C3
South End TS25. . . . . . **13** D1
Southfield Cres
　TS20 . . . . **26** C2
Southfield La
　Middlesbrough TS1. . . . **85** C2
　Middlesbrough TS1. . . . **87** A2

Southfield Rd
　Marske-by-t-S TS11 . . . **75** A
　Middlesbrough TS1. . . . **87** A
　Stockton-on-T TS20. . . **26** B°
Southgate
　Eston TS6 . . . . **44** B°
　Hartlepool TS24 . . . .**7** B
South Gn 🫥 TS6 . . . . . **18** B
　South Lackenby TS6 . . **44** B°
Southland Ave TS26. . . .**9** A°
Southlands Dr TS7. . . **62** B°
Southmead Ave TS3 . . **52** A
South Mount Pleasant
　St 🔟 TS20 . . . . **26** B°
South Par TS25 . . . .**9** C°
South Park Ave TS6 . . **53** C
Southport Cl TS18 . . . **37** B°
South Rd
　Hartlepool TS24 . . . .**9** C°
　Stockton-on-T TS20. . . . .**9** C°
South Side Ret Pk
　TS18 . . . . **37** C°
South St
　Eston TS6 . . . . **44** A°
　Guisborough TS14 . . . . **79** A°
South Tees Bsns Ctr
　TS6 . . . . **32** B°
South Terr
　Redcar TS10 . . . . **71** B°
　South Bank TS6. . . . . . **32** A°
South View
　Billingham TS23 . . . . . **21** B°
　Egglescliffe TS16 . . . . . **63** B°
South View Terr TS3. . **41** A°
Southwark Cl TS6. . . . **53** B°
South Way TS20 . . . . . **26** C°
Southwell Rd TS5. . . . **40** A°
Southwell Sq TS5. . . . **40** A°
Southwick Ave TS4 . . **51** A°
Southwold Cl TS10. . . **72** A°
Southwood TS8. . . . . . **68** A°
Sowerby Way TS16. . . **54** B°
Spain Hill TS11 . . . . . . **75** A°
Spalding Rd TS25 . . . . **14** B°
Spalding Wlk TS20. . . **26** C°
Spark Sq TS19 . . . . . . **25** A°
Sparrow La TS14. . . . . **79** C°
Spaunton Cl TS8. . . . . **58** C°
Spearman Wlk TS27 . . .**2** C°
Speeding Dr TS24. . . . . .**3** A°
Speeton Ave TS5. . . . . **50** A°
Speeton Cl TS23 . . . . . **17** B°
Spell Cl TS15 . . . . **64** C°
Spellman Gr TS10. . . . **69** B°
Spenborough Rd
　TS19 . . . . **25** A°
Spencerbeck Farm
　TS7 . . . . **53** A°
Spencercroft Farm
　Cotts TS7. . . . . **53** A°
Spencerbeck Ho 🫥
　TS7 . . . . **53** A°
Spencer Cl TS11. . . . . . **74** C°
Spencerfield Cres
　TS3 . . . . **52** A°
Spencer Rd TS6 . . . . . . **43** B°
Spennithorne Rd
　TS18 . . . . **80** B°
Spenser Gr TS25 . . . .**9** B°
Spilsby Cl TS25 . . . . . . **14** B°
Spinnaker Ho TS24. . . **10** B°
Spinney The
　Hartlepool TS26 . . . .**8** A°
　Stockton-on-T TS18. . . **45** C°
Spital Fields TS15. . . . **63** C°
SPITAL FLATT. . . . . . . **67** A°
Spital Gate TS15 . . . . . **66** C°
Spital The TS15 . . . . . . **63** C°
Spitfire Cl 🫥 TS11 . . **74** B°
Springbank Rd TS7 . . **53** A°
Spring Cl TS17 . . . . . . **47** B°
Springfield Ave TS18. . **46** A°
Springfield Cl TS16 . . **54** B°
Springfield Gr TS15. . **67** B°
Springfield Rd TS16. . **54** B°
Spring Garden Cl
　TS7 . . . . **53** A°

Spring Garden La
TS7 . . . . 53 A1
Spring Garden Rd
TS25 . . . . 9 C1
Springhill 2 TS7 . . . . 53 A3
Springhill Gr TS17 . . . . 65 B3
Springholme
3 Ormesby TS7 . . . . 53 A3
Stockton-on-T TS18 . . . . 81 C1
Springholme Yd
TS18 . . . . 81 C1
Springlea 6 TS7 . . . . 53 A3
Springmead 5 TS7 . . . . 53 A3
Spring Rise TS6 . . . . . . 53 B3
Spring St
Middlesbrough TS2 . . . . 86 A4
Stockton-on-T TS18 . . . . 81 C1
Springston Rd TS26 . . . . 4 C1
Springvale Terr TS5 . . . . 38 C1
Springwalk 4 TS7 . . . . 53 A3
Spring Way TS18 . . . . . . 46 A4
Springwell Cl TS23 . . . . 17 C4
Springwell Flatlets
TS26 . . . . 5 A2
Springwell Sch TS26 . . 5 A2
Spring Wood Rd
TS14 . . . . 79 B3
Spruce Rd TS19 . . . . . . 25 B3
Spurn Wlk 14 TS24 . . . . 10 A3
Spurrey Cl TS17 . . . . . . 56 B2
Squadron Ct TS17 . . . . 47 B1
Square The
5 Eston TS6 . . . . . . 44 A2
Stockton-on-T TS18 . . . . 82 B3
Stable Mews TS10 . . . . 71 A3
Stadium Ct TS6 . . . . . . 42 B4
Stafford Cl TS17 . . . . 47 A4
Stafford Rd
Eston TS6 . . . . 44 A4
Guisborough TS14 . . . . 79 A2
Stafford St TS18 . . . . . . 83 A1
Staincliffe Rd TS25 . . . . 13 C3
Staindale TS14 . . . . . . 78 A2
Staindale Cl TS15 . . . . 64 B1
Staindale Gdns TS19 . . 25 B1
Staindale Pl TS25 . . . . 12 A4
Staindale Rd TS17 . . . . 47 C2
Staindrop Ct TS23 . . . . 16 C3
Staindrop Dr TS5 . . . . 49 B1
Staindrop St TS24 . . . . 10 A3
Stainforth St TS3 . . . . 51 C3
Stainforth Gdns
TS17 . . . . 56 C1
Stainmore Cl TS19 . . . . 80 C3
Stainsby Gate TS17 . . 48 B3
Stainsby Grange Ho
TS17 . . . . 48 A1
Stainsby Rd TS5 . . . . 49 A4
Stainsby St TS17 . . . . 47 B4
STAINTON 58 B1
Staintondale Ave
TS10 . . . . 69 C1
Stainton Gr TS20 . . . . 26 A2
Stainton Rd TS22 . . . . 16 C1
Stainton St TS3 . . . . . . 41 A3
Stainton Way
Coulby Newham
TS8 . . . . 60 B1
Nunthorpe TS7 . . . . . . 61 C3
Stainton St8 . . . . 58 C1
Staithes Ct TS24 . . . . . . 10 B3
Staithes Rd TS10 . . . . . . 70 A1
Stakesby Cl TS14 . . . . 79 A5
Stakesby Ho TS14 . . . . 79 B5
Stamford Ct TS23 . . . . 17 C3
Stamford St TS1 . . . . . . 87 B2
Stamford Wlk TS25 . . 12 A1
Stamp St TS18 . . . . . . 82 A3
Stanford Cl TS17 . . . . 83 C1
Stanhope Ave TS26 . . . . 9 B3
Stanhope Gdns TS4 . . 40 C1
Stanhope Gr TS5 . . . . 49 C3
Stanhope Rd
Billingham TS23 . . . . . . 17 C1
Stockton-on-T TS18 . . . . 80 B4
Stanhope St 1 TS12 . . 76 C3
Stanley Cl 3 TS17 . . . . 47 B4

Stanley Gr TS10 . . . . . . 71 A3
Stanley Rd TS25 . . . . 12 C4
Stanley St TS20 . . . . . . 26 A4
Stanley Wlk TS18 . . . . 82 A3
Stanmore Ave TS4 . . 50 C3
Stanmore Gr TS25 . . . . 13 B2
Stannage Gr TS17 . . . . 47 B2
Stanstead Way TS17 . . 48 A1
Stapleford Rd TS3 . . . . 52 C4
Stapleton Rd TS20 . . . . 20 B2
Stapylton Ct TS6 . . . . 33 A2
Stapylton St TS6 . . . . . . 33 A2
Starbeck Way TS7 . . . . 53 A4
Starbeck Wlk TS7 . . . . 57 B3
Startforth Rd TS2 . . . . 29 A3
Station App 3 TS24 . . 10 A4
Station Ave TS25 . . . . 14 B2
Station Cl 5 TS11 . . 74 C1
Station Cres TS23 . . . . 21 B3
Station La TS25 . . . . 13 C2
Station Par TS22 . . . . 21 A3
Station Rd
Billingham TS23 . . . . . . 21 A3
Eaglescliffe TS16 . . . . 54 C3
Eston TS6 . . . . 43 C1
Greatham TS25 . . . . . . 14 C1
Redcar TS10 . . . . 70 C4
Stockton-on-T TS20 . . . . 20 B2
Station Sq TS12 . . . . . . 76 C3
Station St
Middlesbrough TS1 . . . . 84 C4
2 Saltburn-by-t-S
TS12 . . . . 76 C3
Stockton-on-T TS18 . . . . 82 A4
Thornaby-on-T TS17 . . 83 C1
Staveley Ct TS3 . . . . 41 A2
Staveley Gr TS19 . . . . 25 B2
Staveley Wlk TS7 . . . . 52 C3
Stavordale Rd TS19 . . 80 C4
Stead Meml Hospl
TS10 . . . . 70 B3
Steele Cres TS6 . . . . 32 B2
Steer Ct TS23 . . . . 17 A3
Stephenson Ct TS6 . . 42 B4
Stephenson Ho
Middlesbrough TS1 . . . . 84 C3
Yarm TS15 . . . . 63 B2
Stephenson St
Middlesbrough TS1 . . . . 87 A2
Thornaby-on-T TS17 . . 83 C1
Stephenson Way
TS18 . . . . 83 B2
Stephens Rd TS6 . . . . 32 B2
Stephen St TS26 . . . . . . 5 B1
Stevenage Cl TS17 . . 64 B1
Stevenson Cl TS15 . . 64 B1
Stewart Rd TS20 . . . . 26 B1
Stileston Cl TS26 . . . . 4 C1
Stirling Rd TS10 . . . . 71 B2
Stirling St TS25 . . . . . . 9 C1
Stirling Way TS17 . . . . 57 A3
Stockdale Ave TS10 . . 69 C1
Stockton Bsns Ctr
TS18 . . . . 83 A2
**STOCKTON
GRANGE** 80 A3
**STOCKTON-ON-
TEES** 80 B3
Stockton Rd
Hartlepool, Bellevue
TS25 . . . . 9 C2
Hartlepool, Foggy Furze
TS25 . . . . 12 C4
Middlesbrough TS5 . . . . 38 B3
Thornaby-on-T TS17 . . 38 A2
Stockton Riverside Coll
TS17 . . . . 83 C2
Stockton Sixth Form
Coll TS19 . . . . 80 A4
Stockton St
Billingham TS23 . . . . . . 21 B2
Hartlepool TS24 . . . . . . 9 C3
Middlesbrough TS2 . . . . 29 B3
Stockton Sta TS18 . . 82 A4
Stockwell Ave TS17 . . 57 A2
Stockwith Cl TS3 . . . . 52 C4
Stokesley Cres TS23 . . 21 B3

Stokesley Rd
Guisborough TS14 . . . . 78 A2
Hartlepool TS25 . . . . . . 13 C2
Marton TS7 . . . . 61 A4
Nunthorpe TS7 . . . . . . 62 B1
Stoneacre Ave TS17 . . 65 B4
Stonebridge Cres
TS17 . . . . 56 A3
Stonechat Cl
Hartlepool TS26 . . . . . . 5 B3
Ingleby Barwick TS17 . . 56 A1
Stonecrop Cl TS18 . . 81 A1
Stonedale Wlk TS5 . . 58 C4
Stonegate TS6 . . . . . . 44 B2
Stonehouse Cl TS15 . . 67 A4
Stonehouse St TS6 . . 39 C2
Stoneleigh Ave TS5 . . 49 A3
Stone St TS6 . . . . 86 B3
Stonethwaite Cl TS24 . 6 A3
Stoneyhurst Ave TS5 . 48 C4
Stonor Wlk TS3 . . . . 52 A3
Stornaway Cl TS19 . . 34 B3
Stotfold St 1 TS26 . . 9 C3
Stotfold Wlk TS5 . . . . 58 B4
Stoupe Gr TS10 . . . . 73 C4
Stourport Cl TS18 . . 82 C4
Stowe St TS1 . . . . . . 85 C2
Stowmarket Cl TS25 . 14 C4
Strait La TS8 . . . . 58 B1
Straker St 7 TS26 . . . . 9 B4
Strand The TS10 . . . . 73 C4
Stranton TS25 . . . . . . 9 C2
Stranton Prim Sch
TS25 . . . . 9 C2
Stranton St TS17 . . . . 47 B4
Stratford Cres TS5 . . 38 C2
Stratford Rd TS25 . . . . 13 A2
Strathaven Dr TS16 . . 54 C1
Strauss Rd TS6 . . . . 44 A3
Strawberry Apartments
TS26 . . . . 4 B4
Streatlam Rd TS23 . . 18 A2
Strome Cl TS17 . . . . 65 C4
Strona Wlk TS14 . . . . 79 A2
Stuart St 9 TS24 . . . . 6 A1
Stubbs Cl TS23 . . . . 17 A3
Studland Dr TS24 . . . . 2 C2
Studland Rd TS10 . . . . 73 C3
Studley Rd
Hartlepool TS25 . . . . . . 9 C2
Middlesbrough TS5 . . . . 39 A1
Stockton-on-T TS19 . . 80 C4
Thornaby-on-T TS17 . . 47 C2
Stump Cross TS14 . . . . 79 A3
Sturt Dr TS20 . . . . . . 25 C4
Sudbury TS8 . . . . 61 B2
Sudbury Rd TS20 . . . . 26 C4
Suffield St TS2 . . . . . . 29 B3
Suffolk Cl TS25 . . . . . . 9 C1
Suffolk Rd TS5 . . . . 40 A1
Suffolk St TS18 . . . . 81 C2
Sugar Loaf Cl TS17 . . 64 C4
Suggitt St TS26 . . . . . . 9 A4
Sulby Ave TS3 . . . . 41 B1
Summerfield Gr 10
TS17 . . . . 47 C1
Summerhill Ctry Pk★
TS25 . . . . 8 A1
Summerhill Visitor
Ctr★ TS25 . . . . 8 B2
Summerhouse Sq 7
TS20 . . . . 26 A4
Sundell Ct TS18 . . . . 81 C2
Sunderland Rd TS22 . . 16 A4
Sundew Ct TS18 . . . . 46 C1
Sundial Mews TS22 . . 16 C4
Sun Gdns TS17 . . . . 47 A4
Sunley Ave 3 TS4 . . 40 B1
Sunningdale Ct 3
TS6 . . . . 43 C1
Sunningdale Dr
TS16 . . . . 54 C1
Sunningdale Gr TS7 . . 2 C1
Sunningdale Ho 4
TS6 . . . . 43 C1
Sunningdale Rd TS4 . . 50 B3

Sunningdale Wlk
TS16 . . . . 54 C1
Sunniside TS24 . . . . . . 7 B2
Sunnybank Rd TS7 . . 53 A2
Sunnybrow Ave TS23 . 21 B2
Sunnyfield TS7 . . . . 52 C3
Sunnygate TS6 . . . . 44 B2
Sunnyside TS8 . . . . . . 60 A2
Sunnyside Ave TS4 . . 50 B4
Sunnyside Gr TS18 . . 45 B4
Sunnyside Prim Sch
TS8 . . . . 60 A2
Sun St
Stockton-on-T TS18 . . . . 81 C1
Thornaby-on-T TS17 . . 47 A4
Sunstar Gr TS7 . . . . 60 C4
Surbiton Rd TS19 . . . . 34 A3
Surgery La TS24 . . . . 5 C4
Surrey Rd TS20 . . . . 26 C3
Surrey St TS1 . . . . . . 85 B1
Surrey Terr TS23 . . . . 21 C3
Surtees St
Hartlepool TS24 . . . . . . 10 A3
Stockton-on-T TS18 . . . . 83 A2
Sussex St
Hartlepool TS25 . . . . . . 9 C1
Middlesbrough TS2 . . . . 84 C4
Sussex Wlk TS20 . . . . 26 C2
Sutherland Gr TS20 . . 20 B2
Sutton Pl TS23 . . . . . . 17 C1
Sutton Way TS4 . . . . 50 B3
Swainby Cl TS5 . . . . 50 A2
Swainby Rd
Hartlepool TS25 . . . . . . 13 C1
Stockton-on-T TS20 . . . . 26 B1
Swainson Pl 3 TS26 . . 9 C4
Swainson St TS24 . . . . 6 A2
Swainston Cl TS5 . . . . 49 A1
Swale Ave TS17 . . . . 47 C2
Swalebrooke Ave
TS25 . . . . 11 C4
Swale Cl TS16 . . . . 63 B3
Swaledale TS17 . . . . 65 B3
Swaledale Cres TS23 . 21 B3
Swaledale Ho 10
TS4 . . . . 50 B3
Swale Rd TS20 . . . . 26 A4
Swallow Cl
Guisborough TS14 . . . . 78 A3
Hartlepool TS26 . . . . . . 4 C3
Swallowfields TS8 . . 68 A4
Swallow La TS20 . . . . 20 B1
Swanage Cl TS8 . . . . 60 B4
Swanage Dr TS10 . . . . 73 C3
Swanage Gr TS24 . . . . 2 C2
Swift Gr TS25 . . . . . . 11 C4
Swinburne Rd
Eaglescliffe TS16 . . . . 54 C3
Hartlepool TS25 . . . . . . 11 C4
Swinburn Rd TS20 . . 26 A2
Swinburn's Yd TS15 . . 63 B2
Swinton Rd TS18 . . . . 45 A4
Sycamore Ave
Saltburn-by-t-S
TS12 . . . . 76 A2
Thornaby-on-T TS17 . . 47 B2
Sycamore Cres TS6 . . 43 A3
Sycamore Rd
Eaglescliffe TS16 . . . . 54 C3
Middlesbrough TS5 . . . . 39 C1
Ormesby TS7 . . . . . . 53 A2
Redcar TS10 . . . . 70 B3
Stockton-on-T TS19 . . . . 25 B2
Sycamores The TS20 . . 20 B2
Sycamore Terr TS2 . . 23 C1
Sycamore Way TS19 . 24 C3
Sydenham Rd
Hartlepool TS25 . . . . . . 9 C1
Hartlepool TS25 . . . . . . 11 C4
Stockton-on-T TS18 . . . . 81 C1
Sydney Cl TS5 . . . . 38 C1
Sydney Rd TS7 . . . . 61 A3
Sydney St TS18 . . . . 82 A3
Sylvan Wlk TS3 . . . . 52 A3
Symons Cl TS18 . . . . 34 B2
Syon Ct 3 TS5 . . . . 38 C1
Syon Gdns TS20 . . . . 19 C1

Tai Hua Ct TS4 . . . . . . 86 B3
Tailrigg Cl TS19 . . . . 80 C4
Talbenny Gr TS17 . . . . 64 C3
Talbot Mews TS6 . . . . 43 B4
Talbot St
Middlesbrough TS1 . . . . 87 B2
Stockton-on-T TS20 . . . . 26 B1
Talgarth Rd TS20 . . . . 20 C1
Talisker Gdns TS10 . . 73 A3
Talisman Cl TS14 . . . . 58 B1
Talland Cl TS27 . . . . 2 B1
Talybont Gr TS17 . . . . 64 C4
Tamarisk Cl TS17 . . 56 B2
Tame Rd TS3 . . . . . . 30 C1
Tamworth Rd TS23 . . 17 B2
Tanfield Rd TS25 . . . . 12 B4
Tanhill Wlk 11 TS3 . . 43 A4
Tankerville St TS26 . . 9 B4
Tanner Cl TS17 . . . . 64 C4
Tanner's Bank TS16 . . 63 B3
Tansley Ave TS3 . . . . 41 C2
Tanton Gr TS22 . . . . 16 A1
Tanwell Cl TS19 . . . . 24 B1
Tanya Gdns
Middlesbrough TS5 . . . . 59 B4
Stockton-on-T TS19 . . . . 35 A3
Taransay View TS17 . . 47 C4
Tarell Ct TS17 . . . . . . 64 C3
Tarnston Rd TS26 . . . . 4 C1
Tarran St TS5 . . . . . . 85 A1
Tarring St TS18 . . . . 83 A2
Tarr Stps TS17 . . . . 65 B2
Tasman Dr TS18 . . . . 34 C1
Tasmania Sq TS7 . . . . 61 B3
Tatham Ct TS7 . . . . 62 A2
Taunton Cl TS8 . . . . 60 B4
Taunton Gr TS26 . . . . 5 A2
Taunton Vale TS14 . . 79 B1
Tavistock Cl TS27 . . . . 2 B1
Tavistock Rd TS5 . . . . 39 B2
Tavistock St TS5 . . . . 39 B2
Tawney Cl TS6 . . . . 43 B4
Tawney Rd TS6 . . . . 43 B4
Taybrooke Ave TS25 . . 9 A1
Teak St TS1 . . . . . . 87 A2
Tealby Wlk TS3 . . . . 42 B1
Teal Ct TS10 . . . . . . 69 B4
Teare Cl TS1 . . . . . . 85 B2
Teasel Ct TS19 . . . . 24 C1
Tebay Cl TS7 . . . . . . 52 C3
Tedder Ave TS17 . . . . 57 B4
Tedder Avenue Prim
Sch TS17 . . . . 57 B4
Tedworth Cl TS14 . . 79 B1
Tees Bank Ave TS16 . . 55 A3
Tees Barrage★ TS17 . 37 C3
Tees Barrage Way
TS17 . . . . 37 C3
Tees Bay Ret Pk
TS25 . . . . 13 A3
Teesbrooke Ave
TS25 . . . . 12 A4
Tees Ct TS6 . . . . . . 42 A4
Teesdale Ave
Billingham TS23 . . . . . . 21 B2
Hartlepool TS26 . . . . . . 9 A3
Teesdale S TS17 . . . . 83 B1
Teesdale Terr 4
TS17 . . . . 47 C4
Tees Dock Rd TS6 . . . . 33 B3
Teesgate TS17 . . . . 48 B3
Tees (newport) Bridge
Approach Rd
Middlesbrough
TS18 . . . . 28 A1
Stockton-on-T TS18 . . . . 28 A1
Teesquay Millennium
Footbridge The
TS18 . . . . 83 B2
Tees Rd
Guisborough TS14 . . . . 78 C2

Tees Rd *continued*
Redcar TS10 .... 70 B2
Teesside High Sch
TS16 .... 55 A2
Teesside Ind Est
TS17 .... 57 A1
Teesside Park Dr
TS17 .... 38 A1
Teesside Pk
Middlesbrough
  TS17 .... 38 B2
Thornaby-on-T TS17 .. 38 A1
Teesside Tertiary Coll
TS4 .... 87 B1
Tees St
Billingham TS23 ...... 23 B2
1 Hartlepool TS24.... 9 C4
TEESVILLE 43 A3
Teesville Inf Sch
TS6 .... 42 C3
Teesway TS18 .... 27 C1
Teignmouth Cl TS27 ..2 B1
Telford Cl TS24 ....6 B3
Telford Rd TS3........ 31 B1
Tempest Rd TS24 ..... 3 A1
Temple Ct TS20 ...... 82 B4
Templeton Cl TS27 ....2 B1
Tenby Cl TS6 .... 43 C3
Tenby Rd TS10 ...... 72 A4
Tenby Way TS16 ..... 63 C4
Tenby Wlk TS26....... 5 A3
Tennant St TS18 ..... 82 A3
Tennyson Ave
Eston TS6 .... 43 C4
Hartlepool TS25 ...... 9 A1
Tennyson Cl TS6 ..... 43 C4
Tennyson Rd TS23 ... 17 A4
Tennyson St TS1..... 85 C1
Ternbeck Way TS17 .. 57 B3
Tern Gr TS10........ 73 B4
Tetcott Cl TS14 ...... 24 C1
Tewkesbury Ave TS7 . 61 B2
Thackeray Gr TS5..... 50 A4
Thackeray Rd TS25....8 B1
Thames Ave
Guisborough TS14 .... 78 C2
Hartlepool TS24 ...... 5 C3
Thornaby-on-T TS17 .. 47 C2
Thames Rd
Billingham TS22 ..... 16 B2
Redcar TS10 .... 70 A2
Thatch La TS17 ...... 56 C2
Theakston Gr TS18.... 34 B1
Thetford Ave TS3 .... 52 B4
Thetford Rd TS25 .... 14 B4
Thinford Gdns TS5... 59 A4
Thirlby Cl TS3 .... 41 A1
Thirlby Way TS14 .... 79 B5
Thirlmere Ave TS5 ... 49 B3
Thirlmere Cres TS6 .. 43 B1
Thirlmere Ct TS23 ... 21 C1
Thirlmere Rd TS10 ... 70 B2
Thirlmere St TS26.....9 B2
Thirlwall Dr TS17 .... 65 A3
Thirsk Gr TS25....... 12 C3
Thirsk Rd TS15 ...... 66 C4
Thistle Gn TS18...... 82 B3
Thistle Rd TS19 ..... 25 B3
Thistle Rise TS8 ..... 59 C3
Thistle St TS1....... 87 A2
Thomas St
Middlesbrough TS3.... 41 A4
Stockton-on-T TS18.... 82 B4
Thomlinson Rd TS25. 10 A1
Thompson Gr TS24.... 5 C2
Thompsons Cl TS22.. 16 C4
Thompson St
2 Hartlepool TS24 ... 9 C2
Stockton-on-T TS18.... 82 A4
Thomson Ave TS5.... 38 C2
Thomson St TS14 .... 79 A3
Thorgill Cl TS4....... 50 B4
Thorington Gdns
TS17 .... 65 C4

Thornaby Com Sch
TS17 .... 48 A2
THORNABY-ON-
TEES 48 A2
Thornaby-on-Tees CE
Prim Sch TS17....... 47 C1
Thornaby Pl TS17 .... 83 B1
Thornaby Rd TS17 ... 47 B2
Thornaby Sta TS17... 83 C1
Thornberry Ct TS5.... 39 A1
Thornbrough Cl
TS18 .... 45 A4
Thornbury Cl
Hartlepool TS27 ...... 2 B2
Redcar TS10 .... 73 C2
Thorn Cl TS17....... 56 B2
Thorndike Rd TS6..... 43 C3
Thorndyke Ave TS4 .. 50 C4
Thornfield Cl TS16.... 54 A1
Thornfield Gr TS5.... 49 B4
Thornfield Rd TS5 ... 39 A1
Thornhill Gdns TS26 .. 5 A1
Thornhill Pl TS26 .... 5 A1
Thornley Ave TS23 ... 17 B4
Thorn Rd TS19 ...... 25 B3
Thorn Side TS17 ..... 56 B2
Thornthwaite TS7 ... 58 B3
THORNTON 58 C1
Thornton Garth
TS15 .... 66 C4
Thornton Gr TS20 ... 26 A2
Thornton Rd TS8 .... 58 B1
Thornton St
Hartlepool TS26 ...... 9 B3
Middlesbrough TS3.... 41 A4
THORNTREE 42 C2
Thorntree Ave TS3 ... 41 C2
Thorntree Ct TS17 ... 47 C2
Thorntree Ho TS3 .... 41 C2
Thorn Tree La TS25... 14 C1
Thorntree Prim Sch
TS3 .... 42 B2
Thorntree Rd TS17... 47 B2
Thornville Rd TS26....9 B4
Thornwood Ave
TS17 .... 56 B2
Thorpe Mews 8
TS20 .... 26 B4
Thorpe St TS24...... 7 A3
Thorphill Way TS25 .. 27 B3
Throckley Ave TS5 ... 49 B1
Thropton Cl TS23 ... 16 C3
THROSTON 7 A1
Throston Cl TS26......5 B3
Throston Grange La
TS26 .... 5 A3
Throston Prim Sch
TS26 .... 5 A2
Throston St TS24 .... 7 B2
Thrush Rd TS10 ..... 71 A3
Thrushwood Cres 4
TS11 .... 75 B1
Thruxton Way TS20 .. 25 C4
Thurlestone TS8 ..... 61 C2
Thurnham Gr TS7.... 61 B3
Thursby Dr TS7 ..... 52 C4
Thursby Gr TS25 .... 14 A4
Thurso Cl TS19 ...... 34 A3
Thwaites La TS10 .... 71 A2
Thweng Way TS14 ... 78 C1
Tibbersley Ave TS23 . 21 C1
Tibthorpe TS7 ...... 61 C3
Tidkin La TS11...... 78 C2
Tilbury Rd TS6....... 32 A3
Tilery Prim Sch
TS18 .... 82 C4
Tilery Rd TS20 ...... 26 B1
Tilery Way TS20...... 26 B1
Timberscombe Cl
TS17 .... 65 A2
Timothy Ct TS18 .... 83 A1
Tindale Cl TS4 ...... 78 A2
Tindale Cl TS15..... 66 B3
Tindale Wlk TS5 .... 58 C4
Tintagel Cl TS27 ......2 B1
Tintern Ave TS23..... 17 A1

Tipton Cl TS17....... 48 A2
Tirril Way TS7 ...... 61 C2
Tithe Barn Rd TS19 .. 24 B2
Tiverton Gr TS26..... 5 A2
Toddington Dr TS20.. 25 B4
Tod Point Rd TS10 ... 69 C4
Tofts Cl TS11 .... 75 B2
Tofts Rd W TS25 ..... 15 C3
Tollerton Cl TS19 .... 80 A4
TOLLESBY 60 B4
Tollesby Bridge TS8.. 60 B3
Tollesby La TS7 ..... 60 C3
Tollesby Rd TS5..... 50 A3
Tollesby Sch TS4 ... 50 B3
Tomlinson Way TS3 .. 42 A3
Topcliffe Dr TS5 .... 58 C4
Topcliffe Rd TS17 ... 48 A1
Topcliffe St TS26..... 9 A4
Topcroft Cl TS3 ..... 52 A3
Topham Gn TS3...... 41 A2
Topping Cl TS24 ..... 6 C4
Torbay Cl TS8....... 51 A1
Torbay Gr TS26 ..... 5 A2
Torbay Wlk TS26..... 5 A2
Torcross Cl TS27 .....2 B1
Torcross Way TS10... 73 B3
Toronto Cres TS4 .... 40 B2
Torquay Ave TS25 ... 12 A1
Torver Mount TS7.... 61 C2
Torwell Dr TS19..... 34 C4
Tothill Ave TS3...... 42 B1
Totnes Cl TS27....... 2 B1
Tovil Cl TS19........ 24 A2
Tower Ct 6 TS12 .... 77 A3
Tower Gn TS2....... 29 C3
Tower St
Hartlepool TS24 ..... 10 A3
Stockton-on-T TS18... 83 B2
TOWN FARM....... 41 C2
Towngate Bsns Pk
TS23 .... 22 A4
Town Ho TS18 ...... 83 A2
Town Sq TS23....... 21 B4
Town Wall TS24......7 B2
Towthorpe TS7 ..... 61 C3
Trafalgar Ct TS6 .... 32 A2
Trafalgar Terr TS10... 70 B4
Tranmere Ave TS3 ... 41 C2
Tranter Rd TS4 ..... 50 B3
Travellers Gate TS25 . 12 C3
Trecastell TS17 ..... 64 C3
Tredegar Wlk TS26... 4 C2
Trefoil Cl TS14 ..... 78 B2
Trefoil Ct TS20..... 26 A2
Trefoil Wood TS7 ... 51 B1
Tregarth Cl TS4..... 50 B4
Tremaine Cl TS27 .....2 B1
Trenchard Ave TS17 . 57 A4
Trenholme Cl TS17... 56 B2
Trenholme Rd TS4 ... 87 C1
Trent Ave TS17 ..... 47 C2
Trentbrooke Ave
TS25 .... 12 A4
Trentham Ave TS3 ... 42 A1
Trent Rd TS10....... 70 B2
Trent St TS20 ...... 26 B2
Tresco Wlk TS14 .... 79 A2
Trevarrian Dr TS10... 73 B3
Trevine Gdns TS17 .. 64 C3
Trevino Ct TS16..... 55 A1
Trevithick Cl TS16.... 54 A2
Trevose Cl TS10..... 73 A3
Triangle The TS14.... 78 B3
Trident Bsns Ctr TS2. 29 A3
Trident Cl TS24 ..... 10 B4
Trigo Cl TS7 .... 60 C4
Trimdon Ave TS5..... 49 A1
Trinity Cres TS3...... 30 C1
Trinity Gdns TS18 ... 83 A2
Trinity Mews TS17 .. 83 C2
Trinity St
Hartlepool TS24 ...... 7 B3
Stockton-on-T TS18.. 83 A2
Tristram Ave TS25.... 9 A1
Tristram Cl TS6 ..... 43 A1
Troisdorf Way TS10 .. 72 A2

Troon Cl
Billingham TS22 ..... 16 A1
Middlesbrough TS4.... 50 B3
Troutbeck Rd TS10 .. 70 C1
Troutpool Cl TS24......6 B3
Troutsdale Cl TS15... 66 B3
Trunk Rd
Eston, Teesside
  TS6 .... 43 A4
Redcar TS10 .... 69 A1
Truro Dr TS25....... 12 A1
Tudor Ct TS3 .... 42 B2
Tunstall Ave
Billingham TS23 ..... 17 C4
Hartlepool TS26 ...... 9 A4
Tunstall Gdns TS10... 73 C2
Tunstall Gr TS26 ..... 5 A1
Tunstall Rd TS18 .... 45 A4
Tunstall St TS3 ..... 41 A4
Turford Ave TS3 .... 41 C3
Turnberry Ave TS16 . 63 C4
Turnberry Gr TS27 ....2 B2
Turnberry Way TS8 .. 61 B1
Turnbull St TS24..... 6 A1
Turner Cl TS23...... 17 A3
Turner St TS10..... 70 C4
Turner Wlk TS25 .... 11 B4
Turnstile The TS5 ... 85 B1
Turton Rd TS15 ..... 66 B4
Tuson Wlk TS24..... 6 A1
Tweed Ave TS17 .... 47 C2
Tweed Ho 8 TS18 .. 82 C4
Tweedport Rd TS18 . 82 C4
Tweed Rd TS10 ..... 70 A2
Tweed St TS12...... 76 C3
Tweed Wlk TS24 .... 5 C1
Tynebrooke Ave
TS25 .... 12 A4
Tyne Cl TS6....... 42 A4
Tynedale St TS18 ... 81 C2
Tyneport Gn 11 TS18 .82 C4
Tyne Rd TS10...... 70 B2
Tyne St 10 TS6 ..... 32 A2
Tyrone Rd TS19 .... 34 B4

U

Uldale Dr TS16...... 63 C4
Ullapool Cl TS19 .... 34 A3
Ulla St TS1 .... 85 C1
Ullswater Ave TS5 ... 49 B3
Ullswater Cl TS6..... 44 A4
Ullswater Gr TS10... 70 C2
Ullswater Rd
Billingham TS23 ..... 21 C1
Hartlepool TS25 ..... 10 A1
Stockton-on-T TS18... 80 B3
Union Rd TS24 ......6 B4
Union St E TS18..... 82 C4
Union St
Guisborough TS14 ... 79 B4
Hartlepool TS24 ..... 7 B2
Middlesbrough TS1... 85 B2
Unity City Acad TS3. 41 B1
University Bvd TS17 . 83 C2
University Hospl of
North Tees TS19 ... 24 C2
Univ Hospl of
Hartlepool TS24 .... 5 B3
Univ of Teesside
TS1 .... 87 A2
Upleatham St TS12 . 76 C3
Upleatham Gr TS19 . 34 C2
Upper Albion St 15
TS6 .... 32 A2
Upper Branch St 7
TS6 .... 32 A2
Upper Church St 5
TS24 .... 9 C4
Upper Garth Gdns
TS14 .... 79 B4
Upper Graham St 14
TS6 .... 32 A2
Upper Green La
TS17 .... 47 B1
Upper Jackson St 16
TS6 .... 32 A2

Upper Napier St TS6 . 32 A2
Upper Oxford St TS6 . 32 A1
Upper Princess St
TS6 .... 32 A2
Uppingham St TS25... 9 B1
Upsall Gr TS19 ...... 34 C1
Upsall Rd
Middlesbrough TS3.... 41 B1
Nunthorpe TS7 ..... 62 B2
Upton Ct TS17 ...... 65 B4
Upton St TS1 ...... 87 A2
Upton Wlk TS25 .... 14 B4
Urford Cl TS15...... 67 B4
Urlay Gr TS5........ 49 C2
Urlay Nook Rd TS16.. 63 B4
Urswick Cl TS4 ..... 40 A1
Usk Ct TS17........ 64 C4
Usway Ct 1 TS17... 65 A3
Usworth Ent Pk
TS25 .... 12 C2
Usworth Rd TS25 ... 12 C1
Usworth Road Ind Est
TS25 .... 12 C1
Uvedale Rd TS6..... 32 B1

V

Vale Dr TS17........ 48 A2
Vale The
Hartlepool TS26 ..... 8 B3
Middlesbrough TS4.... 40 A1
Stockton-on-T TS19... 25 A3
Valiant Way TS17 ... 56 C3
Valley Cl
Hartlepool TS26 ..... 8 A3
Marske-by-t-S TS11 .. 75 A3
Yarm TS15.......... 64 A2
Valley Dr
Hartlepool TS26 ..... 8 A3
Yarm TS15.......... 64 B2
Valley Gdns
Egglescliffe TS16 .... 63 A4
Stockton-on-T TS19... 25 A3
Valley Rd TS4....... 40 A2
Vancouver Gdns TS4. 87 B1
Vane St
Hartlepool TS24 ..... 7 A3
Stockton-on-T TS18... 82 A3
Vanguard Ct TS18... 46 B2
Van Mildert Way
TS18 .... 46 B4
Varo Terr TS18 ..... 81 C2
Vaughan Ct TS16.... 33 A2
Vaughan Sh Ctr The
TS3 .... 42 B2
Vaughan St TS1..... 84 C3
Vaynor Dr TS17 .... 64 C4
Venables Rd TS14.... 79 A4
Ventnor Ave TS25 .. 12 B4
Ventnor Rd TS5..... 39 B3
Verner Cl TS24......2 B1
Verner Rd TS24 .....2 B1
Vernon St TS6 ..... 58 C2
Veronica St TS3..... 87 C2
Verwood Cl TS19.... 24 A2
Veryan Rd TS23 .... 17 C1
Viburnum Cl 11 TS10. 73 B2
Vicarage Ave TS19 .. 80 C3
Vicarage Ct 6 TS25.. 9 C2
Vicarage Dr TS11 ... 75 A2
Vicarage Row TS25 . 14 B2
Vicarage St TS19.... 80 C4
Vickers Cl
Marske-by-t-S TS11 .. 74 B3
Stockton-on-T TS18... 46 B2
Victoria Apartments
TS1 .... 87 A2
Victoria Ave
Redcar TS10 .... 71 A2
Stockton-on-T TS20... 26 B2
Victoria Cl TS6 ..... 32 A1
Victoria Gdns 3 TS3. 52 B4
Victoria Gr TS19 .... 35 A4
Victoria Homes TS5..9 B2
Victoria Pl TS24.....7 B2
Victoria Rd
Egglescliffe TS16 .... 54 C2

Victoria Rd *continued*
Hartlepool TS24, TS26 . . 9 C4
Middlesbrough TS1. . . . 87 A2
Saltburn-by-t-S TS12. . . 76 C2
Stockton-on-T TS19. . . . 35 A3
Thornaby-on-T TS17 . . . 47 B4
Victoria St
Hartlepool TS24 . . . . 7 B2
Middlesbrough TS1. . . . 85 B2
Seaton Carew TS25 . . . 13 C2
South Bank TS6. . . . . . . 32 A1
Stockton-on-T TS18. . . . 82 A3
Victoria Terr
Billingham TS2 . . . . 29 C4
Hartlepool TS24 . . . . . . 10 A4
Saltburn-by-t-S TS12. . . 76 C2
Victor Way TS17 . . . . . 57 A4
Victory Terr TS10. . . . . 70 B4
Vienna Ct TS10 . . . . . . 72 A2
Viewley Centre Rd
TS8 . . . . 59 B2
Viewley Ctr The TS8 . . 59 B2
Viewley Hill Ave TS8 . . 59 C2
Viewley Hill Prim Sch
TS8 . . . . 59 B2
Village Paddock
TS18 . . . . 45 C4
Village Prim Sch The
TS17 . . . . 47 B2
Village The TS7 . . . . . . 61 A4
Villa Rd TS3 . . . . 42 A3
Villiers St TS24 . . . . . . 9 C3
Vincent Rd
Billingham TS23 . . . . . . 17 A3
Middlesbrough TS5. . . . 40 A1
Vincent St TS24. . . . . . .6 B4
Vine Cl TS14 . . . . 79 C2
Vine St TS2 . . . . 84 C4
Viola Cl TS26 . . . . 4 C4
Violet Cl TS20. . . . . . . 26 A2
Virginia Cl TS19. . . . . . 25 A2
Virginia Gdns TS5. . . . 59 A4
Viscount Cl TS24. . . . . . 6 A3
Vollum Rise TS24 . . . . . 7 A3
Vulcan St TS2. . . . . . . 29 C3
Vulcan Way TS17 . . . . 57 A3

W

Wade Ave TS18 . . . . . . 82 B4
Wainfleet Rd TS25 . . . 14 A4
Wainwright Cl TS25. . . 13 C4
Wainwright Wlk
TS25 . . . . 13 C4
Wakefield Rd TS5. . . . 39 C2
Wake St TS3 . . . . 41 A4
Waldridge Gr TS23. . . 18 A4
Waldridge Rd TS19 . . 24 B3
Walkers Row TS14 . . . 79 B4
Walker St
Redcar TS10 . . . . 70 C4
Thornaby-on-T TS17 . . . 47 B4
Walkley Ave TS17 . . . . 47 B2
Waller Ct TS24. . . . . . . 5 C4
Wallington Ct TS23 . . 17 B3
Wallington Rd TS23 . . 17 B4
Wallington Way
TS23 . . . . 17 B3
Wallis Rd TS6. . . . . . . 42 A4
Walnut Cl TS17 . . . . . . 47 B2
Walnut Gr TS10 . . . . . 71 C2
Walpole Rd TS25. . . . . . 8 C1
Walpole St TS1 . . . . . 85 C2
Walsham Cl TS19 . . . . 24 C1
Walsingham Ct TS23 . 21 B1
Walter St TS11 . . . . . . 81 C1
Waltham Ave TS18 . . . 35 A2
Walton Ave TS5. . . . . 49 C4
Walton Ct TS18 . . . . . 37 B4
Walton St TS18 . . . . . 37 B4
Walton Terr TS14. . . . . 79 B3
Walworth Cl TS10. . . . 71 B1
Walworth Gr TS5 . . . . 49 B2
Wansbeck Gdns TS26 . .9 B3

Wansford Cl TS23. . . . 17 C4
Wanstead Cl TS11. . . . 74 C3
Warbler Cl TS17 . . . . . 56 A1
Warcop Cl TS21 . . . . . 61 C2
Wardale Ave TS5. . . . 58 C4
Ward Cl TS18 . . . . 83 A2
Wardell Cl TS15. . . . . . 67 A4
Warden Cl TS19. . . . . . 24 C3
Ward Jackson Prim Sch
TS24 . . . . 10 A3
Wardley Cl TS19 . . . . . 24 C3
Wardman Cres TS10 . . 71 B2
Warehouse The
TS17 . . . . 83 B1
Warelands Way TS4 . . 87 C1
Ware St TS20 . . . . 26 B1
Warkworth Dr TS26 . . .8 B4
Warkworth Rd TS23. . 16 C2
WARRENBY 69 B3
Warrenby Ct TS10. . . . 69 B4
Warren Cl TS24. . . . . . .5 B3
Warren Ct TS24. . . . . . . 5 C3
Warrenport Rd TS18 . 37 B4
Warren Rd TS24 . . . . . . 5 C4
Warren St
Hartlepool TS24 . . . . 7 A3
Middlesbrough TS1. . . . 85 B2
Warrior Dr TS25 . . . . . 13 B3
Warrior Terr 8
TS12 . . . . 77 A3
Warsett Rd TS11 . . . . 75 B2
Warton St TS3 . . . . . . 41 A4
Warwick Cl TS16. . . . . 63 B3
Warwick Cres TS23 . . 22 A3
Warwick Gr
Hartlepool TS26 . . . . 9 A3
Stockton-on-T TS20. . . 26 C2
Warwick Pl TS24. . . . . 10 A3
Warwick Rd
Guisborough TS14 . . . . 79 A2
Redcar TS10 . . . . 71 B1
Warwick St
Middlesbrough TS1. . . . 85 B1
South Bank TS6. . . . . . . 32 A1
Wasdale Cl TS24 . . . . . 6 A3
Wasdale Gr TS15. . . . . 25 B2
Wasdale Gr TS19. . . . . 25 B2
Washford Cl TS17 . . . . 65 A2
Washington Gr TS20 . 25 C4
Washington St TS2. . . 84 C4
Waskerley Cl TS19 . . . 24 C3
Wass Way TS16 . . . . . 54 B2
Watchgate TS7 . . . . . 62 A2
Water Avens Way
TS18 . . . . 46 C1
Watercress Cl TS26 . . . 4 C4
Waterford Rd TS20. . . 26 A2
Waterford Terr TS1. . . 85 A1
Waterlily Ct TS26 . . . . . 5 A4
Waterloo Rd
Middlesbrough TS1. . . 85 C2
Middlesbrough TS1. . . 87 A2
Waterside Way TS26 . .4 B2
Watersmeet Cl TS17 . 65 B1
Watling Cl TS20 . . . . . 25 C4
Watson Gr TS17. . . . . 47 A4
Watson St TS1 . . . . . . 86 A3
Watton Cl TS25 . . . . . 14 B3
Watton Rd TS17. . . . . 48 B2
Waveney Rd TS10. . . . 70 A1
Waverley St
Middlesbrough TS1. . . . 85 B2
Stockton-on-T TS18. . . . 81 C1
Waverley Terr TS25. . . . 9 A1
Waymar Cl TS5 . . . . . 39 A1
Wayside Rd TS3 . . . . . 42 B3
Wear Cres TS16. . . . . . 63 B3
Wear Ct TS6 . . . . 42 A4
Weardale TS14 . . . . . . 78 A1
Weardale Cres TS23. . 21 B2
Weardale Gr TS5. . . . . 59 A4
Weardale Pl TS18. . . . 80 B4
Wearport Gn 12
TS18 . . . . 82 C4
Weastell St TS5 . . . . . 39 C2
Weatherhead Ave
TS5 . . . . 49 A4

Weaver Cl TS17 . . . . . 56 C2
Weaverham Rd TS20 . 25 C4
Weaverthorpe TS7 . . . 61 C3
Webb Rd TS6 . . . . 31 C1
Webster Ave TS5. . . . . 40 A1
Webster Cl TS18 . . . . . 83 A2
Webster Rd
Billingham TS22 . . . . . . 16 C1
Eston TS6 . . . . 43 C1
Webster St TS18 . . . . . 83 A2
Welburn Ave TS4 . . . . 40 B1
Welburn Gr TS7. . . . . . 52 C3
Welbury Cl TS18 . . . . . 34 C1
Welland Cl TS5 . . . . . . 58 C4
Welland Cres TS19 . . . 24 B1
Welland Rd
Hartlepool TS25 . . . . . . 14 B4
Redcar TS10 . . . . 70 A1
Wellbrook Cl TS17 . . . 65 C4
Wellburn Ct TS19 . . . . 34 C3
Wellburn Rd TS19. . . . 34 C3
Welldale Cres TS19 . . 34 C4
Welldeck Gdns TS26 . . 9 A4
Welldeck Rd TS26. . . . . 9 A4
Wellesley Rd TS4 . . . . 87 B2
Wellfield Gn TS19. . . . 24 B3
Wellington Cl
Marske-by-t-S TS11 . . . 74 B2
Middlesbrough TS2. . . . 84 C4
Wellington Ct TS18 . . 46 A2
Wellington Sq TS18. . 82 A3
Wellington St
Middlesbrough TS2. . . . 84 C4
Stockton-on-T TS18. . . . 82 A3
Wellmead Rd TS3 . . . . 42 A3
Wells Ave TS24 . . . . . . 5 C4
Wells Cl TS6 . . . . 43 C2
Well's Cotts TS16 . . . . 63 C3
Wells Gr TS10. . . . . . . 71 C1
Wellspring Cl TS5. . . . 49 A1
Wells St TS24 . . . . .7 B3
Welton Ho TS3. . . . . . 42 B1
Wembley Ct TS18 . . . . 81 C2
Wembley St TS1 . . . . 85 A2
Wembley Way
Normanby TS6 . . . . 53 B3
Stockton-on-T TS18. . . . 81 C2
Wembury Ct TS10. . . . 73 B3
Wensleydale Gdns
TS17 . . . . 48 A2
Wensleydale Gr
TS17 . . . . 65 B2
Wensleydale St TS25. . 9 C1
Wensley Rd TS18. . . . . 80 A3
Wentworth Ct 1
TS6 . . . . 43 C1
Wentworth Gr TS27 . . 2 C1
Wentworth Ho 2
TS6 . . . . 43 C1
Wentworth St TS1 . . . 85 B2
Wentworth Way
TS16 . . . . 63 C4
Wesley Mall TS1 . . . . 84 C3
Wesley Pl TS20 . . . . . 26 B3
Wesley Row TS1 . . . . 84 B3
Wesley Sq 4 TS24 . . . . 9 C4
West Ave
Billingham TS23 . . . . . . 21 B1
Saltburn-by-t-S TS12. . . 76 B3
Westbank Rd TS7 . . . . 53 A2
Westbeck Gdns TS5. . 50 A4
West Beck Way TS8 . . 60 C3
Westborough Gr
TS18 . . . . 34 B1
Westbourne Gr
Eston TS6 . . . . 42 C3
Middlesbrough TS3. . . . 87 C2
Redcar TS10 . . . . 70 C4
Westbourne Rd
Hartlepool TS25 . . . . 9 B2
Middlesbrough TS5. . . . 39 A1
Westbourne St TS18 . 83 A1
Westbrooke Ave
TS25 . . . . 12 B4
Westbrooke Gr TS25 . 12 B4
Westbury St TS17 . . . . 47 B4

West Coatham La
TS10 . . . . 69 A1
Westcott Ho TS3. . . . . 41 A2
Westcott St TS18. . . . . 83 A1
West Cres TS5 . . . . . . 38 C1
Westcroft 1 TS3 . . . . . 41 A2
Westcroft Rd TS6 . . . . 33 B2
Westdale Rd TS17. . . . 47 C1
West Dyke Rd TS10. . . 72 C4
West End TS14. . . . . . . 79 A3
West End Ave TS14. . . 79 A3
West End Gdns TS15 . 63 B3
West End Way TS18 . . 46 A4
Westerby Rd TS3 . . . . 31 A1
Westerdale Ave
Redcar TS10 . . . . 70 A1
Stockton-on-T TS19. . . . 80 B4
Westerdale Ct TS14 . . 79 A3
Westerdale Rd
Hartlepool TS25 . . . . . . 13 B1
Middlesbrough TS3. . . . 41 A2
Westerham Gr TS4. . . 50 C3
Westerleigh Ave
TS19 . . . . 34 C3
Westerton Gn 5
TS19 . . . . 24 B3
Westerton Rd 9
TS23 . . . . 17 B4
WESTFIELD 70 A2
Westfield Cl TS16 . . . . 42 C1
Westfield Cres TS19. . 25 B2
Westfield Ct
Redcar TS10 . . . . 69 B1
Stockton-on-T TS19. . . . 25 B1
Westfield Rd
Eston TS6 . . . . 43 A1
Marske-by-t-S TS11 . . . 74 A2
Westfield Way TS10. . 69 B1
Westgarth Cl TS11 . . . 74 C2
Westgarth Prim Sch
TS11 . . . . 74 C2
Westgate
Guisborough TS14 . . . . 79 B3
Yarm TS15. . . . . 63 B2
Westgate Rd
Guisborough TS14 . . . . 79 B3
Middlesbrough TS5. . . . 49 B4
West Hartlepool Rd
TS22 . . . . 16 C4
Westholme Ct TS23 . . 17 C2
West La
Eston TS6 . . . . 33 A2
Middlesbrough TS5. . . . 38 C2
Westland Ave TS26. . . . 9 A2
Westlands Ave 7
TS20 . . . . 26 B3
Westlands Rd TS16. . . 63 B4
Westlands Sch TS17 . . 57 B3
Westland Way TS18 . . 46 C3
West Lane Hospl
TS5 . . . . 39 A2
Westlowthian St TS2 . 29 C4
West Mews TS15. . . . . 63 B2
Westminster Cl TS6. . 43 C2
Westminster Oval
TS20 . . . . 20 B2
Westminster Rd TS5 . 39 C2
West Moor Cl TS15. . . 64 B1
Westmoreland Gr
TS20 . . . . 20 A2
Westmoreland St 3
TS25 . . . . 9 C2
Westmoreland Wlk 14
TS25 . . . . 9 C2
Westmorland Rd
Middlesbrough TS5. . . . 39 B2
Redcar TS10 . . . . 70 C1
Weston Ave TS3 . . . . . 42 A4
Weston Cres TS20. . . . 26 C2
WEST PARK 8 A3
West Park Prim Sch
TS26 . . . . 8 B4
West Pk TS25 . . . . 12 B4
Westpoint Rd TS17. . . 83 C2
Westport Cl TS18 . . . . 82 C4
West Prec TS23 . . . . . 21 B4
Westray TS8 . . . . 61 B1

West Rd TS23 . . . . 21 B1
West Row
Eston TS6 . . . . 44 A2
Greatham TS25. . . . . . 14 B1
Middlesbrough TS5. . . . 38 C1
Stockton-on-T TS18. . . . 83 A2
West Scar TS10 . . . . . . 73 A4
West Side TS7 . . . . 61 A4
West St
Billingham TS2 . . . . 29 C4
8 Eston, California
TS6 . . . . 44 A2
Eston, Normanby TS6 . . 43 B1
Marske-by-t-S TS11 . . . 75 A3
Middlesbrough TS2. . . . 29 B3
Yarm TS15. . . . . 63 B2
West Terr
Middlesbrough TS3. . . . 87 C2
Redcar TS10 . . . . 70 C4
WEST VIEW 3 A1
West View TS10 . . . . . 71 A3
West View Cl 4
TS16 . . . . 54 B1
West View Prim Sch
TS24 . . . . 5 B4
West View Rd TS24. . . . 3 C1
West View Terr
Eaglescliffe TS16 . . . . . 54 B1
Seaton Carew TS25 . . . 13 C2
Westward Cl TS1. . . . . 84 C3
Westwick Terr TS4 . . . 51 A1
Westwood Ave
Middlesbrough TS5. . . . 50 A4
Nunthorpe TS7 . . . . . . 62 B3
Westwood La TS17. . . 65 C4
Westwood Way TS27 . .2 B1
Westworth Cl TS15. . . 50 B2
Wetherall Ave TS15 . . 66 B3
Wetherby Cl TS18. . . . 27 B1
Wetherby Gn TS3 . . . . 52 C4
Wetherell Cl TS11 . . . . 75 B1
Wetherfell Cl TS17. . . 65 A2
Weymouth Ave TS8 . . 60 B4
Weymouth Dr TS21 . . 62 C2
Weymouth Rd TS18 . . 35 A2
Whaddon Chase
TS14 . . . . 79 C2
Whale Hill Prim Sch
TS6 . . . . 44 A3
Wharfdale Ave TS3 . . 42 B2
Wharfedale Cl TS17 . . 65 B3
Wharf St TS18 . . . . . . 83 B2
Wharton Cl TS15. . . . . 67 B4
Wharton St TS24. . . . . . 9 C4
Wharton Terr TS24 . . . 6 A2
Wheatacre Cl 1
TS11 . . . . 75 B1
Wheatear Dr TS10 . . . 73 A3
Wheatear La TS17 . . . 56 A1
Wheatfields Ho TS6. . 53 C4
Wheatlands Cl TS14. . 79 C2
Wheatlands Dr TS11 . 74 C2
Wheatlands Pk TS10 . 73 A3
Wheatlands Prim Sch
TS10 . . . . 73 B4
Wheatley Cl TS5 . . . . . 59 A4
Wheatley Rd TS19 . . . 24 B3
Wheatley Wlk TS19 . . 24 C3
Wheeldale Ave TS10 . 73 A3
Wheeldale Cres
TS17 . . . . 47 C1
Wheldrake Cl TS14. . . 79 B5
Whernside TS7 . . . . . . 61 C2
Whernside Cres
TS17 . . . . 65 B2
Whessoe Rd TS19. . . . 24 C3
Whessoe Wlk TS19 . . 24 C3
Whickham Cl TS3. . . . 30 C1
Whickham Rd TS19 . . 24 A3
Whinchat Cl
Hartlepool TS26 . . . . 5 A3
Ingleby Barwick TS17. . 56 B1
Whinchat Tail TS14. . . 78 B3
Whinfell Ave TS16 . . . 54 B2

Whinfell Cl TS7 . . . . . 61 C2
Whinfield Cl TS19. . . . 24 A1
Whinflower Dr TS20 . 20 A1
Whingroves TS17 . . . . 48 B3
Whinlatter Cl TS19. . . 80 C3
Whin Mdws TS7 . . . . 3 A1
WHINNEY BANKS . . 48 C4
Whinney Banks Prim
  Sch TS5 . . . . 49 A4
Whinney Banks Rd
  TS5 . . . . 38 C1
Whin St TS1 . . . . 84 C3
Whinston Cl TS26 . . . . .4 B1
Whinstone Dr TS8 . . 58 C1
Whinstone Prim Sch
  TS17 . . . . 56 B2
Whisperdale Ct TS3 . . 41 C2
Whitburn Rd TS19 . . . 24 B3
Whitburn St TS24 . . . . . 9 C2
Whitby Ave
  Eston TS6 . . . . 43 C3
  Guisborough TS14 . . . 79 C3
Whitby Cres TS10 . . 71 C1
Whitby Gr **4** TS24 . . 10 A3
Whitby Rd TS7. . . . . . 62 B3
Whitby St
  Hartlepool TS24 . . . . . 10 A3
  Hartlepool TS26 . . . . . 10 A2
Whitby Wlk TS24. . . . 10 A3
Whitchurch Cl TS17. . 65 A2
Whitebeam Ct **4**
  TS4 . . . . 50 B4
Whitehaven Ct TS10 . 72 B4
Whitehouse Dr TS19 . 80 A4
Whitehouse Prim Sch
  TS19 . . . . 25 A1
Whitehouse Rd TS22. 16 B1
White House Rd
  TS17 . . . . 47 A1
Whitehouse St TS5 . . 85 A2
Whiteoaks Cl TS10. . . 73 C3
White St TS3 . . . . 41 A3
Whitestone Bsns Pk
  TS4 . . . . 87 B2
White Stone Cl TS10 . 73 C4
Whitfield Ave TS4. . . . 87 B2
Whitfield Bldgs
  TS4 . . . . 87 B2
Whitfield Cl TS16 . . . 54 B1
Whitfield Dr TS25. . . 12 C4
Whitfield Rd TS20. . . 20 A1
Whithorn Gr TS8. . . . 59 B3
Whitley Rd TS17 . . . . 57 A4
Whitrout Rd TS24 . . . . 3 A1
Whitstable Gdns
  TS10 . . . . 72 A3
Whitton Cl TS5 . . . . . 49 A2
Whitton Rd TS19. . . . 35 A3
Whitwell Cl TS18. . . . 83 A1
Whitwell Terr TS14 . . 79 B4
Whitworth Gdns
  TS25 . . . . 12 A3
Whorlton Cl TS14 . . . 79 A1
Whorlton Rd
  Billingham TS22 . . . . . 16 B1
  Middlesbrough TS2. . . 29 A4
  Stockton-on-T TS19. . 24 B3
Wibsey Ave TS3. . . . . . 52 A3
Wickets The
  Marton TS7. . . . . 60 C4
  Seaton Carew TS25 . . 11 C4
Wicklow St TS1. . . . . 85 B1
Widdrington Ct TS19. 24 A4
Wigton Sands TS5 . . 58 B3
Wilder Gr TS25 . . . . 8 B1
Wilken Cres TS14 . . . 79 C5
Willerby Gn TS5 . . . . 49 B4
Willey Flatt La TS15. . 66 B4
Williams Ave TS5 . . . 38 C1

William St
  7 Eston TS6 . . . . 44 A2
  Hartlepool TS24 . . . . . 10 A3
  Middlesbrough TS2. . . 84 C4
  Redcar TS10 . . . . 71 A3
  Stockton-on-T TS18. . 83 A2
William Terr **2** TS20 . 26 B2
Willington Rd TS19 . . 24 B4
Willowbank TS8 . . . . 60 B1
Willow Cl
  Saltburn-by-t-S
  TS12 . . . . 76 A2
  Thornaby-on-T TS17 . . 47 B2
Willowdene Ave
  TS18 . . . . 46 A4
Willow Dr TS6 . . . . . . 53 B4
Willow Gr TS24 . . . . . . 5 C2
Willow Rd
  Guisborough TS14 . . . 79 B4
  Stockton-on-T TS19 . . 25 C1
Willow Sage Ct TS18 . 46 C1
Willows Ct TS17 . . . . 57 B1
Willows Rd TS5 . . . . . 39 C1
Willows The
  Marton TS7 . . . . 61 B4
  Redcar TS10 . . . . 71 B2
  Stockton-on-T TS19. . 25 A1
Willow Terr TS2 . . . . . 23 C1
Willow Wlk **2** TS24 . . 5 C2
Wilmire Rd TS22 . . . . 16 C1
Wilson St
  Guisborough TS14 . . . 79 A3
  Hartlepool TS26 . . . . . . 9 A4
  Middlesbrough TS1. . . 84 C4
  Thornaby-on-T TS17 . . 37 B1
Wilstrop Gn TS3 . . . . 51 C3
Wilton Ave
  Hartlepool TS26 . . . . . . 9 A3
  Redcar TS10 . . . . 69 A1
Wilton Bank TS12 . . . 76 A2
Wilton Rd TS26 . . . . . . 9 B3
Wilton St
  Middlesbrough TS1. . . 85 C2
  Redcar TS10 . . . . 70 C4
Wilton Way TS6. . . . . 44 A4
Wiltshire Way TS26 . . . 5 A2
Wiltshire Wlk TS20. . 26 C2
Wimbledon Cl TS15 . . 49 A4
Wimbledon Rd TS5 . . 49 B4
Wimpole Rd TS19 . . . 34 B4
Wincanton Rd TS10 . 71 A1
Winchester Rd
  Middlesbrough TS5. . . 40 A2
  Redcar TS10 . . . . 71 C1
  Winchester Wlk TS15 . . 5 A2
Windermere Ave
  Billingham TS23 . . . . . 21 C1
  Redcar TS10 . . . . 71 A1
Windermere Rd
  Hartlepool TS25 . . . . . 12 C4
  Hartlepool TS25 . . . . . 13 A4
  4 Middlesbrough
  TS5 . . . . 39 B1
  Stockton-on-T TS18. . 80 B3
Windleston Cl **1**
  TS19 . . . . 24 B3
Windleston Dr TS3. . 51 C2
Windlestone Ho
  TS23 . . . . 17 C1
Windlestone Rd
  TS23 . . . . 17 C2
Windmill Terr TS10. . 26 B2
Windmill Way TS17 . . 65 C2
Windsor Cres TS7. . . 62 A3
Windsor Ct
  Eston TS6 . . . . 43 C4
  5 Saltburn-by-t-S
  TS12 . . . . 77 A3
Windsor Oval TS17. . 47 B2
Windsor Rd
  Eston TS6 . . . . 43 B1
  Middlesbrough TS5. . . 39 B1

Windsor Rd continued
  Redcar TS10 . . . . 71 B1
  Saltburn-by-t-S TS12. . 76 C3
  Stockton-on-T TS18. . 81 B2
  Thornaby-on-T TS17 . . 47 B2
Windsor St
  Billingham TS23 . . . . . 23 B2
  Hartlepool TS26 . . . . . . 9 C3
  Middlesbrough TS1. . . 85 C2
Windward Way TS1, TS2,
  TS3 . . . . 86 B4
Windy Hill La TS11 . . 75 B2
Wingate Ave TS23. . . 17 C3
Wingate Rd TS19 . . . 24 B3
Wingate Wlk TS4 . . . 52 A2
Wingrove TS15 . . . . . 63 B2
Winlaton Cl **2** TS19. . 24 B3
Winpenny Cl TS15 . . 67 B4
Winsford Cl TS17 . . . 65 B2
Winslade Ave TS3. . . 42 A4
Winston Ave TS23. . . 17 B3
Winston Churchill Cl
  TS17 . . . . 57 A4
Winston Ct TS24 . . . . . 6 C4
Winston Dr TS6. . . . . 44 A2
Winston St TS18 . . . . 81 C1
Winterbottom Ave
  TS24 . . . . 5 C4
Winter Cl
  Hartlepool TS25 . . . . . 12 C4
  Yarm TS15. . . . . 66 B3
Wintersweet Gdns
  TS20 . . . . 25 C3
Winthorpe Gr TS5. . . 14 A4
Wisbech Cl TS25 . . . . 14 A3
Wiske Cl TS19 . . . . . . 24 B1
Witcombe Cl TS17 . . 55 B2
Witham Ave TS16 . . . 54 C3
Witham Gr TS25 . . . . 14 B4
Witham Ho TS16 . . . 54 C3
Witham Lo TS16 . . . . 54 C3
Witton Ct TS23. . . . . 17 C1
Witton Pk TS18 . . . . 83 A1
Woburn Gr
  Hartlepool TS25 . . . . . 12 B1
  2 Middlesbrough
  TS3 . . . . 52 B4
Woking Cl TS14 . . . . 53 C3
Wolfe Rd TS20 . . . . . 26 A3
Wollaton Rd TS23 . . . 17 C1
Wolsey Dr TS20 . . . . 19 C1
Wolsingham Cl TS19 . 34 B4
Wolsingham Dr
  Middlesbrough TS5. . . 59 A4
  Thornaby-on-T TS17 . . 48 A1
WOLVISTON 16 B4
Wolviston Back La
  Billingham TS23 . . . . . 17 B4
  Billingham TS23 . . . . . 18 A3
Wolviston Ct TS22 . . 16 B1
Wolviston Mill La
  TS22 . . . . 16 A2
Wolviston Prim Sch
  TS22 . . . . 16 C4
Wolviston Rd
  Billingham TS23 . . . . . 16 C1
  Hartlepool TS25 . . . . . . 9 B1
Wolviston Wlk TS19. . 24 B3
Woodbank Rd TS7 . . . 53 A2
Woodbine Cotts
  TS23 . . . . 18 B2
Woodbine Terr TS25. . 14 B2
Woodborough La
  TS19 . . . . 25 A1
Woodburn Cl TS8 . . . 59 B3
Woodchester Gr
  TS17 . . . . 55 C2
Woodcock Cl TS14 . . 53 C4
Woodford Cl TS11. . . 74 B3
Woodford Gn TS16. . 63 C4
Woodford Wlk TS17 . 56 C3
Woodgarth TS6. . . . . 43 C2

Woodgate Cl TS25 . . . 14 B3
Woodhall Gr TS18. . . 45 A4
Woodham Gn TS19. . 24 B3
Woodham Rd TS23 . . 17 B3
Woodhay Ave TS5. . . 49 A4
Woodhouse Rd TS14 . 78 C4
Woodlands Dr
  Normanby TS6 . . . . . . 53 C4
  Yarm TS15. . . . . 64 A1
Woodlands Gr TS26 . . 8 B4
Woodlands Rd
  Middlesbrough TS1. . . 87 A2
  Normanby TS6 . . . . . . 53 C3
  Woodland St TS18 . . . 81 C1
Woodlands The
  Nunthorpe TS7 . . . . . . 62 B1
  Thornaby-on-T TS17 . . 47 B1
Woodlea TS8 . . . . 60 B1
Woodley Gr TS7 . . . . 53 A1
Woodmere Rd TS19. . 80 A4
Woodrow Ave
  Marton TS7 . . . . 61 A3
  Saltburn-by-t-S TS12. . 76 A2
Woodrush TS8. . . . . . 68 B3
Woodside
  Ingleby Barwick
  TS17 . . . . 56 B2
  Ormesby TS7. . . . . 52 B3
  Redcar TS10 . . . . 73 A3
Woodside Gr TS18 . . 45 B4
Woodside St TS1. . . . 86 B3
Wood St
  Eston TS6 . . . . 33 A2
  Hartlepool TS24 . . . . . . 7 C2
  Middlesbrough TS1. . . 86 A4
Woodstock Ct TS18 . . 47 A3
Woodstock Way TS27 . .2 B2
Woodvale TS8 . . . . . . 61 A2
Woodvale Cl TS14. . . 79 C5
Woodville Ave TS4. . . 50 B4
Woolcotts Cl TS17 . . 65 B2
Wooler Cres TS23 . . . 21 C1
Wooler Rd TS26. . . . . . 8 C4
Worcester Gdns **5**
  TS25 . . . . 9 C1
Worcester St TS1. . . . 85 B1
Wordsworth Ave TS25 .9 B1
Wordsworth Cl TS23 . 17 B3
Wordsworth Rd TS6. . 43 B3
Wordsworth Vale
  TS5 . . . . 49 A2
Works Rd TS3 . . . . . . 31 A2
Worsall Cl TS15. . . . . 63 B2
Worsall Gr **5** TS18. . 35 A1
Worsall Rd TS15 . . . . 66 A4
Worset Gr **1** TS10 . . 73 B2
Worset La TS26, TS27 . . 4 A2
Worsley Cl TS16 . . . . 45 C1
Worsley Cres TS7 . . . 61 A2
Worthing Ct TS18. . . 83 A2
Worthing St TS18 . . . 83 A2
Wray St TS4 . . . . 88 B3
Wrekenton Cl TS19 . . 24 B3
Wren Cl TS18. . . . . . . 81 C2
Wrensfield Rd TS19 . . 80 C3
Wren St TS18. . . . . . . 81 C2
Wrentree Cl TS10 . . . 73 A3
Wrightson Ho **6**
  TS3 . . . . 41 B1
Wrightsons Ho **11**
  TS17 . . . . 47 C1
Wrightson St **4**
  TS20 . . . . 26 B3
Wroxham Cl TS19 . . . 24 C1
Wroxton Ave TS5 . . . 49 B4
Wroxton Cl TS15 . . . . 49 B4
Wrynose Gdns TS19. . 80 C3
Wycherley Ave TS5. . 49 B4
Wycherley Cl TS7 . . . 53 A1
Wychgate TS6 . . . . . . 44 B2
Wychwood Cl TS17 . . 57 A4
Wycliffe Ct TS15 . . . . 67 A4

Wye Cl TS19 . . . . 24 B1
Wykeham Ave TS14 . . 79 A1
Wykeham Cl
  Billingham TS22 . . . . . 16 A4
  Redcar TS10 . . . . 72 B1
Wykeham Way TS8. . . 60 B1
Wylam Rd TS20 . . . . 26 A3
Wylam St TS1. . . . . . 85 B1
Wynde The TS19 . . . . 24 A1
Wynd The
  Marske-by-t-S TS11 . . 75 A2
  Stainton TS8 . . . . 58 B1
Wynnstay Gdns TS24. . 9 C1
Wynyard Mews TS25. 11 C2
Wynyard Rd TS25 . . . 11 B2
Wynyard St TS20. . . . 25 B4
Wynyerd Ho TS22 . . . 16 C4
Wyverne Ct TS25. . . . 12 B3

Y

Yale Cres TS17 . . . . . . 83 C2
YARM 63 A2
Yarm Back La TS19,
  TS21 . . . . 34 A2
Yarm Cl TS25 . . . . 12 B4
Yarm La TS18 . . . . . . 83 A2
Yarmouth Cl TS25. . . 14 B3
Yarmouth Dr TS10 . . 72 B4
Yarm Prep Sch TS15 . 66 C4
Yarm Prim Sch TS15 . 66 C4
Yarm Rd
  Eaglescliffe TS16 . . . . 54 C3
  Stockton-on-T TS18. . 46 A1
Yarm Sch TS15 . . . . . 63 C2
Yarm St TS18 . . . . 83 A2
Yarm Sta TS15 . . . . . . 66 C4
Yarrow Dr TS18 . . . . . 46 C1
Yeadon Gr TS17. . . . . 48 A1
Yearby Cl
  Eston TS6 . . . . 43 C2
  Middlesbrough TS5. . . 49 A2
Yearby Cres TS11 . . . 75 B2
Yenton Cl TS23 . . . . . 21 B1
Yeoman St TS10 . . . . 71 A1
Yeoman Terr TS11 . . . 74 C2
Yeovil Wlk TS26. . . . . . 5 A2
Yew St TS1. . . . . 84 C2
Yew Tree Ave TS10 . . 72 A3
Yew Tree Gr TS7 . . . . 61 C4
Yoredale Cl TS17 . . . 65 B3
York Apartments
  TS17 . . . . 47 B1
York Cres TS23 . . . . . 21 C2
York Pl TS24 . . . . 7 B2
York Rd
  Hartlepool TS26 . . . . . . 9 C3
  Middlesbrough TS5. . . 40 A2
  Nunthorpe TS7 . . . . . . 62 B3
  Redcar TS10 . . . . 69 C4
York St TS18. . . . . . . 83 A2
Yorkway TS17 . . . . . . 83 C1
Young St TS26 . . . . 9 C4
Yukon Gdns TS4 . . . . 87 B1

Z

Zetland Ct **2** TS12. . 77 A3
Zetland Mews **1**
  TS12 . . . . 77 A3
Zetland Mus * TS10. . 71 A4
Zetland Pl TS1. . . . . . 85 A4
Zetland Prim Sch
  TS10 . . . . 71 A3
Zetland Rd
  Hartlepool TS26 . . . . . . 9 A4
  Marske-by-t-S TS11 . . 75 A2
  Middlesbrough TS1. . . 86 A4
  Redcar TS10 . . . . 71 C1
  Stockton-on-T TS19. . 25 C1
Zetland Terr TS12 . . . 76 C2
Zetland The **7** TS12. . 77 A3

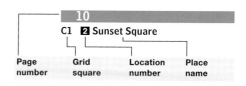

In some busy areas of the maps it is not always possible to show the name of every place.

Where not all names will fit, some smaller places are shown by a number. If you wish to find out the name associated with a number, use this listing.

The places in this list are also listed normally in the Index.

```
         10
C1   2  Sunset Square
     |     |              |              |
   Page   Grid       Location        Place
  number  square      number          name
```

2

2 **1** Copperwood Cl
2 Amberwood Cl
3 Middlewood Cl
4 Pannell Pl
5 Pannell Cl
6 Birkdale Cl
7 Gleneagles Rd

5

1 **1** Ernest Wlk
2 Blake Wlk
3 Hopps St
4 Carr St
5 Richardson St
6 Jobson St
7 Hawkridge Cl
8 Ridley Ct
2 **1** Jesmond Est
2 Willow Wlk
3 Cedar Wlk
4 Challoner Sq
5 Chatham Sq
6 Raby Sq

6

1 **1** Mapleton Rd
2 Brougham Ho
3 Abigail Wlk
4 Breward Wlk
5 Mason Wlk
6 Potter Wlk
7 Herbert Wlk
8 Lynnfield Rd
9 Stuart St

9

4 **1** Roseberry Mews
2 Brafferton St
3 Raeburn St
2 **1** Elwick Grange
2 Flaxton Ct
3 Elwick Ct
4 Grasmere St
3 **1** Mitchell St
2 Alderson St
3 Campion St
4 Benson St
5 Bentley St
6 Lansdowne Ct
4 **1** Collingwood Wlk
2 Hawkridge St
3 Brook St
4 Christopher St
5 Grosvenor St
6 Laburnum St
7 Straker St
8 Morton St
9 Albany Ct
10 Hartley Cl
11 Hunter St
12 Grosvenor Gdns
13 Hutton Ct
14 St Joseph's Ct
1 **15** St Aidan's St

2 Leamington Dr
3 Alverstone Ave
4 Hereford St
5 Worcester Gdns
C2 **1** Bathgate Terr
2 Thompson St
3 Westmoreland St
4 Moyne Gdns
5 Lonsdale Ct
6 Vicarage Ct
7 Maltings The
8 Russell Wlk
9 Northampton Wlk
10 Nottingham Wlk
11 Cumbria Wlk
12 Northumberland Gr
13 Northumberland Wlk
14 Westmoreland Wlk
15 Shropshire Wlk
C3 **1** Stotfold St
2 Johnson St
3 Jubilee Ho
4 Gainford St
5 Gill St
6 Gainford Ho
7 Brewery St
C4 **1** Tees St
2 Middleton Grange La
3 Swainson Pl
4 Wesley St
5 Upper Church St
6 Old Municipal Blgs

10

A3 **1** Brunswick St
2 Andrew St
3 Newhaven Ct
4 Whitby Gr
5 Hucklehoven Ct
6 Fastnet Ct
7 St Abbs Wlk
8 St Bees Wlk
9 Lambton St
10 Musgrave Wlk
11 Burbank Ct
12 Lizard Wlk
13 Longscar Wlk
14 Spurn Wlk
15 Goodwin Wlk
A4 **1** Church Sq
2 Central Bldgs
3 Station App
4 Avondene Flats
5 Scarborough St
6 Jersey St
7 Britannia Cl

11

B2 **1** Kilmory Wlk
2 Kebock Wlk
3 Juniper Wlk
4 Jarvis Wlk
5 Glencairn Gr
6 Guthire Wlk

7 Forres Wlk
C2 **1** Farr Wlk
2 Holyrood Wlk

17

B4 **1** Betjeman Cl
2 Dryden Cl
3 Lowell Cl
4 Sandhall Cl
5 Wallington Wlk
6 Halton Ct
7 Butsfield Way
8 Newbiggin Rd
9 Westerton Rd

24

B2 **1** Cassop Wlk
2 Coundon Gn
3 Cleadon Wlk
4 Carville Ct
5 Corbridge Ct
6 Crookhall Wlk
7 Cowshill Gn
B3 **1** Windleston Cl
2 Winlaton Cl
3 Dunford Ct
4 Cornriggs Wlk
5 Westerton Gn
C4 **1** Egglescliffe Ct
2 Edmondsley Wlk
3 Ilkeston Wlk
4 Irstead Wlk
5 Iveston Wlk
6 Inskip Wlk
7 Reepham Cl
8 Ruberry Ave
9 Rillington Cl
10 Rockall Ave

25

A3 **1** Ruswarp Ave
2 Raskelf Ave
3 Ridsdale Ave
4 Rugeley Ct
5 Kirknewton Cl
6 Kininvie Wlk
7 Killerby Ct
8 Kimblesworth Wlk
A4 **1** Ribchester Cl
2 Ryhope Ave
3 Rosedale Gdns
4 Retford Cl

26

A4 **1** Gilpin Ho
2 Anstey Ho
3 Ragworth Pl
4 Cameron St
5 Newby Ct
6 Colpitt Cl
7 Summerhouse Sq
B1 **1** Danby Ct
2 Compton Cl
3 Haswell Ct
4 Christopher St

5 Headlam Ct
6 Carlile Wlk
7 Newton Wlk
8 Douglas Wlk
B2 **1** Dorlcote Pl
2 William Terr
3 St Michaelis Ct
4 Grey St
5 St Michael's Gr
6 Edgar St
7 Prospect Pl
8 Lexington Ct
9 North Mount Pleasant St
10 South Mount Pleasant St
11 Belle Vue Ho
12 Norton Ct
13 Hillhouse Farm
B3 **1** Harland Pl
2 Chapman St
3 Holly St
4 Wrightson St
5 Chesterton Ct
6 Oaklands Ave
7 Westlands Ave
B4 **1** Fox Almshouses
2 Picton Pl
3 Malden Rd
5 Maybray King Wlk
6 Ridley Mews
7 Smirks Yd
8 Thorpe Mews
9 Dragon Ct
10 Mill Meadow Ct

32

A2 **1** Oxford St
2 Napier St
3 Milbank St
4 Jackson St
5 Middlesbrough Road E
6 Market St
7 Upper Branch St
8 Shepherdson Ct
9 Coulthard Ct
10 Tyne St
11 Alan St
12 South Ct
13 Fenton Ct
14 Upper Graham St
15 Upper Albion St
16 Upper Jackson St

34

C4 **1** Lauder Ho
2 Markham Sq
3 Midfield View
4 Maplin View
5 Madison Sq
6 Melksham Ct
7 Marwood Sq
8 Morven View
9 Meldrum Sq
10 Mallaig View

35

A1 **1** Hawkesbury Cl
2 Gisborne Gr
3 Masterton Dr
4 Hudswell Gr
5 Worsall Gr

38

C1 **1** Riverdale Ct
2 Sherborne Wlk
3 Syon Ct
4 Rousham Gdns
5 Scotney Ct
6 School Ave

39

B1 **1** Askwith Rd
2 Patey Ct
3 Dresser La
4 Windermere Rd
5 Pilkingtons Bldgs
6 Airedale Ho
7 Lunefield Ho
8 Crescent Lo

40

A1 **1** Palladium Bldgs
2 Crofton Ave
3 Hawthorne Ave
4 Rosecroft Ave
5 Jackson Ho
B1 **1** Brough Ct
2 Hedingham Cl
3 Sunley Ave
4 Barnard Ct
5 Belvedere Rd
6 St Lukeis Cotts
7 Newby
8 Maltby
9 Loftus
10 Kildale
C1 **1** Ingleby
2 Flamborough
3 Escomb
4 Durham
5 Corby
6 Bamborough
7 Alnwick
8 Guisborough
9 Harewood

41

A1 **1** Langsett Ave
2 Rossett Wlk
3 Samuelson Ho
4 Askrigg Wlk
A2 **1** Westcroft
2 Eastcroft
3 Gilling Wlk
4 Barsby Gn
B1 **1** Tanhill Wlk
2 Brunner Ho
3 Mond Ho
4 Dunster Ho

5 Luttrell Ho
6 Wrightson Ho
7 Colleton Wlk
8 Breckland Wlk
B2 1 Hadlow Wlk
2 Firsby Wlk
3 Malling Wlk
4 Gatwick Gn
5 Garsdale Gn

43

B1 1 Coronation Ct
2 Mason St
3 Patten St
4 Crossbeck Terr
5 Hastings The
C1 1 Wentworth Ct
2 Wentworth Ho
3 Sunningdale Ct
4 Sunningdale Ho
5 Lindrick Ho
6 Morris Rd

44

A1 1 Curson St
2 Imeson St
3 Hodgson Ct
4 Medbourne Cl
5 Bartol Ct
6 Bankside Ct
7 Jubilee Ct
A2 1 Ruswarp Cl
2 Prospect Terr
3 East Row
4 Cross St
5 Square The
6 Old Row
7 William St
8 West St
9 Guisborough Ct
A3 1 Rudland Wlk
2 Lealholm Wlk
3 Deepgrove Wlk
4 Colburn Wlk
5 Brackenberry Wlk
6 Ainthorpe Pl
7 Boulby Wlk
8 Lythe Wlk
9 Mulgrave Wlk
10 Farndale Wlk

46

B4 2 Arncliffe Ave
3 Maxwell Ct
4 Richard Hind Wlk

47

B4 1 Cardwell Wlk

2 Palmerston Ct
3 Stanley Cl
4 Russell Wlk
5 Francis Wlk
6 St Cuthbert Ct
7 Hartington Cl
8 Crosby Wlk
9 Dorothy Terr
10 Scarborough St
11 Silverwood Ct
C1 1 St Margarets Gr
2 Anson Ho
3 Hudson Ho
4 Appleby Ho
5 Brus Ho
6 Manning Way
7 Fawcett Way
8 Butterworth Ho
9 Elkington Cl
10 Summerfield Gr
11 Wrightsons Ho
C4 1 Eldon Wlk
2 Elizabeth St
3 Derby Cl
4 Teesdale Terr
5 Heslop St
6 Salisbury St
7 Ellerburne St
8 Cheltenham Ave
9 Camelon St
10 Sandringham Rd
11 Belvedere Rd

50

B4 1 Crosthwaite Ave
2 Mulberry Ct
3 Keithwood Cl
4 Whitebeam Ct
5 Elderwood Ct
6 Evergreen Wlk
7 Limetree Ct
8 Brookside Ave
9 Hollyhurst Ave
10 Swaledale Ho
11 Frome Ho
12 Mowbray Ho
13 Pickering Ho

51

C4 1 Kirkland Wlk
2 Ilston Gn
3 Coryton Wlk
4 Corsham Wlk
5 Copley Wlk
6 Copnor Wlk
7 Chadwell Ave
8 Cheadle Wlk
9 Chatton Cl
10 Phyllis Mohan Ct
11 Ludford Ave

12 Margrove Wlk
13 Langley Ct
14 Barnford Wlk

52

A4 1 Anglesey Ave
2 Dunmow Ave
3 Bushmead Terr
4 Ormston Ave
5 Ordsall Gn
6 Chetwode Terr
7 Croxden Gr
8 Glastonbury Ho
9 Keynsham Ave
B4 1 Alvingham Terr
2 Woburn Gr
3 Sawtry Rd
4 Kirkstall Ave
5 Victoria Gdns
6 Park Ave N
7 Somerville Ave

53

A3 1 Oakridge
2 Springhill
3 Springholme
4 Springwalk
5 Springmead
6 Springlea
7 Ashwood Cl
8 Hornbeam Cl
9 Birch Tree Cl
10 Cherry Tree Cl
11 Lobelia Cl
12 Dalston Ct
13 Spencerbeck Ho

54

B1 1 Birchfield Cl
2 Broomfield Ave
4 West View Cl
5 Cleveland Gdns

56

B1 1 Goldcrest Cl
2 Pheasant Cl
3 Partridge Cl
4 Saddler Cl
C1 1 Longshaw Cl
2 Scarthwood Cl
3 Penshaw Cl
4 Oakhurst Cl
6 Chalfield Cl

61

C3 1 Rufford Cl
2 Hulton Cl

3 Ribbleton Cl
4 Scotforth Cl

63

B4 2 Butterfield Gr
3 Butterfield Cl
4 Newsam Cres
5 Norlyn

65

A3 1 Usway Ct
2 Redesdale Gr
3 Kirknewton Gr
4 Elishaw Gn
5 Greenlee Cl
B4 2 Berrington Gdns
3 Alfriston Cl
4 Florence Ct

73

B2 1 Worset Gr
2 Cragston Ct
3 Millstone Cl
4 Juniper Cl
5 Azalia Gr
6 Finchdale Cl
7 Bramble Dykes
8 Amberley Cl
9 Abercorn Cl
10 Rillstone Way
11 Viburnum Cl
12 Acacia Ct
13 Magnolia Ct
14 Didcot Cl

74

B2 1 Highfield Rd
2 Northfield Rd
3 Spitfire Cl
4 Lancaster Dr
5 Lysander Dr
6 Brabazon Dr
C1 1 Rossendale Cl
2 Inglewood Ave
3 Charnwood Cl
4 Chapel Cl
5 Station Cl
C2 1 Kerridge Cl
2 St Mark's Cl
3 Greenacres Cl
6 Adelaide Pl

75

A2 1 King Edward Terr
2 Crescent The
3 Fitzwilliam Ct
B1 1 Wheatacre Cl

2 Barnaby Cl
4 Thrushwood Cres
5 Errington Garth

76

C3 1 Stanhope St
2 Station St
3 Macnay St
4 Cambridge St
5 Ingleside Mews
6 Glenhow
7 Claire Ho
8 Gables The
C4 1 Marine Ct
2 Convalescent St
3 Langbaurgh Ct
4 De Brus Ct
5 Hanover Ho
6 Albert Ct
7 Amber Ct

77

A3 1 Zetland Mews
2 Zetland Ct
3 Cleveland St
4 Balmoral Terr
5 Windsor Ct
6 Tower Ct
7 Zetland The
8 Warrior Terr

82

C4 1 Ladyport Gn
2 Baronport Gn
3 Dukeport Ct
4 Cliffport Ct
5 Ellenport Ct
6 Seatonport Ct
7 Burtonport Wlk
8 Tweed Ho
9 Sandport Wlk
10 Kentport Ct
11 Tyneport Gn
12 Wearport Gn

83

A1 1 Ellicott Wlk
2 Pearson Wlk
3 Penny La
4 Parliament Wlk
5 North Gn
6 South Gn
7 Parkfield Way
8 Bickersteth Wlk